# The Complete Idiot's Refere

## Characteristics of the Successful Chea

**Cheapskates—**

➤ Value their relationships with people more than money
➤ Continually educate themselves about personal finances
➤ Are creative and resourceful when it comes to saving
➤ Are organized in their saving approach
➤ Ask lots of questions to make sure they understand everything and are never afraid to ask for a discount
➤ Avoid excessive amounts of debt
➤ Always shop around, and around, and around
➤ Have the discipline to say "no" to a bad deal
➤ Have the willpower to delay purchases they don't need
➤ Save and invest on a regular basis
➤ Have powerful, written plans of action to achieve their financial dreams
➤ Respect everyone they have dealings with
➤ When they can, buy used instead of new
➤ Understand the basics of the investment markets

## Top Twenty Biggest Wastes of Money

1. Buying lottery tickets and entering sweepstakes
2. Purchasing a new car every two years
3. Investing in whole life insurance, commodities, options, land in Transylvania, or anything else you are clueless about
4. Buying credit life insurance
5. Purchasing extended warranties on appliances and electronics
6. Taking action on a "hot" stock tip
7. Lending money to friends
8. Shopping on QVC or the Home Shopping Channel
9. Claiming the wrong amount of deductions on your W-4s
10. Getting suckered into "get rich quick" opportunities
11. Paying fees on your checking account
12. Using credit cards like a regular loan
13. Buying name brands on a regular basis
14. Keeping money in low-interest savings accounts
15. Buying anything at convenience stores
16. The car dealer extras
17. Shopping at ritzy clothes and grocery stores
18. Paying an annual fee on a credit card
19. Eating at upscale restaurants
20. Buying food and drinks at the movies or ball games

*tear here*

## alpha books

## Top Twenty Best Money Moves

1. Saving a set amount of money month after month
2. Avoiding illness by eating right and exercising regularly
3. Shopping at warehouse clubs
4. Buying term life insurance instead of whole life insurance
5. Taking a Saturday morning and going to a few neighborhood garage sales
6. Doing your taxes yourself
7. Investing through mutual funds
8. Buying generic and store brands at the grocery store
9. Double-checking the word of a commissioned salesperson
10. Buying clothes at thrift stores
11. Getting wired to the Internet to find the best deals on everything
12. Investing in income-producing real estate
13. Being your own travel agent
14. Finding out the dealer cost of a car before you start negotiations
15. Being debt-free and buying most everything with cash
16. Educating yourself about investing and being your own adviser
17. Finding a no-fee checking account
18. Shopping at outlet stores
19. Eating meals at home rather than out
20. Making "extra principal" payments on your mortgage

## The Cheapskate's Quick Calculator

How long does it take to double your money in an investment? Just divide the number 72 by your expected return on your dollars, and the result is the number of years it would take to double your money. It's that simple.

For example, let's say you invested $5,000 in a mutual fund, and you expect a 10 percent return over the next several years. You divide 72 by 10, which yields 7.2. So after 7.2 years you will have $10,000. Cheapskates use this simple and fast formula to calculate how much money they can accumulate for their future.

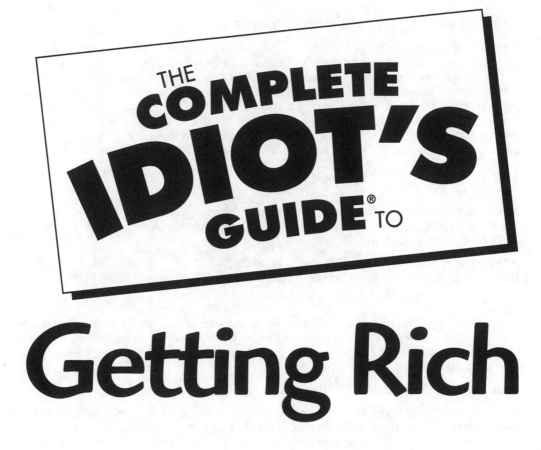

# THE COMPLETE IDIOT'S GUIDE® TO

# Getting Rich

*by Larry Waschka*

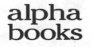

alpha
books

A Division of Macmillan General Reference
A Simon & Schuster Macmillan Company
1633 Broadway, New York, NY 10019-6785

# Alpha Development Team

**Publisher**
*Kathy Nebenhaus*

**Editorial Director**
*Gary M. Krebs*

**Managing Editor**
*Bob Shuman*

**Marketing Brand Manager**
*Felice Primeau*

**Development Editors**
*Phil Kitchel*
*Amy Zavatto*

# Production Team

**Development Editor**
*Joan Paterson*

**Production Editor**
*Donna Wright*

**Copy Editor**
*Kris Simmons*

**Cover Designer**
*Mike Freeland*

**Photo Editor**
*Richard H. Fox*

**Illustrator**
*Jody P. Schaeffer*

**Designers**
*Scott Cook and Amy Adams*
*of DesignLab*

**Indexer**
*Craig Small*

**Layout/Proofreading**
*Angela Calvert*
*Mary Hunt*
*Megan Wade*

# Contents at a Glance

# Contents

## 4  How to Become a Saver — 39

## 5  The Secrets of Millionaires — 59

## 6  An Employee's Guide to Building Wealth — 75

# Foreword

In his day, steel magnate Andrew Carnegie was the wealthiest man on the planet. In response to a question from a young man who wanted to know the secret to becoming wealthy, Carnegie responded, "You want to know if you will be rich?" He followed with, "Can you save money?"

You can't do anything if you don't have anything to do anything with. This is the point Larry drives home over and over again in his terrific book, *The Complete Idiot's Guide to Getting Rich*. Only investors, those who own assets that increase in value, have the chance to become rich. But they can't become investors unless they have something left over after every paycheck. They have to become savers first. The more they save and the more they invest using Larry's sound principles, the richer they'll be.

I was hooked immediately when I read the first chapter where Larry makes it clear that you're never too old to get started on the road to becoming rich and that you, and only you, are in control of your financial destiny because nobody cares more about your money than you do. He says that if you want to become rich, truly rich, you have to be willing to learn and to develop the habits and characteristics necessary for riches, you have to believe that it can be done, and you have to know that wealth is a journey, a process, that does not happen overnight.

Larry starts by explaining the secrets of millionaires and leads you quickly, easily, and painlessly through short chapters that lay not only the foundation but also the complete structure of a wealth-building program that really works. This program is not a get-rich-quick scheme. Rather, it's a proven, practical way to get you from where you are today to where you want to be financially.

Understanding and mastering the law of compound interest is one of the secrets to amassing great wealth. Benjamin Franklin described compounding as money making money on which it makes more money. Einstein thought that compound interest is humanity's greatest invention because it allows for the systematic, reliable increase of wealth. Albert Einstein, when asked to name the eighth wonder of the world, remarked, "I believe that the eighth wonder is compound interest."

Larry says wealthy people have great CPAs. They also have great bankers. I might add that wealthy people need a great money manager like Larry Waschka. Anne Frank said, "How wonderful it is that nobody need wait a single moment before starting to improve the world." Larry Waschka would revise that to say that nobody need wait a single moment before starting to dramatically improve his or her financial status. And that he will be with them every step of the way.

Bill Staton
America's Money Coach

# Introduction

Until I was 25 years old, my dream of getting rich led me to believe that wealth was something you could achieve quickly. Like most people in their teens and twenties, I looked for the lottery win or the windfall that I believed was out there. This illusion becomes reality for only an exclusive handful of people who do actually win the lottery or inherit big sums of money. By the way, if you want to learn how to achieve either of these two dreams, this is not the book for you.

The book you're holding in your hand is not about getting rich fast. It's about gradually building wealth that, if cared for properly, can last for years and even generations to come.

Over the past 13 years, I've spent countless hours studying wealthy people—and not so wealthy people. What I've learned is that the difference has more to do with decisions and habits than it does talent, skill, and intelligence. I know multi-millionaires who never went to college, and I know multi-talented, highly intelligent people who will never become millionaires.

The decision to build wealth is easy to make but may be difficult at times to maintain. It doesn't take a brilliant idea, but it often takes the ability to change your habits and ways of thinking. Old habits are hard to break, and I've seen many times how bad habits ruin a person's chances of ever building significant wealth. The journey takes some effort, and for whatever reason, many people are just not willing to put out the effort necessary to make the change.

What exactly is a strong enough power to change a person's habit? The answer is decision and passion. The decision to build wealth must be accompanied by and aligned with your passion. The first part is easy to do, but the second takes some people a lifetime. You must know your passions. What do you enjoy the most? What excites you? What makes you smile? What would you be willing to do for free? These are the types of questions you must ask yourself. Within the answers you should find several items that will motivate you enough to build the wealth you've always dreamed of. This book will help you find your own passion and motivation.

Let me comment on the concept of wealth, which has many definitions. Each of us has our own definition, as well as an idea of how to accomplish it. This book focuses on financial wealth, which may be important to you, but it shouldn't be your only goal. It is a tragedy to be financially wealthy, but personally empty. I've met hundreds of very wealthy people who have spent all their lives trying to get rich with little or no focus on what's really important. They have enough money to buy whatever they want, but their families suffer, they have no spiritual life, they have little or no real friends, they have no social skills, and they are miserable—some almost suicidal. That may be difficult for you to imagine, but I assure you, this is reality for many wealthy people. Fortunately, I've been blessed with very happy wealthy people as clients.

The best advice I can give you before you read this book is that the wealthiest person in the world is someone who has healthy relationships with family and friends, looks for the good in every situation, endeavors to follow his or her passions, and lives well within his or her means. I've also found that a spiritual foundation certainly helps as well—no matter what religion you follow. These are the people you want to follow and emulate (and if you're an investment advisor, these are the kinds of people you want as clients).

You can build significant financial wealth with the lessons in this book. I've seen thousands of people do it. However, be sure to focus on the other facets just as much. True wealth involves a balanced life. It's a journey, not a destination.

# My Personal Story of Wealth

I first learned about wealth at the age of four when my mother persuaded me to meet another child my age. I noticed that the other family's house was much larger than mine, and they had many wonderful things such as beautiful furniture, fancy cars, and above all else, an incredible selection of toys. Of course, what really excited me was the trampoline. They even had a treehouse in the backyard that a carpenter had built. Until this time, I had never seen a lifestyle like this.

My friend always had a nice new bicycle, and gosh, did I want a bike like his. It was a Schwinn Orange Krate that had three gears. At that time, I didn't even know what a gear was, but I sure didn't let him know that.

For nearly four years, I spent almost every afternoon with my best friend at this wonderful home. Don't think that I had a poor childhood; I lived in a comfortable home with the most wonderful family. My mother and father loved me and gave me everything I needed. Even my brother loved me in spite of all the noogies, wet willies, and other harassment I gave him. My childhood was wonderful, and for that, I'm grateful. It was just obvious as I grew older that my friend's family was much wealthier than mine.

I knew my friend's father was a doctor, and back then, my other young friends told me that if you were a doctor, you were rich. Once I realized this, I wanted to be a doctor, but this dream was only temporary. Occasionally, I spent the night at my friend's house, and almost every time, I heard my friend's father take a call at 3:00 in the morning. I decided that being a doctor was just a little too difficult.

What I continued to dream about, however, was being rich. I wanted to live in the house of my dreams and have enough money to buy whatever I wanted, which at that time was a Schwinn Orange Krate bicycle with three gears.

It has taken me 25 years to realize just how much this friendship affected my life. It was one of the catalysts that helped drive my desire for wealth. However, my family was the backbone of this drive. I was (and still am) the luckiest child in the world. My parents and step-parents raised me in an environment of love and support. Whether I deserved it or not, they supported my adventures as a child (and now that I'm an adult, they do the same). I knew that one day, I would have enough money to buy whatever I wanted for myself and family, but I also knew that it was going to take a lot of work.

Soon, I learned that building wealth would require even more than sweat. One day while in college, I learned from some classmates that a company called HBO sold software to hospitals. This company was growing fast, and its stock was going up. After researching the company in the library for hours, I called my father and told him about it. He agreed to buy 200 shares.

At first, the stock went up. My immediate thought was "Wow! Here's a way to make money with my brain doing what I love to do." This meant that I didn't have to necessarily work hard; I just had to work smart. I could use my brain power to build wealth. All this stupid research my professors required really could help me.

When the stock fell back below our purchase price, my heart sank. I was embarrassed that I had talked my dad into buying the stock. His money was lost, and I felt horrible. However, I learned some very valuable lessons about the market and about making money with my brain. That brief time the stock was up was just enough to make me realize that wealth was not just born of hard work, but of smart work. I knew that my mind was the key here and not my hands. From that moment, I dedicated part of my life to studying the stock market. That one single experience changed my entire concept of work and the vision I had of building wealth. Thanks, Dad! I love ya, but please don't ask me to pay you back for the HBO loss.

After college, my ultimate professional dream was to start my own fee-based money-management company. Fee-based means that the company's income is derived from a fee charged to the client, which is based upon a percentage of assets in the account (1 percent). After interviewing with several firms, I realized that I had nothing to offer except a desire to learn. They all told me that Merrill Lynch had the best training program on Wall Street. However, working at Merrill Lynch meant that I would have to sell securities for a commission, which was completely different from my dream of managing money for a fee. Nonetheless, it was a great place to start. When I interviewed with Merrill Lynch, the interviewers said they primarily cared about my ability to sell. In fact, the manager told me to get a year's worth of sales training with a national company and he would hire me. I got a job with Warner Lambert selling consumer goods to retail and wholesale stores. Exactly one year later, I returned to Merrill Lynch.

My plan was to spend 10 years at Merrill Lynch learning the business and then start my own firm. However, some clients encouraged me to leave just prior to my five-year anniversary. In 1990, at the age of 28, I started my company with 13 clients and $3 million under my company's management. By the middle of 1996, I had 350 clients and $73 million under management. My company, Waschka Capital Investments, is a fee-only money management firm that specializes in global diversification using no-load mutual funds. I've also hosted a state-wide radio show for three years called "Arkansas' MoneyTalk" and have written a monthly column for several publications in Arkansas. I'm truly living my dream and grateful for it all.

I recently spoke to 400 high school sophomores about building wealth. One student asked me, "Are you rich?" This was a fair question to ask. If I can't claim some degree of wealth, what gives me the authority to speak on the matter? I explained that by the time I was 34 years old, my company's gross revenue annualized over $900,000, and my net worth exceeded $2 million. Then, I explained that to some people, that makes me wealthy. Other people would say I'm far from it. It just depends upon how each person defines wealth.

The drive to build wealth can come from many sources. Having supportive parents like mine may increase your chances, but it's not necessary. I know of many wealthy people who were not quite as fortunate. Many of them used tough circumstances as a motivational factor. For some people I know, the desire to be wealthy came from being brought up in a terribly poor family. The simple challenge of making it completely on their own drove them forward. They wanted to prove that they could do it. Many of them never had a father around. The lesson is that *whatever* your circumstances are, *wealth is achievable*.

Through my experiences, I've learned that there is no real "get rich quick" method to achieve the wealth you want. My goal with this book is to teach you long-term techniques to build and maintain wealth. My hope is that this book does just that for you. With persistence, patience, and diligence, your work will pay off, enabling you to achieve the level of wealth that you want. Thank you for buying the book, and I hope you enjoy reading it.

## How to Use This Book

This book is carefully organized to present the tools and techniques you can use to set and reach your goals for wealth. I've defined five levels of wealth to make it easier for you to plan your journey to wealth, and the book leads you through each level.

**Part 1, The Basics of Getting Rich—Wealth Stages 1 and 2**, is all about the basics of getting rich. It breaks down the definition of wealth into five measurable levels and shows you how to design a plan to achieve the first two levels. This part covers the habits and characteristics of wealthy people, as well as how to get rich as an employee.

**Part 2, Becoming an Investor—Wealth Stages 3 and 4**, shows you how to become financially independent. It focuses on the investment tools and strategies you need to beat the market.

**Part 3, Building Wealth with Your Own Business**, will explain the basic details of starting, growing, and selling your own business. It will show you how to achieve the top two levels of wealth using your own business.

**Part 4, The Advanced Strategies for Building Wealth,** lists all the basic tax strategies, mental paradigms, and planning secrets you need to build your wealth. It will also teach you why so many people fail to achieve wealth.

You also get a glossary of wealth-related terms and definitions that will help you better understand the words of the wealthy. These terms will also help you keep up a conversation with any wealthy person.

# Extras

The text in each chapter provides full coverage of each topic. However, while I wrote each chapter, certain related topics came to mind that were just too good not to include. I've placed these extras in four different types of informational boxes within each chapter:

### That Reminds Me...

It seems that every significant lesson I've learned about building wealth has been the result of my own experience or the experiences of others. These boxes explain such lessons for you in the form of a story or observation so that you get a better understanding of the concepts within this book.

### Words of the Wealthy

These terms and definitions are part of the language of the wealthy. If you know and understand these words, you are well on your way to building wealth. These terms will also help you have more meaningful discussions with your financial advisors.

### Wealth Warning

If you know what to avoid in your financial life, you can significantly reduce your chances of experiencing problems. These warning boxes help you do just that. Consider these the caution signs on your journey toward wealth. They are common errors or things to be aware of.

### Treasure Tip

These helpful little hints make life easier. If you prefer the "path of least resistance," be sure to read them.

Some chapters include software packages and Web sites that are helpful in organizing and keeping track of your investments. Be sure to check out Appendix A and Appendix B for additional resources to get you started on the road to financial success.

# Acknowledgments

My clients have been the single most influential source of information for this book. I am grateful for all you've taught me over the last 10 years. Thanks for sharing your lessons in wealth with me. I dedicate this book to all of you.

Special thanks to my associates who spent so much time helping me write this revised edition. Special thanks to Jason Carlton who worked very hard on this project. Thank you, Linda Giles, Angie Johnson, Sharon Kolb, Michael Love, Jill Cox, and Pat Minyard for supporting me on this project.

I'd like to thank Christy Heady for referring me to Macmillan Publishing. This book would not have been possible for me if it weren't for you and your advice. You've been a huge source of inspiration.

Thank you, Jessica Faust, for asking me to write the revised edition. Thank you, Debbie Englander, for giving me the opportunity to write the first edition. Special thanks to Joan Paterson, Kris Simmons, and Donna Wright for your help in editing all my work. I'd also like to thank Stanley Chadsey for being such an outstanding technical editor. Thank you Bill Staton for the wonderful foreword.

I would also like to thank my parents Beverly and Tom Brewer and Lawrence and Julie Waschka for all your love, advice, and tolerance. I owe a great deal of thanks to all my family, especially my Mamoo, for all your love and spiritual guidance. Thank you, Joe Paul, for being the big brother I never had.

Many of my friends have been instrumental in helping me with ideas for this book, especially Mary Ann Campbell, Greg Hatcher, Stewart Welch, III, Rob Rikoon, Ron Yolles, Ted Grace, Pete Maris, George Worthen, Don Munro, Stuart Bowles, Gordon Rathbun, Samantha Cross, Brandon Rogers and his family, and Brian Tracey. Thank you. I sincerely appreciate everything you've done for me.

# Special Thanks from the Publisher to the Technical Reviewer

*The Complete Idiot's Guide to Getting Rich, Second Edition* was reviewed by an expert who checked the technical accuracy of what you'll learn and provided insights and guidance to help ensure that this book gives you everything you need to build wealth. We extend our special thanks to Stanley Chadsey.

With over 20 years of experience in the area of finances and investments, Mr. Chadsey is now an Associate in Capital Planning Associates, Inc. a portfolio management firm specializing in equities and fixed income investments for private accounts. A guest columnist for *The Planner* magazine and a guest lecturer at Columbia University, he is frequently interviewed and quoted in the national media. He has also lectured at New York University. In addition to holding an MBA from Columbia University, he is a Certified Public Account (CPA), a Chartered Financial Analyst (CFA), and a Certified Financial Planner (CFP).

# Special Thanks from the Publisher to the Foreword Writer

An expert in the field of helping people handle their finances, Bill Staton reviewed *The Complete Idiot's Guide to Getting Rich* and gave it his stamp of approval. "It's never too late to get started on the road to financial success and the principles that Larry sets out will guide you."

Bill Staton, America's Money Coach, became a millionaire investor at age 31 and a multimillionaire by age 35. He is the founder and chairman of The Staton Institute Inc., which empowers people to take charge of their personal finances through entertaining and easy-to-understand educational materials and wealth-building seminars. Staton publishes the internationally circulated *Staton Institute Advisory*.

Staton is a chartered financial analyst with an MBA in finance from The Wharton School. He has been quoted in *The Wall Street Journal, The Washington Post, The New York Times, USA Today, U.S. News & World Report,* and *Kiplinger's Personal Finance* and has been profiled in *Money* magazine, *Bottom Line/Personal, The Charlotte Observer,* and *The Business Journal.* Staton is interviewed frequently on radio and television across America.

Staton is the author of *The America's Finest Companies Investment Plan: Double Your Money Every Five Years, 60 Minute Investing, How to Become a Multimillionaire on Just $50 a Month,* and *Never Invest in Anything That Eats or Needs Repairing,* and creator of "The Staton 100 Performance" stock-market index.

Staton lives in Charlotte, North Carolina, with his wife and four children.

For more information, call 800-779-7175 or visit the Staton Web site at www.StatonInstitute.com.

# Part 1

# The Basics of Getting Rich— Wealth Stages 1 and 2

*Wouldn't it be nice to win a million-dollar lottery? Just the thought of it might seem nice, but if you really examine how a lottery is paid, you'll probably be surprised. Lottery winners think that they're going to get all the money at one time. Not true. If you win a million-dollar lottery, in most states your payout will be sent to you in yearly increments, minus federal and state taxes, based on your life expectancy. Once you really examine the truth about winning the lottery, you'll find that it's not all that attractive anymore.*

*The opposite is true with building wealth. I have found that once you really examine the truth about building wealth, it's not only more attractive, it's also a lot easier to achieve than you might think. You just have to break it up into different levels and design a plan to achieve the first level first, then the second, and so on. That's exactly what I've done in this part of the book for you. All you have to do is read and implement the steps, habits, and characteristics needed, and you will be on your way to building wealth.*

# Chapter 1

# Are You Going to Be Rich?

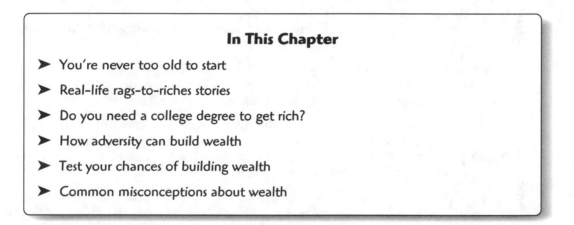

### In This Chapter

➤ You're never too old to start

➤ Real-life rags-to-riches stories

➤ Do you need a college degree to get rich?

➤ How adversity can build wealth

➤ Test your chances of building wealth

➤ Common misconceptions about wealth

Who would you say is the wealthiest person you know personally? How did he or she achieve the wealth? Is it possible for you to achieve similar wealth? It's as possible as you think it is. Most of the wealthy people I know built their fortunes with their own hands. This is self-made wealth: It's not inherited, acquired through marriage, or won in the lottery. It's built with hard work, determination, and passion.

Self-made wealth is often invisible. You don't see it or recognize it because it's owned by people who don't flaunt it or talk about it. You can learn a lot from these people, but they aren't often featured in magazines or television. They may live next door to you and have an incredible knowledge about building wealth, but you'd never know to ask.

This chapter is about these people. Although I discuss a few wealthy people featured in magazines, most of this chapter is focused on the invisible wealthy people. I dedicate this book to them because they taught me the secrets of building wealth. This chapter will also enable you to find out whether you have what it takes to be wealthy.

# Lives of the Rich and Affluent

Most dictionaries define rich as "having an abundance of money." The Commerce Department uses the term *affluent* instead of rich. According to it, if you make more than $75,000 per year, you are considered affluent. Every year, you can find numerous magazine articles featuring people who have achieved affluence.

*Time Magazine* (2/19/96, p. 42) featured five guys who really scored big in the technology industry. Software designer Marc Andreessen at the age of 24 was worth an estimated $131 million after his company Netscape went public. Netscape's Internet browser called the Navigator was a huge success.

At age 40, Steve Jobs was worth an estimated $728 million after his company Pixar Animation Studios went public. The other three men were worth $22, $79, and $86 million, and all were under the age of 45.

A story in *Cosmopolitan* (5/96, p. 214) featured eight women who became millionaires before the age of 30. Each one did it in a unique way in eight different industries—parking garages, clothing, marketing, stock trading, asbestos abatement, frozen yogurt, computers, and medical screening.

Thirty-four year-old Lisa Renshaw of Baltimore controls 51 parking garages in Maryland, Washington, D.C., and Virginia with $25 million in revenues. She started at 21 years old by renting a parking garage and leasing out spaces herself.

While in Italy studying printmaking and fashion, Jennifer Barclay missed the beginning of her college semester and decided to start a business tie-dying and block-printing cotton clothing and scarves. She went from her parents' garage to a company with $10 million in sales before she turned 29.

### Words of the Wealthy

**Wealth** is defined by *Webster's Dictionary* as an "abundance of valuable material possessions or resources," and the word wealthy is defined as "extremely affluent." The definition of **affluent** sounds even better, "having a generously sufficient and typically increasing supply of material possessions."

Former nurse and aerobics instructor, Karen Behnke, became a millionaire before her 30th birthday by starting a company called Execu-Fit. Her company offered medical screenings of executives and analyses of employee health. She built sales by calling on personnel departments and signing large companies such as Pacific Gas & Electric. When bank loans were impossible, she used credit cards at 22 percent interest. Later, she traded 10 percent of her company for additional capital. In 1993, Karen sold her company to PacifiCare HMO for nearly $5 million.

The *Cosmopolitan* article has more examples such as these. Wealthy people all started their own businesses. However, you don't have to start your own business to be wealthy. Plenty of wealthy people never had their own companies. Sure, starting your own business definitely increases your chances, but it's not a requirement.

## *Do You Identify with Wealthy People?*

Most people can't identify with extremely wealthy people. Either the story is too complicated or it just seems too overwhelming. However, most people can easily identify with real people who built fortunes out of almost nothing. I'm talking about wealthy people who earned every dime they made. Most of them don't wear flashy clothes or drive fancy cars. They don't live in mansions or travel to Paris for a vacation. They live next door to you, and you may not even know their names. Most of my clients fit this description. Some of these people drive old trucks with worn-out tires. If I pointed them out to you on the street, you would never believe they had any money. They earned every dime, and they're darn proud of it.

# You're Never Too Old to Start

Most people in their 40s think it's too late to build wealth. They claim they don't have the energy they once had. They feel as if their peak earnings potential is behind them. They've missed out on too many opportunities. My response to these people is simply, "What about Anne Scheiver?"

Frank Lalli wrote an article about Anne Scheiver in *Money Magazine* ("How She Turned $5,000 into $22 Million," p. 64, January 1996, *Money*, Copyright 1996 Time, Inc.) that I found to be priceless. It read

> *In the depths of the Depression, when she was already 38 years old and earning only a little more than $3,000 a year, Anne invested a major portion of her life savings in stocks. She entrusted the money to the youngest of her four brothers, Bernard, who was getting started at 22 as a Wall Street broker. He did well picking issues for her as the market drifted upward in 1933 and '34, but his firm did not. It went bust suddenly, and Anne lost all her money. In 1944, 10 years after her big loss, she started fresh with a $5,000 account at Merrill Lynch Pierce Fenner & Bean and slowly built the nest egg up to $20 million by the time she died last January, loveless and alone at 101. It's now worth $22 million.*

**Wealth Warning**

In spite of the fact that the chances of winning the lottery are usually worse than a million to one, it seems that most Americans use lottery tickets to plan for their retirement. The irony is that a large percentage of people who win the lottery end up in serious trouble, if not dead broke.

The article stated that her performance of 17.5 percent per year exceeded some of the best-known investment professionals in the world, including John Neff and Ben Graham. In 51 years, this incredible lady built a fortune using simple strategies that anyone can follow.

## Investing with Passion

Those who knew Anne Scheiver said she lived a terrible existence as a recluse who never enjoyed her money. My bet is that investing was her passion, her love, and her life. I'm also willing to bet that this woman enjoyed her money more than most people ever will. She enjoyed managing it, not spending it. As a result, she turned near-disaster into an almost unbelievable fortune with nothing more than patience, interest in the market, research, and a little planning. So what if she didn't take vacations or eat out! This woman left a legacy behind that all of us can learn from. She was able to outperform trained professionals in their own field for more than 50 years. The story of Anne's life is what I call an invisible rags-to-riches story.

# The Wealthy Postman

Here is a true story from which everyone can learn something; I know I did. The story involves a modest couple who attended my investment workshop in 1993. This couple, let's call them Mr. and Mrs. Post, met with me after the workshop to discuss some specific questions they had regarding their *no-load* fund portfolio. As usual, I asked some questions and found that Mr. Post had worked all his life for the United States Postal Service and was considering retirement the next year. His wife raised their children and had never earned any additional income. Mr. Post told me that the most they had ever made in one year was $30,000. They were conservatively dressed, simple in their ways, and almost shy about talking to me.

They wanted me to review their no-load mutual fund portfolio to see if I thought anything needed to be sold. As Mr. Post began to show me his portfolio, I put my pen down and prepared to see a small portfolio of funds.

### Words of the Wealthy

**No-load** funds are mutual funds that can be purchased, sold, and owned without any commission charges (or loads). The only charges involved are yearly management fees. A commission-paid broker or salesperson would never offer to sell you a no-load fund because there is no commission available for him.

Wrong! Their portfolio had more than 35 different no-load mutual funds worth more than $800,000. To say the least, I was dumbfounded. How could this couple have so much money? Well, of course, I made all kinds of assumptions. First, I asked if any of the money was inherited. They replied quickly and firmly, "No, not one dime." I asked if they owned any real estate other than their home. They replied, "No." I was impressed.

They quickly told me that they had also purchased homes for each of their two daughters as wedding presents, both of which cost $120,000. They paid cash, of course. They had also prefunded their four grandchildren's college education with a total of $100,000. If you add that up, the total is $1,140,000. I gave up and asked how they did it. They came to me for advice, and I turned the appointment around and asked for theirs. What I learned from them that day I will never forget. I share their secrets of wealth in Chapter 5, "The Secrets of Millionaires." Their story immediately made me want to write a book so I could share what I learned. (By the way, you are holding that book in your hands, and I hope it helps you achieve the wealth you dream of.) This couple told me later in the most humble tone, "If we can do it, anybody can." They were invisibly wealthy.

### That Reminds Me...

I've learned over the last 12 years in the wealth-management business that most of the really wealthy people do not own fancy cars, jet planes, or huge mansions. Most of the wealthy people I know are more like Sam Walton. They drive older cars or trucks, fly coach seats on commercial airlines, and wear simple clothes. To my surprise, most of them live well within their means in simple homes. They tend to avoid anything flashy and avoid large mortgages and car payments by paying cash. My point is that you would never think these people had any more money than the average citizen. As a matter of fact, they keep their wealth confidential.

## Is a College Education Necessary?

Contrary to popular belief, a college education is not necessary for you to build great wealth. The world is full of super-intelligent people who never built any significant amount of wealth. What may surprise you is that many wealthy people never finished college.

My second favorite story about wealthy people is about a man who built a $10 million net worth from the ground up without a college education. He worked hard and earned his net wealth. He decided to retire last year in his early 50s.

When he was 18, he decided to skip college and work in a soft drink distribution company. He was dedicated and worked harder than anyone in the company. In fact, he worked so hard that a truck driver at the company once told him, "Don't work so hard. You'll make all of us look bad." This didn't even faze him. He soon became a truck driver and then a supervisor for all the truck drivers.

### Treasure Tip

No matter what your education or resources, the key to building financial wealth is to compose and follow a plan of action you design to meet your specific needs and goals. Your plan should identify and combat your weaknesses.

After four years, a national soft drink company saw what he had done for his employer and asked him to be a division manager. This position gave him the opportunity to help other soft drink distributors in several states. In only a few years, one of his distributors offered him 20 percent of the company to manage his distributorship. He agreed, and they soon bought other distributorships and added other brands to their line. The original owner wanted to retire, so he offered the remaining stock to my client. The transaction involved a lot of money for my client at that time, so he took on a partner to make the transaction. Soon, they bought other distributorships in five states, including Hawaii.

The business became larger than my client ever dreamed. I asked him to sum it up in a few sentences how he built his wealth. He said, "Dedication, hard work, and going that extra mile." I asked him where he got his motivation to work so hard. He replied, "Believe it or not, it had a lot to do with the fact that I didn't have a college education. I felt like everyone else did, and I had this complex about not finishing college."

I really believe that a college education is a great idea, but it certainly is not a requirement for building wealth. My client proved that determination, hard work, and the willingness to go that extra mile are more important than a college education. By the way, the truck driver who told him to not work so hard is still a truck driver. I bet my client's wealth isn't invisible to him.

## The Rich Couple Next Door

One day, a retired couple in their 60s came to my office for some help. They were a tiny couple, both about 5 feet tall, and wore clothes that had to be 10 years old. You couldn't ask for a nicer couple. They asked almost bashfully if I would take a look at their "little" portfolio and make some suggestions. They both apologized for the "small" size of their holdings. The husband said, "I know that you are accustomed to dealing with much larger amounts, but would you please give us some advice?" I explained that size didn't matter and that I would be glad to help them in any way I could. I nearly fell out of my chair when I opened the portfolio to find more than $1 million in stocks, bonds, and mutual funds. You would never think that these people had any money. It never ceases to amaze me how people such as this can be so humble and simple, yet be completely sophisticated with their investment knowledge.

I asked them a little about their background. They said that the most they ever made in income in one year was $27,000 and that they didn't inherit anything. I just love these people! I'm willing to bet that you know people just like this in your neighborhood, church, or synagogue. They are the salt of the earth, and if you can ever get them to tell you their story, you may learn more than you ever thought you could from these people.

## That Reminds Me...

While working at a national discount brokerage firm, my associate Sharon Kolb got to know many wealthy people who earned their money from non-glamour businesses such as scrap metal salvage, electrical supply companies, used car lots, and other such endeavors. Sharon said, "It's really true that you don't need a formal education or work in a glamour field to earn a good living and build wealth."

# Wealth and Adversity

It's strange how adversity can change the life of a person for the better. I've heard it said that the strongest pine lumber comes from trees that have been subject to windy environments. The same is true for people. The strongest people I know have struggled the most in life. Some of the wealthiest people I know have done the same. The difference between them and most people is their perseverance. The value of courage, persistence, and perseverance has rarely been illustrated more convincingly than in the life story of this man.

| Event | Age |
| --- | --- |
| Failed in business | 22 |
| Ran for legislature—defeated | 23 |
| Again failed in business | 24 |
| Elected to legislature | 25 |
| Sweetheart died | 26 |
| Had a nervous breakdown | 27 |
| Defeated for speaker | 29 |
| Defeated for elector | 31 |
| Defeated for Congress | 34 |
| Elected to Congress | 37 |
| Defeated for Congress | 39 |
| Defeated for Senate | 46 |
| Defeated for Vice President | 47 |
| Defeated for Senate | 49 |
| Elected President of the United States | 51 |

That's the record of Abraham Lincoln.

# Don't Be a Hodad!

Just because someone makes a lot of money, it doesn't mean they're wealthy. If their expenses equal or exceed their income, they don't qualify as wealthy. Just because someone works hard, earns a great salary, and has nice things, it doesn't make him or her wealthy. The person may look like wealth and smell like wealth, but it's all a big show. In Texas, they call these people *hodads*. They're all hat and no cattle. They wear fancy hats and talk the talk, but they don't even have a pasture or a cow to put in it.

Somewhere along the way, these seemingly wealthy people didn't learn the habits and characteristics necessary to build real wealth. No one taught them the concept of saving for a rainy day, much less retirement. They don't have what it takes to be wealthy.

**That Reminds Me...**

I knew a business owner once who didn't have any capital, so he leased every single thing in his business. He leased his car, his condo, his office furniture, his office equipment, his office, and all his manufacturing equipment. Leases typically are ridiculously expensive, and therefore, he didn't make enough money for his business to survive, so he returned all his leased items, moved out of that industry, and went to another state. For a while there, he looked like a rich young man. Almost every guy in town envied him. He looked rich, but after a closer look, you could tell he was a hodad.

# The Wealth Quiz

I know what you're saying, "So Larry, how do I become wealthy?" Most everyone I know would like to be rich. They may not all be willing to admit it, but it's the truth. If this is the case, then why do so few people get rich? What do these people do to become so wealthy? Why can't everyone do that? We are going to discuss the answers to all these questions throughout this book, but first, we must ask the most important question.

# Do You Have What It Takes to Be Rich?

Let's see if you do. I have designed a test based solely on my own experience and the experiences of wealthy people I have met. Almost all of them share certain habits and characteristics. This test is not scientifically perfect, but the scoring levels measure your probability of achieving wealth.

The purpose of the wealth test is to get a picture of yourself today based upon what you have learned in the past and what you are doing now to achieve wealth. If you answer honestly, you will see what your chances would have been if you hadn't purchased this book and made the necessary adjustments. You don't have to show your results to anyone. Remember, your chances will increase once you've finished the book and implemented what you've learned. For now, let's focus on the "old you," and after the test, we'll focus on the "new you."

## The Wealth Quiz

1.  Do you enjoy your work?  Yes  No

2.  Do you often visualize yourself achieving something bigger than what you are currently doing?  Yes  No

3.  Do you save money every month?  Yes  No

4.  Do you invest at least some of your money directly in the stock market either through a 401(k), individual stocks, or mutual funds?  Yes  No

5.  Do you shop before you buy most of the time, especially for big-ticket items?  Yes  No

6.  Do you take care of your home or apartment, performing regular maintenance as well as repairs?  Yes  No

7.  Do you perform regular maintenance on your car and other expensive items?  Yes  No

8.  Do you pay off the full balance on your credit cards each month?  Yes  No

9.  Are you comfortable buying used big-ticket items such as cars and appliances?  Yes  No

10. Have you ever started your own business? (Even a lemonade stand counts.)  Yes  No

11. Have you ever estimated how much money you would need in a portfolio to produce enough income to cover your current living expenses?  Yes  No

12. Do you measure the performance results of your portfolio at least yearly?  Yes  No

13. Do you maximize your personal contribution to your IRA or company's 401(k) plan?   Yes   No

14. Is your mortgage payment less than 20 percent of your total gross household income? (If you do not own a home, is your rent less than 20 percent of your total gross household income?)   Yes   No

15. Do you spend less than you make?   Yes   No

16. Have you ever read a book about building wealth or an autobiography about someone who was wealthy?   Yes   No

17. Do you have your own business now that produces a positive net income?   Yes   No

18. Have you ever worked all night or more than 24 hours on a project?   Yes   No

For each question that you answered yes, give yourself one point.

Total these points and then compare the total to the scale below to check the probability of becoming wealthy.

| Score | Probability of Becoming Rich |
| --- | --- |
| 1–5 | Low |
| 6–10 | Average |
| 11–15 | Very likely |
| 16–18 | You are on your way! |

Even if you scored low on the test, don't worry about it. A low score simply means that if you don't change some things in your life, the probability of becoming wealthy is low. All you have to do is be willing to make some changes. Regardless of your score, you can achieve wealth. Your score just identifies your weak points. Take a moment and look at the questions to which you answered "No."

These are your areas of weakness. By identifying these areas now, you will recognize the solutions as you study this book. They reflect the areas that you need to change.

# Why Are Most People Not Wealthy?

Why is it so difficult to get rich? Most people lack the willingness to change their ways. Building wealth is a way of life. It's a mindset or paradigm that few people are willing to accept. Achieving the mindset often requires only a few simple changes in the way we think about and view life.

Most people also lack the discipline to maintain the changes. It's not easy to change, much less make the change permanent. Most people don't have the tenacity or "stick-to-it-ness" necessary to build wealth. They give up too easily.

Brian Tracy, in his famous cassette tape series, "The Psychology of Achievement," mentioned a study that was done several years ago involving a group of people who were worth more than $1 million before the age of 30. They were all asked, "How many different businesses were you involved in before you became a millionaire?" The average answer was 18. Can you imagine? What does this tell you? It tells me that achieving wealth takes a heck of a lot of tenacity and patience. You have to be willing to stick to this goal and be willing to fail more than once. I speak from experience. When I don't enjoy what I'm doing, the chances are good that I'm going to give up after failing the first few times. My money-management firm lost money during the first three years of business, but this didn't get me down. I had a passion for building my firm that would never let me quit. Now, my profit margin exceeds 50 percent.

**Wealth Warning**

Two other common ways to become wealthy include inheritance and marriage. Most people who achieve wealth in that manner do not become good stewards of their money.

**That Reminds Me...**

Motivation and accomplishment can come from adversity. The first company I worked for just out of college did not pay me bonuses I earned. When I quit, my boss yelled, "You're a quitter, a loser. You'll never get a job anywhere. You'll never achieve anything." This motivated me. All I could think about was making enough money one day to buy the company and have him work for me. Quitting enabled me to go into the investment industry—my true passion. I have no interest in buying that company any more. Maybe I should thank the guy for motivating me so much at an early age.

# The Misconceptions of Wealth

Now that I've seen both sides of the story, I've learned that there are many misconceptions regarding wealth. People simply misunderstand what wealth is and how you get it. It may sound simple, but it's the truth. I've seen it all my life. I remember that growing up as a child, I heard people make hundreds of comments about their concept of wealth. These misconceptions may hold these people back from wealth for the rest of their lives. If you hold any of these misconceptions, one of the things you should do immediately is stop using them as an excuse not to build your wealth. Here are a few of the most common misconceptions. I call them the fallacies of wealth:

➤ If I had a lot of money, my problems would go away.

➤ It would be easy to decide how to spend my money and whom to leave it to.

➤ More people will like me if I am more successful.

➤ Getting rich is something that only happens to other people.

➤ If I just had a little more money, I'd be happy.

➤ If I were wealthy, I could buy anything I want.

➤ I wish I were wealthy so I wouldn't have to worry about money anymore.

➤ I'm young; I've got plenty of time to become wealthy. Why save money now?

➤ I'm too old to start saving money.

➤ I wish I had saved more money when I was younger.

➤ There's no chance of me ever becoming wealthy. I only make $20,000 a year.

➤ The only way to get rich is inheriting the money, winning the lottery, owning commercial real estate, or starting a business.

➤ If I were really wealthy, I wouldn't care how much I paid in taxes.

I think it all boils down to one thing: Most people aren't willing to make the decisions or sacrifice it takes to become wealthy. The whole process seems too overwhelming to them. Admittedly, if you are starting with little or no money, this process of building wealth might seem overwhelming. *But it's not impossible!* If you think becoming wealthy is impossible, well, you can bet it will be. You'll never make it. Someone once said, "Argue your limitations and they're yours." Therefore, if you want to get rich, stop arguing your limitations and get busy.

# Wealth Is a Journey

Building wealth is basically a lifestyle change, just like losing weight or starting a new hobby. It's a journey, not a destination. We change our lives by changing our attitudes and perceptions. Whether you believe you *can* or you *can't*—you're right. In the end, we become exactly what we think about. If you think about what you lack, you will always lack. If you have an attitude of abundance, you will have abundance.

You will often get trapped in a comfort zone that could ultimately stalemate your efforts. Remember to be aware of these zones and don't get too comfortable. Don't be afraid of making mistakes. Mistakes will teach you everything you need to know if you're willing to learn from them.

**That Reminds Me...**

Every year, I ask my associates to give me three answers to this question: What one great thing would you dare to attempt if you knew you could not fail? My associate Angie Johnson said that she wanted to run a full marathon (26 miles). She ran a little almost everyday but had never gone beyond 5 miles at that time. Less than a year later, she ran her first marathon in 3 hours and 50 minutes. She worked very hard, never gave up, and sacrificed a lot of time to train for the event. Who knows what she'll be doing next!

Occasionally, you'll have setbacks. You can plan for most of them in advance. However, if you do fall back, all you have to do is retrace your steps and continue your journey. Remember that wealth is a journey and not a destination. When you make the decision to seek wealth, you have taken the first step on a life-long journey. Let's get started.

**The Least You Need to Know**

➤ Wealth can be built by anyone at any age who is willing to learn and develop the habits and characteristics necessary.

➤ The habits and characteristics are simple to understand and easy to implement but grossly overlooked by so many people.

➤ Start identifying the common misconceptions of wealth, and don't let them hold you back from achieving your fortune.

➤ To build real wealth, you have to believe that it can be done.

➤ Wealth is a journey that requires a high level of tenacity and determination to overcome the occasional setbacks.

# Eleven Tools for Building Wealth

Before you start any project, you must know what tools to use and how to use them. Once you know the proper tools and how they work together, the project is much easier to finish. This chapter will teach you the basic tools you need to build wealth. These tools are easy to understand and easy to use. Every industry has its own unique language, which consists of the jargon and concepts that are used every day. Because almost everyone deals with at least some financial issues, most of the terms should already be somewhat familiar. Even so, it's important to make sure that we are all using the same language for our discussions.

The concept of wealth is unique for everyone. Each person has his own definition that may or may not emphasize financial wealth. As you know, for the purpose of this book, we are focusing on financial wealth. The tools discussed in this chapter are specifically for building financial wealth.

## Tools to Build Your Wealth

Before discussing the specific definition of wealth in the next chapter, let's go over the 11 necessary tools for building wealth:

1. Investments
2. Time
3. Compounding growth
4. Living expenses
5. Risk management
6. Inflation awareness
7. Taxes minimization
8. Debt
9. Target savings goal (TSG)
10. Salary or income
11. Net worth

If you don't understand these tools, you will have trouble understanding the logic of the next chapter.

# Investments

An investment is something you can buy that has the potential of returning to you more money than you spent to buy it originally. Therefore, before you buy an investment, you have to think like an investor. Your biggest concern should be the amount of money you'll get back in the future from the investment. The second biggest concern should be the risk of volatility in the investment's value while holding it. Will the price fluctuate over time? Can you handle that? What's the risk of the investment becoming worthless? When you make a decision to buy an investment, these are the questions to ask.

**Words of the Wealthy**

An asset can be liquid or illiquid property that can be sold for cash. This can include stocks, bonds, and real estate. **Liquid assets** include those assets that can be instantly converted into cash. **Illiquid assets** are just the opposite; they are not easily converted into cash.

For the purpose of this book, the term investments primarily refers to *liquid assets*, which are securities that are traded in a regulated market such as the banking or stock markets. An asset is considered liquid if it can be easily sold for cash within an established financial market. This includes stocks, bonds, CDs (certificates of deposit), mutual funds, and foreign securities. The most common liquid assets are checking and money market accounts. You can sell or liquidate these assets and get your money within 24 hours.

A portfolio could also include *illiquid assets* such as privately held securities or commercial real estate. These assets are not easily sold for cash because you have to find a buyer yourself. However, there is absolutely nothing wrong with illiquid assets. For example, the most commonly held illiquid asset is a home. It can be sold and converted to cash, but the process can take some time. Another example of an illiquid asset is privately held stock (which is not listed on an exchange such as the New York Stock Exchange).

What's the problem with owning illiquid assets? Establishing a price tag. Illiquid assets are not always easy to value. Therefore, they must be evaluated by an expert to establish a fair market value.

Many wealthy people have built their fortunes using illiquid assets such as land, commercial buildings, and *privately held company* stock. However, these people understood the characteristics and risks unique to each particular illiquid asset. Do not attempt to get involved with illiquid assets without doing some serious homework. If you understand what you own and the market you participate in, you can make money by investing in illiquid assets.

**Words of the Wealthy**

A **privately held company** is one in which its shares are not publicly traded. Privately held stock is issued to a small number of shareholders, and the value or price of the stock is usually determined by comparisons with other similar companies using factors such as company earnings and gross income.

## The Value of Time

Most people don't realize the value of time and its effect on an investment. Time is a powerful tool. If you are in your 20s or 30s, you have an advantage over someone in her 40s or 50s. When I think of the time component, I think of an old expression, "Give me a lever long enough and I can move the world." Time works the same way with wealth. Give me enough time and I can build a fortune. The opposite is also true. The less time you have, the less likely it is that you will build any significant wealth. It's not impossible, however, to use this tool later in life. Remember Anne Scheiver in the first chapter, who began saving at the age of 50 and died with a $20 million portfolio. If she can do it, so can you.

Let's take a closer look at how important time is in the accumulation of wealth. The following table illustrates the progress of a portfolio for an early saver versus a portfolio for someone who starts saving later.

**Wealth Warning**

The tool of time can also work in reverse. The longer you wait to start your portfolio, the harder it is to build any significant wealth. A good place to start your investment portfolio is a $2,000 IRA, which can grow tax deferred until all the money is drawn out during retirement. This account allows you to combine the tools of time, compound growth, and tax deferral.

## The Early Saver Versus the Late Saver

| Age | Early Start | | | Late Start | | |
|-----|------|---------|----------|--------|---------|----------|
| 22 | $2,000 | $180 | $2,180 | $0 | $0 | $0 |
| 23 | $2,000 | $376 | $4,556 | $0 | $0 | $0 |
| 24 | $2,000 | $590 | $7,146 | $0 | $0 | $0 |
| 25 | $2,000 | $823 | $9,969 | $0 | $0 | $0 |
| 26 | $2,000 | $1,077 | $13,047 | $0 | $0 | $0 |
| 27 | $2,000 | $1,354 | $16,401 | $0 | $0 | $0 |
| 28 | $2,000 | $1,656 | $20,057 | $0 | $0 | $0 |
| 29 | $2,000 | $1,985 | $24,042 | $0 | $0 | $0 |
| 30 | $2,000 | $2,344 | $28,386 | $0 | $0 | $0 |
| 31 | $0 | $2,555 | $30,941 | $2,000 | $180 | $2,180 |
| 32 | $0 | $2,785 | $33,725 | $2,000 | $376 | $4,556 |
| 33 | $0 | $3,035 | $36,761 | $2,000 | $590 | $7,146 |
| 34 | $0 | $3,308 | $40,069 | $2,000 | $823 | $9,969 |
| 35 | $0 | $3,606 | $43,675 | $2,000 | $1,077 | $13,047 |
| 36 | $0 | $3,931 | $47,606 | $2,000 | $1,354 | $16,401 |
| 37 | $0 | $4,285 | $51,890 | $2,000 | $1,656 | $20,057 |
| 38 | $0 | $4,670 | $56,561 | $2,000 | $1,985 | $24,042 |
| 39 | $0 | $5,090 | $61,651 | $2,000 | $2,344 | $28,386 |
| 40 | $0 | $5,549 | $67,200 | $2,000 | $2,735 | $33,121 |
| 41 | $0 | $6,048 | $73,248 | $2,000 | $3,161 | $38,281 |
| 42 | $0 | $6,592 | $79,840 | $2,000 | $3,625 | $43,907 |
| 43 | $0 | $7,186 | $87,025 | $2,000 | $4,132 | $50,038 |
| 44 | $0 | $7,832 | $94,858 | $2,000 | $4,683 | $56,722 |
| 45 | $0 | $8,537 | $103,395 | $2,000 | $5,285 | $64,007 |
| 46 | $0 | $9,306 | $112,701 | $2,000 | $5,941 | $71,947 |
| 47 | $0 | $10,143 | $122,844 | $2,000 | $6,655 | $80,603 |
| 48 | $0 | $11,056 | $133,900 | $2,000 | $7,434 | $90,037 |
| 49 | $0 | $12,051 | $145,950 | $2,000 | $8,283 | $100,320 |
| 50 | $0 | $13,136 | $159,086 | $2,000 | $9,209 | $111,529 |
| 51 | $0 | $14,318 | $173,404 | $2,000 | $10,218 | $123,747 |
| 52 | $0 | $15,606 | $189,010 | $2,000 | $11,317 | $137,064 |
| 53 | $0 | $17,011 | $206,021 | $2,000 | $12,516 | $151,580 |
| 54 | $0 | $18,542 | $224,563 | $2,000 | $13,822 | $167,402 |
| 55 | $0 | $20,211 | $244,774 | $2,000 | $15,246 | $184,648 |
| 56 | $0 | $22,030 | $266,803 | $2,000 | $16,798 | $203,446 |

| Age | Early Start | | | Late Start | | |
|---|---|---|---|---|---|---|
| 57 | $0 | $24,012 | $290,815 | $2,000 | $18,490 | $223,936 |
| 58 | $0 | $26,173 | $316,989 | $2,000 | $20,334 | $246,271 |
| 59 | $0 | $28,529 | $345,518 | $2,000 | $22,344 | $270,615 |
| 60 | $0 | $31,097 | $376,614 | $2,000 | $24,535 | $297,150 |
| 61 | $0 | $33,895 | $410,510 | $2,000 | $26,924 | $326,074 |
| 62 | $0 | $36,946 | $447,456 | $2,000 | $29,527 | $357,601 |
| 63 | $0 | $40,271 | $487,727 | $2,000 | $32,364 | $391,965 |
| 64 | $0 | $43,895 | $531,622 | $2,000 | $35,457 | $429,422 |
| 65 | $0 | $47,846 | $579,468 | $2,000 | $38,828 | $470,249 |
| **Total Deposited by Each: $18,000** | | | | **$70,000** | | |

*\*Please note that this illustration is for comparison purposes only.*

*\*Taxes are not calculated into the equation.*

The first investor deposits $18,000 between the ages of 22 and 30 and ends up with a $579,468 account. The second investor gets a later start and deposits $70,000 between the ages of 31 and 65—almost four times as much money—but his account grows to only $470,249. That's a difference of $109,219. How is this possible? The first investor simply had the advantage of more time to compound the growth. Notice that by the time the second investor began saving money, the first investor's gain exceeded the second investor's deposit. Time is powerful stuff and is often completely overlooked. Use the power of time.

Time is also important during times of volatility. In a bear market, many investors lose sight of the value of time, and they focus on the short term and not the long term.

**Words of the Wealthy**

**Total return,** also known as portfolio performance, refers to the percentage return of an investment or portfolio that includes dividends, interest, and capital gains. By the way, when the total return is reinvested into the investment or portfolio, the result is compound growth.

# Compound Growth

Compound growth is different from compound interest. It is achieved when you invest in stocks (or anything that appreciates in value) over a long period of time while allowing the capital gains and dividends to reinvest into the original investment. The combination of your dividends, interest, and capital gains is also known as *total return*.

### Treasure Tip

Dr. Albert Einstein left Germany to come to the United States to escape potential conflict with Hitler. It has been said that a young reporter met Einstein when he arrived at the Port of New York and asked him what he believed was the eighth wonder of the world. Einstein replied, "I believe it is compound interest."

### Words of the Wealthy

**Harvesting** is a term I use to describe a more unconventional method of deriving income that includes not only dividends and interest, but also capital gains. You can easily obtain capital gains occasionally selling (harvesting) pieces of a portfolio that have appreciated.

Over the past seven years, I have spoken to more than two thousand investors—both successful and unsuccessful. What idea seems to be common among those who are successful is simple: Successful investors understand that compound growth is the most powerful investment tool—second only to research.

What makes compound growth so attractive is the added effect of price appreciation with reinvested interest or dividends.

The next concept is the total return on your capital. Total return consists of dividends, interest, and capital gains. A capital gain is the price appreciation realized from the sale of an asset. If you invest in real estate, your portfolio might also produce rental income. Total return is also known as portfolio gains, portfolio performance, and portfolio growth.

The most confusing concept about total return involves taking regular monthly income from your portfolio, which is most commonly necessary once retirement begins. When taking income from a liquid portfolio for living expenses, most investors look only at dividends and interest (cash flow). They pay little, if any, attention to capital gain because they claim it's not reliable. This is conventional thinking.

In the long run, capital gains can be reliable from a properly diversified portfolio. Whether you are building wealth in the early years or maintaining wealth in the later years, you should not ignore capital gains. You should harvest them over time and consider them part of the cash flow. This unconventional concept of *harvesting* might be new to you; that's okay. To build and maintain the levels of wealth this book discusses, you must think unconventionally.

### That Reminds Me...

The rule of 72 estimates how fast money can compound over time. Divide the number 72 by the rate of return you expect to receive. The result is the number of years it will take for your money to double. If you get 6 percent, your money would double in 12 years. If you get 8 percent, your money would double in 9 years; if 10 percent, 7.2 years; if 12 percent, 6 years. It also works in reverse. Divide the number 72 by the number of years you have to invest. The result is the percentage of total return you need to double the portfolio. This equation measures pure compound growth without the effect of any taxes. Therefore, it works best in measuring the growth of tax deferred accounts such as 401(k)s and qualified plans.

## Living Expenses

There are many different categories of expenses. Variable expenses cover entertainment, clothing, and travel. Fixed expenses are rent or mortgage payments. Living expenses might seem like a relatively boring subject, but most people don't understand just how important the expense component can be in building wealth. When you are just beginning to build your portfolio, the amount of money you spend monthly for expenses directly affects the speed of your journey to wealth. If you are accustomed to a high standard of living with no willingness to be flexible, your chances of saving money in the early years are small.

I truly believe that the main reason people don't save money is that they are unwilling to limit their standard of living. I mostly see this unwillingness in young couples but also notice it in older retired couples. In the later years, especially during retirement, if you spend more than your portfolio produces, you deplete your capital source or principal. I now have a client who started with a $100,000 retirement account. For the past two

### Wealth Warning

Ignoring your spending habits relative to your income will quickly get you into hot water.

### Wealth Warning

You must be willing to make some sacrifices now to build wealth in the future.

years, this client has lived beyond his means, and the account is now worth only $33,000. His portfolio grew faster than the world stock market index but didn't grow fast enough to keep up with his spending habits. This scenario is a nightmare that didn't have to happen. The client did not measure spending habits, ignored his resources, and now has a big problem. Don't let this scenario happen to you. It's important to understand that systematic measurement of your monthly expenses is vital to the wealth-building process. (I show you how to do this in Chapter 3, "The Five Stages of Wealth.")

# Risk Management

I discuss the many different types of risk in more detail later. For our purposes in this chapter, the two basic types of risk are portfolio and situational. Portfolio risk can be defined as the volatility (the potential to rise or fall quickly) of the total portfolio value. Some investors are willing to accept higher levels of volatility for higher rates of return. Return is your reward for your willingness to assume risk. In general, risk can increase your potential for return, but it can also lead to more potential for loss. Setting proper return goals involves determining your acceptable level of risk.

**Wealth Warning**

Risk tolerance is the degree to which an investor can live with the volatility of his or her portfolio. When asked, most investors tend to overestimate their tolerance for risk. However, when confronted with significantly poor performance or losses from an investment, they fully understand their true tolerance.

Situational risk is the chance you'll experience health problems, premature death, a disability, an automobile accident, or another liability. Each of these risks has the potential of ruining your journey toward building serious financial wealth. However, you can manage each of these risks using the right insurance tool. A wealthy person understands these risks and manages each type efficiently using the right insurance tools. Therefore, insurance is also an important tool.

# Inflation Awareness

Inflation is what happens when too many dollars chase too little goods. It takes place when the economy is growing strong, wages are high, and consumers are spending a lot of money. For example, during a time of increased consumer spending, retailers can easily raise prices a little without bothering the consumer much. The opposite is also true. If the economy is not growing strongly, wages are low, and consumers are not spending a lot of money, then retailers may have to drop prices. This situation is called disinflation.

Inflation is simply an increase in the price of goods and services. The most important thing to remember about inflation is that it will affect your future living expenses. I remember 10 cent sodas and 25 cent hamburgers. What costs a dollar today may cost five dollars in the future. You must take inflation into account when making projections about the future. The easy way to measure and project inflation is to use the Consumer Price Index (CPI), which is the yearly growth rate of the total price of a basket of consumer goods. All financial publications show this rate as the CPI. It isn't a perfect measurement, but most economists use it. You will need to know this index in Chapter 3 when I show you how to project your future living expenses.

### That Reminds Me...

Tabulated by the U.S. Government's Bureau of Labor Statistics, the CPI measures the cost of a representative basket of consumer goods, which might include a loaf of bread, a gallon of milk, or a hamburger. The price of the basket is not that important. The most important aspect of CPI is the rate of change from one month to another. The amount of change from month to month in the cost of this basket of goods is stated as a percentage of the CPI for the previous month. This percentage is known as the rate of inflation and is usually quoted as an annualized percentage. This measurement appears in the *Wall Street Journal* in Section A at approximately the middle of the month.

## Taxes Minimization

When I mention taxes, I am referring to all federal, state, and local income taxes. Specifically, in the next chapter, you will need to know your overall income tax rate. An easy way to calculate this is to add up the federal, state, and local taxes you paid last year and divide that amount by your gross income. This will give you your income tax rate. If you need help calculating this, ask your CPA.

(Federal + State + Local Taxes) ÷ Gross Annual Income = Your Income Tax Rate

For example, if you had a gross income of $30,000 with federal taxes of $3,540 and state taxes of $1,344, your average income tax rate equals 16.28 percent.

Taxes can be avoided or deferred using certain investment vehicles. However, the most important goal of an investor should be to make money, not avoid taxes. If you focus primarily on avoiding taxes, you might accomplish your goal, but I can promise you that you will not make much money in the process. Later in this book, I discuss some ways you can defer taxes without sacrificing total return.

# Debt

Debt is simply a loan, which can include a home mortgage, personal loans, business loans, and lines of credit. Don't get me wrong: Debt can be a big problem in the wealth-building process. However, it can also be a great tool. If you want to build serious wealth, you need a good relationship with a banker who can service your needs properly. The most common healthy debt tools include a home mortgage, business loans, and lines of credit. All of these tools can help you leverage your wealth (or cash flow) in order to afford a home, invest in a business, or cushion cash-flow problems.

### Words of the Wealthy

You're **upside down** when you borrow money to buy a car and the value of the car drops below the total value of the loan.

I have a few notes of caution that I discuss fully later in the book. I do not recommend the use of margin in an investment account. A margin loan is simply a loan against the securities in your account. I also do not recommend loans for purchases that improve your self-image, such as fancy cars and boats. My hope is that this book helps you look at everything you buy, especially when you borrow money to buy it, as an investment. As I said previously, your biggest concern is the amount of money you'll get back in the future from the investment. The risk gets worse if you get *upside down*. You're upside down when you borrow money to buy something, and it falls in value so much that the money you owe exceeds the value of the item.

# Target Savings Goal

An important concept for building wealth is the amount of money you save every month or every year. The two terms I use in this book are *target savings goal (TSG)* and actual savings. Your target savings goal (TSG) is the amount of money you need to save

### Words of the Wealthy

Your **target savings goal,** or **TSG,** refers to the amount of money required each year to build a portfolio large enough to support your preferred standard of living at retirement.

every year in order to build a portfolio large enough to produce a total return by a certain date (usually retirement) that will sustain your standard of living plus keep up with inflation. I realize that this definition might be a mouthful, but, don't worry, it's simpler than it seems. I discuss this concept step-by-step in Chapter 4 and make it easy for you.

Your actual savings amount is just what it says: the difference between your total household income and expenses. This surplus is what goes into your investment account. If there is money available for savings, you are living within your means and that's great. If you have a negative actual savings amount, you are living beyond your means, and that's not good at all.

The actual savings amount is important in the early stages of your life. Therefore, your focus should be on saving and investing as much as you can when you are young. During the first years of saving when your portfolio is small, total return is relatively less important than the amount of money you save (the deposits you make). The deposits you make at first will dwarf the amount of money you make on your investments (the dividends and gains). Therefore, your early years of saving is a great time to learn about investing. When you are new to the game of investing, you tend to make a lot of mistakes. If you can make those mistakes early, when the returns have less effect on your overall portfolio, you save your portfolio from harm later when your return really counts.

## Salary or Income

Before you can save any money, you have to be making money, which most people refer to as cash flow. The most common source of cash flow is a salary. The idea behind this book is that you spend less than your salary so that after taxes, you have some excess cash flow to save and invest. Your salary is a key tool in the wealth-building process.

Most people believe that your salary is the most important tool. The bigger the salary, the more you have to spend and invest. This is certainly true. However, many people get caught up more in the spending rather than the investing. Increasing your salary is wonderful for the wealth-building process if you can discipline yourself to save more as you make more. As I've illustrated for you in the last chapter, a hefty salary is not necessary to build significant wealth. Don't get discouraged if your salary isn't as high as you want it to be. By all means, do what you can to maximize your salary, but don't get so caught up that you lose sight of other tools such as compound growth, time, and controlling expenses.

**Treasure Tip**

Compound interest refers to fixed income investments where interest is earned and reinvested causing a compounding effect. Compound growth *is* different in that it refers to stocks and other investments that appreciate in value causing a potentially faster compounding effect. Compound growth over time allows even moderate rates of return to produce great wealth.

## Net Worth

Building your net worth is the goal of this book. The definition of net worth is the value of your assets and investments minus your debt or liabilities:

> Assets – Liabilities = Net Worth

The idea is to increase assets and decrease liabilities. In reality, you may find yourself increasing liabilities temporarily in order to increase assets at a future date. The key is to focus on assets that grow over time. The most powerful asset to own is usually stock in your own business, which I discuss in Part 3, "Building Wealth with Your Own Business." The second most powerful tool is stock in someone else's business, which I discuss in the next few chapters.

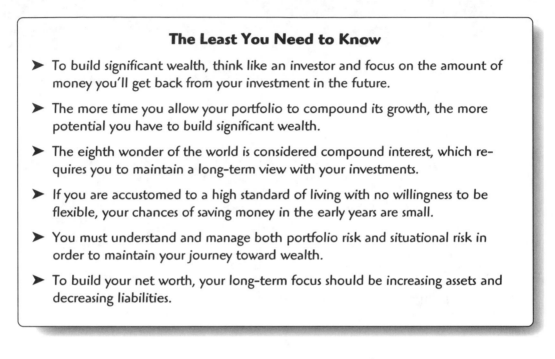

### The Least You Need to Know

➤ To build significant wealth, think like an investor and focus on the amount of money you'll get back from your investment in the future.

➤ The more time you allow your portfolio to compound its growth, the more potential you have to build significant wealth.

➤ The eighth wonder of the world is considered compound interest, which requires you to maintain a long-term view with your investments.

➤ If you are accustomed to a high standard of living with no willingness to be flexible, your chances of saving money in the early years are small.

➤ You must understand and manage both portfolio risk and situational risk in order to maintain your journey toward wealth.

➤ To build your net worth, your long-term focus should be increasing assets and decreasing liabilities.

# Chapter 3

# The Five Stages of Wealth

**In This Chapter**

➤ Calculating your current net worth

➤ How to calculate your stage of wealth

➤ What you should focus on when attempting to achieve each stage

➤ How to get through these stages faster

➤ When saving money becomes less important

Everyone's definition of financial wealth is different. To make things simple, I've defined five specific, measurable stages of wealth. These stages reduce the confusion surrounding the concept of wealth by breaking down the definition into easy-to-understand pieces.

The first thing you must realize in your search for a personal definition of wealth is that your definition will always be a relative term. Relative to what? A poor immigrant family might say that being rich means having an apartment with running water and a roof overhead. You might like to be wealthy relative to your neighbor or friend. I was guilty of this when I was a young man in my 20s. I found myself constantly in a battle to build more wealth than that of other people I knew. The only problem was that I constantly met new people who were wealthier than the last. The benchmark kept moving, and it always seemed out of reach. Your idea of wealth should be defined relative to your desired standard of living—not your neighbor's or your friend's. Be realistic about this standard, and focus on what income stage makes you happy. Your life will be a lot easier, and you will feel more fulfilled in the process.

To learn more about wealth, you must associate yourself with wealthy people. You can do this through clubs, non-profit organizations, church, and friends who can introduce you. An alternative is to read books about wealthy people. You need to learn how they think, how they got there, and what is important to them—their values.

# What Is Your Net Worth?

The most common way to define your current stage of wealth is to measure your net worth. When you go to a bank and apply for a loan, one of the first things they want is a net worth statement. This statement lists both liquid and illiquid assets, subtracts your liabilities (debts you owe, such as your mortgage), and results in a bottom-line net worth amount. Take a moment and copy the following net worth statement. Fill it out and calculate your net worth today. Be sure to date it so you'll be able to look back and compare in the future.

## Net Worth Statement

| Assets | Total Value |
|---|---|
| Cash | _____ |
| Money market funds | _____ |
| Savings account | _____ |
| Real estate (estimated current market value) | _____ |
| Residence | _____ |
| Farm | _____ |
| Other | _____ |
| *Investments* | |
| Individual stocks | _____ |
| Individual bonds | _____ |
| Mutual funds | _____ |
| 401(k) | _____ |
| IRA | _____ |
| Other retirement plans | _____ |
| Closely held business (estimated current market value) | _____ |
| Equity interest | _____ |
| *Personal Assets* | |
| Automobile | _____ |
| Jewelry | _____ |
| Other | _____ |
| **Total Assets** | _____ |

| Assets | Total Value |
|---|---|
| *Liabilities* | |
| Personal line of credit (short term) | _____ |
| Home mortgage(s) | _____ |
| Automobile loan(s) | _____ |
| Other | _____ |
| **Total Liabilities** | _____ |
| **Net Worth (Total Assets Minus Total Liabilities)** | _____ |

Now that you understand the 11 key wealth concepts from Chapter 2, "Eleven Tools for Building Wealth," let's discuss the five stages of wealth. Please understand these stages are my definitions. Each person has his or her own definition of wealth, which might not involve anything financial. Wealth to one person might be extensive wisdom. Wealth to another might be artistic ability. This book focuses on financial wealth.

For this book, I have defined five stages of financial wealth; each stage is defined relative to your current or desired standard of living.

# Wealth Stage 1

The beginning of your journey is Stage 1. At this stage, you are able to maintain your standard of living and save enough money to achieve your target savings goal. This stage is as easy to achieve as you make it. It usually involves only a simple mindset change. When you live within your means and your actual savings amount equals or exceeds your TSG, you've made it to Wealth Stage 1. It's the easiest stage to achieve and can be your wealth safeguard if you fail at other stages.

Don't misunderstand: Wealth Stage 1 has nothing to do with looking wealthy or building a financially wealthy outer image. In fact, in many ways, it means to do just the opposite. If you really want to achieve Stage 1, you may have to simplify your life and reduce expenses in order to achieve your target savings goal. Building wealth is not about buying fancy cars and clothes. It's about living within your means. If you can't handle this concept, you'll never achieve significant wealth.

Most people would love to build wealth. However, many get caught up in the glamour and excitement of spending rather than saving. The end result is that they don't live within their means, and they never even make it to Stage 1.

**Wealth Warning**

The attitude today in the U.S. seems to be "spend now, save later." Although Southeast Asians save more than 30 percent of their income, we only save about 4 percent. If this keeps up, we are going to have a serious problem.

The wealthy people I know each have a passion. They spend their time and energy focusing on what they're passionate about, which usually doesn't cost too much money.

Several of my favorite clients with net worths more than $1 million spend their time doing home-improvement projects. I don't mean just painting. These people redo entire bathrooms and kitchens themselves. They love it, and they make money when they sell the home.

You don't have to be a home-improvement expert to be wealthy. You just need to be aware of how you're spending your time and money. Could you be more productive with your time and still follow your passion? My passion is writing and teaching people how to build and maintain wealth. I can't think of many things that could be more fun. Does it cost a lot of money to do that? No! In fact, the only money I'm spending now is on the electric bill. I talk more in Chapter 5, "The Secrets of Millionaires," about how to find your passion and later how you might be able to make money with that passion.

## What's Your Focus Here?

To make it to Wealth Stage 1, the most important thing is your actual savings amount. This will affect the portfolio much more than the compound growth on your portfolio. For now, compound growth is of secondary importance. The most common mistake made by neophyte investors is that they focus too much on compound growth. Consequently, many of them end up taking too much risk and losing their money. To achieve and maintain this stage, you should focus on maximizing your actual savings amount as much as you possibly can.

During your journey toward Wealth Stage 1, you should also focus on learning as much as you can about investment management and learn from your mistakes now. These mistakes, if made now, will not have nearly the effect they will later when your account is larger and the mistakes are harder to recover from. For example, a common mistake made by neophyte investors is the use of futures and options contracts, which is not a wise way to start investing. I know because I did it and lost a lot of money. However, I'm glad I did this in the early part of my life. It taught me early to stick with stocks, bonds, and mutual funds.

### Wealth Warning

Let's face it: Saving money is boring to most people. Commercial advertisements and our "give it to me now" society makes spending fun. To many people, shopping is an escape. Some people even use this experience to make them feel and look wealthy. Ironically, it takes more energy to shop and spend than it does to save money.

### Treasure Tip

You don't need a college education to earn a high income, but it does help. According to Census Bureau surveys in 1993, less than 6 percent of U.S. households earn more than $100,000 per year, 68 percent of which are headed by college graduates. The median household income of college graduates is $55,000, which is 76 percent higher than the median income for all households.

It may be easier to conquer Stage 1 in steps. For example, you could set your first target savings goal at 5 percent of your net monthly income. The second goal could be 10 percent; third, 15 percent; and so on. The last step is to save your true total TSG. If you save in slowly increasing amounts over time and continue this habit through life as your income increases, you will dramatically increase your chances of reaching Wealth Stages 2 through 5.

Setting and sticking to a savings goal may sound easy, but I know so few people who do. Most are unwilling to cut back their standard of living in order to save the 10 percent, or they are unwilling to try harder for more income. They procrastinate, never save any money, have too much pride to cut back their spending, borrow too much to keep up with the neighbors, or just never think about the future. Whatever the reason, they will never achieve the stage of wealth they desire.

# Wealth Stage 2

At the beginning of Wealth Stage 2, your portfolio is large enough to produce, on its own, compound growth each year equal to your TSG. That means you have now, in essence, doubled your TSG: One part comes from your monthly TSG deposit and the other part from portfolio gains. You've really harnessed the power of compound growth. The combined effect of your TSG deposit and compound growth produces enormous portfolio growth power for you.

## *What's Your Focus Here?*

Because at this stage your actual savings amount and compound growth are equal, they become equally important. You must focus on both components. This is also the stage of wealth where knowledge of risk becomes vital to the remainder of the wealth-building process. Unfortunately, most people wait until this stage to begin learning about risks. Bad investment decisions made in Wealth Stage 2 are more costly than they would have been in Stage 1.

You haven't completed Wealth Stage 2 when your portfolio's annual return equals your TSG. There are actually three steps to this stage. Stage 2 continues as your portfolio produces a compound growth equal to two times your TSG. Therefore, your portfolio is growing by three times your TSG. One part is your actual TSG deposit, and the other two parts come from portfolio performance. The most important component becomes compound growth. Your actual savings amount still helps speed the process, but compound growth is more important and powerful. If compound growth is twice the size of your actual savings amount, then

### Wealth Warning

There are four categories of risks involving stocks: specific issue risk, which involves the risk of the individual company; industry risk, the company's industry; country risk, the risk of the country in which the company resides; and world risk, the risk of the world market.

your downside risk is also twice as big. This makes mistakes more difficult to recover from. Suddenly, compound growth becomes important, and therefore, making the right investment decisions becomes paramount. This certainly also makes risk management vital.

You've reached the third step of Wealth Stage 2 when your portfolio produces a compound growth equal to three times your TSG. The compounding effect is expanding your portfolio three times faster than your own deposit. Now the relative effect of an additional deposit equal to your TSG has little influence on the growth of the portfolio. That doesn't mean you need to stop saving money! It just means that compound growth is vital, and investment management has never before been so important.

# Wealth Stage 3

If your portfolio produces compound growth large enough to cover your desired lifestyle and inflation, then congratulations! You've made it to Wealth Stage 3. Employment is optional, and your money is working hard for you. According to my research, only about 5 percent of the population achieve this stage of wealth by retirement age. Most of my clients have made it to this stage. They enjoy life and they have the option to work. They have more freedom to focus on what they love to do. Ironically, most of them don't retire at this point if they enjoy what they do. If they don't enjoy their work, they often make the changes necessary to get into what they do enjoy the most.

Retirement is only a transition into another passion. Once people make the decision to retire, or at least slow down, their living expenses usually decrease. Maybe they take more vacations and spend more money, but they still live within their means. The habit is so ingrained that they actually feel uncomfortable spending more than normal, even if they can afford it. My "retired" clients are like most wealthy people in the world. They built their wealth over a long period of time by living well within their means, and they maintain their wealth by continuing to do the same.

**Wealth Warning**

Our Social Security system has produced a population of citizens who believe in their right to a subsidized comfortable retirement. After seeing thousands of workers realize their benefits are much less than they expected, I came to the conclusion that my comfortable retirement depends on me and my efforts.

## *What's Your Focus Here?*

The most important component in Wealth Stage 3 is compound growth. The amount of money you're saving is probably dwarfed by the effect of compound growth. Likewise, your potential downside is also significant, which reduces your ability to recover from a loss using additional deposits. Therefore, the second most important tool is risk. This is especially true if you are no longer earning a salary. If you're not comfortable managing your own portfolio when it's this large, you'd better get some help.

If you are relying upon your portfolio for income (such as to pay your living expenses after you retire), you have to focus on two components: compound growth and living expenses. If you spend more than your portfolio produces, over the long run, you'll erode your income-generating capital and drop back into Stage 1 or 2 with no source of income to replace what you lost. The wealthy people I know in this stage prevent this from happening by simply making it a habit to live well within their means. They always spend less than their total income.

# Wealth Stage 4

You have accumulated enough assets to produce compound growth sufficient enough to substantially increase your desired lifestyle, while at the same time keep up with inflation. If you've made it beyond Stage 3 and you've built your portfolio big enough to support your dream lifestyle, you've made it to Wealth Stage 4. You now have the option not to work and, at the same time, raise your standard of living. You might buy a bigger home, travel more, or just spend more money. You not only have enough compound growth to cover your desired lifestyle, but you also have a little extra to build your portfolio further.

### That Reminds Me...

According to official Social Security projections, in 1990 only 4 percent of Americans were over 65. By 2040, the figure will be approximately 25 percent. The number of Social Security beneficiaries will more than double by the year 2040. In 1960, there were 5.1 taxpaying workers to support each Social Security beneficiary. Today, there are 3.3. By 2040, there will be no more than 2, perhaps as few as 1.6. One of four things must happen: We must raise taxes, raise the official Social Security retirement age, radically change the existing Social Security system, or radically change our own personal retirement savings program. The only option we completely control is the last one.

Only about 1 percent of the population make it to Wealth Stage 4. Most people aren't willing to take the time to plan, make the sacrifices, or take the risk. That's right: This stage involves planning, sacrifices, and risk. There's that word risk again! After reading this book, you will understand more about risk and how to manage it properly.

Many of the individuals who make it to this stage are business owners. Their wealth was built from net income, the sale of the business, or both. You can certainly make it to this level without having your own business. This book will show you how.

## What's Your Focus Here?

Your two master components are compound growth and risk management. The portfolio is very large, and you might want to focus on reducing volatility. You can do this yourself, but it must be a hobby you enjoy. Most Wealth Stage 4 people hire help in the investment management process. Chapter 9, "How to Find Help," shows you how.

# Wealth Stage 5

You have accumulated enough assets to produce compound growth well beyond what you would ever spend. You now have the option not to work, raise your standard of living, and bestow large charitable gifts. Once you reach this stage, you need some serious estate-planning help.

If you want to make it to this stage, you could become a famous movie star or corporate executive with a lot of stock options. However, the most common way people make it to this stage is through the sale of a large cash-generating asset such as a business or commercial real estate. You can also get there by building and selling a company. It happens all the time. Just look at the stories in Chapter 1, "Are You Going to Be Rich?"

**Wealth Warning**

Many of the teenagers and 20-year-olds today who are living with their parents in order to save money are actually spending what they save on their image by buying cool clothes and nice cars. This makes them look and feel successful, but they never seem to save enough money to go to college or have their own apartment, much less a home.

## What's Your Focus Here?

What do you think Wealth Stage 5 people focus on in regard to their money? I can tell you from experience that the answer is risk. The master component is risk and more specifically management of risk. When you make it to this stage, you tend to focus on protection of principal. It doesn't matter whether you make 5 percent or 15 percent on your portfolio. Your needs are covered either way. Therefore, you tend to focus on maintenance instead of compound growth. First, you want to reduce the possibility of a substantial loss. Second, you want to maintain an adequate rate of return.

Certainly, it is great to achieve this stage of wealth, but most people would be content with Stage 3 or 4. Therefore, this book focuses primarily on the first four stages. Making Stage 5 your goal is certainly noble, but it's silly when Stage 4 covers all your needs. Most people who achieve this stage focused on their passion and not necessarily the achievement of this stage of wealth. This idea is important, and I discuss it later. Following your passion is an important element in the wealth-building process.

# How Can You Get There Faster?

You can skip some stages completely if you are starting a business that you believe could substantially increase your income and net worth. This process might get you to Stage 3 or 4 faster. If you take this route, get ready for an exciting ride. There's more risk of failure, and recovery time might be slow depending upon the damage done if the business fails. Therefore, you must be willing to accept failure and keep on going. Before skipping stages and starting your own business, you must be willing to accept the worst thing that can happen. I was willing to accept the risk years ago when I started my own business. I'm glad I did. Would I do it again? You bet I would—even if I couldn't manage money. As long as I had a vision and was excited about it, I would do it. Later in Part 3, "Building Wealth with Your Own Business," I discuss how you can develop your own vision and improve your chances of success in your own business. You must be willing to accept big failures and know that you can bounce back in the face of adversity. Remember the story of Abraham Lincoln in Chapter 1.

---

### The Least You Need to Know

➤ Your idea of wealth should be based upon your desired standard of living, not your neighbor's.

➤ If you really want to build wealth, don't buy the fancy cars and clothes; keep things simple and live well within your means.

➤ Take one wealth stage at a time and focus on what's important in each stage.

➤ In Stage 1, focus on the amount you save and then on the amount of return and risk you want.

➤ In the later stages, focus on managing the risk in your portfolio.

# Chapter 4

---

# How to Become a Saver

## In This Chapter

➤ Developing your Wealth Stage 1 formula

➤ How to increase your income

➤ How to decrease expenses

➤ Calculating how much money you need to consider yourself wealthy

➤ How to stay on track with your plan

Mark Twain once said, "The secret of getting ahead is getting started. The secret of getting started is breaking your complex overwhelming tasks into small manageable tasks and then starting on the first one." Most people never achieve any significant wealth because they have no idea how to build wealth or even how to get started. There's no class or television show that really shows you how to do it. You might find a few late-night infomercials that sound pretty convincing, but they're really working on their own get-rich agenda to sell you a product. You might find a few books on the subject, but rarely do you find an actual formula that works. If you do find a formula, it is probably either too complicated or too ambiguous. Therefore, I sat down and designed an easy step-by-step formula that would help others get to Wealth Stage 1. It's simple to complete, and it should be your first step in your journey toward wealth. Let's get started.

# Wealth Is a Journey, Not a Destination

I've learned that wealth achieved over a long period of time tends to be appreciated more and wealth acquired suddenly tends to be squandered. This is especially evident among lottery winners. An article in the *New York Times* (4/23/95) titled "Ticket to Trouble" stated, "There are no statistics on what happens to jackpot winners. But a growing body of evidence suggests that winning big often brings big, if not ruinous trouble." For example, William Post of Oil City, PA, won a $16.2 million jackpot in 1988. Five years later, he was completely broke, and his brother was in jail charged with hiring a hit man to murder William and his wife for the lottery money.

### Treasure Tip

The great wealth hunter Waschka says, "If you always hunt elephants, you may die of starvation. But if you focus on the easier little game like rabbits and birds, you'll be better prepared when the elephant comes along."

### Treasure Tip

Looking back at all the wealthy people I've met in my life, it seems that the ones who built their own wealth slowly over time seem to appreciate and maintain it better than those who inherited or married it.

Why do these lottery winners end up in so much trouble? Think about it a minute. They win the lottery, suddenly they feel like they're rich, they begin spending money like never before, and they pay little attention to planning for the future. Who cares about the future when you're rich and you have all this money coming in? That's the problem. These winners see wealth as a destination, and they feel as if they have definitely arrived. What they don't understand is that wealth is a journey, not a destination. You can't get to Wealth Stage 3 and go nuts. You have to continue to be a good steward of your money, which requires some responsibility.

If you want to achieve and maintain wealth throughout your lifetime, you must see wealth as a journey. How most people view wealth is that you hit it big somehow (get rich quick) and then live the good life. If that's your view, stop right now and erase this vision from your mind. Wealth is a way of life. It is a set of beliefs and habits, rather than something material that you attain and then sit back and relax. For example, wealth is born from the initial habit of living within your means. As you saw in Chapter 3, "The Five Stages of Wealth," this journey has many levels and transitions, and most people don't understand them. If you take the time to plan and prepare for each step or transition, you improve your chances of becoming and staying wealthy. It also helps to be patient along the way, especially at the beginning of your journey.

Let's begin your journey by focusing on accomplishing the first level of wealth. Here are the steps to follow:

1. Analyze your current income—and focus on maximizing it.

2. Analyze your current spending habits—and focus on minimizing spending.

3. Estimate how much you need to cover your future expenses (such as your living expenses after retirement) in before-tax dollars.

4. Project the effect of inflation on expenses.

5. Estimate your target portfolio amount (the amount of money you'll need in your portfolio to retire).

6. Estimate your yearly and monthly target savings goal.

7. Achieve your target savings goal.

8. Maintain your plan.

What you are about to embark on is a simple process of estimating income and expenses to find an approximate target savings goal. You could get really serious here with this exercise and build a complex model of expense analysis and wealth projections. If you have a lot of free time on your hands, go for it. I suggest using computer spreadsheets or personal finance software that will do all the calculations for you. To make things easy for now, let's establish some approximate goals so you can at least get started. This chapter walks you, in detail, through each of the steps in the Wealth Builder Worksheet, particularly those steps that require calculations. Read the chapter before using the worksheet, and then make numerous copies of the tearcard in the front of the book so you can update it from year to year to review your progress toward your goals. If you read this chapter before you complete the worksheet, you will understand everything much better.

I've included two examples for you to use. The first is illustrated in the worksheet and the second is illustrated in the text. Both are different and are only there to help you better understand the process.

## Wealth Builder Worksheet

1. What is your current yearly income?_____

   Let's say it's $30,000

2. What are your monthly and annual expenses?

   Enter your monthly expenses and multiply by 12:

   _____ × 12 = _____

   (Monthly expenses) × 12 = Yearly expenses

   Don't forget to add any additional expenses you see coming in the next year.

   Assuming your monthly expenses are $1,000 a month, that's $12,000 per year.

   *continues*

*continued*

3. Estimate the income needed to cover your expenses in before-tax dollars.

   Calculate the inverse of your total average tax rate by subtracting your average tax rate from one:

   1.00 –_____ =_____

   1.00 – (Total federal, state, and local income tax rate percentage) = Inverse rate

   If your total tax rate was 28 percent, your inverse would be 72% (1.00 – .28 = .72).

   Convert yearly expenses into a before-tax amount by dividing your yearly expenses by the inverse rate.

   _____ ÷ _____ = _____

   (Total yearly expenses) ÷ (Inverse rate) = Pretax yearly expenses

   Your before tax amount would be $16,666 ($12,000 ÷ .72 = $16,666)

4. Project the effect of inflation on expenses.

   _____ × _____ = _____

   (Pre-tax yearly expenses) × (1.00 + Inflation estimate) = Yearly inflated expenses

   Continue this calculation for every year until retirement to get the amount of money you need each year to cover expenses at retirement.

   If you assume the inflation rate to be 2 percent, here's what your calculation would look like for the first ten years (rounded to the nearest tenth):

   | Year 1 | $16,666 × 1.02 = 16,999 |
   | Year 2 | $16,999 × 1.02 = 17,339 |
   | Year 3 | $17,339 × 1.02 = 17,686 |
   | Year 4 | $17,686 × 1.02 = 18,040 |
   | Year 5 | $18,040 × 1.02 = 18,401 |
   | Year 6 | $18,401 × 1.02 = 18,769 |
   | Year 7 | $18,769 × 1.02 = 19,144 |
   | Year 8 | $19,144 × 1.02 = 19,527 |
   | Year 9 | $19,527 × 1.02 = 19,917 |
   | Year 10 | $19,917 × 1.02 = 20,315 |

In ten years, your expenses will be $20,315 assuming an inflation rate of 2 percent. By the way, this is much easier to do on a computer spreadsheet if you have access to one.

5. Estimate your Target Portfolio Goal (TPG).

_____ ÷ _____ =

_____

(Yearly inflated expenses) ÷ (Estimated net rate of return) = Target Portfolio Goal

Let's assume you'll retire in ten years (that may not be realistic, but let's use the numbers above), and you'll need $16,127 in income. If you could make a 12 percent rate of return on your portfolio, your target portfolio goal would be (20,315 ÷ .12 = 169,292) $169,292. However, remember that this assumes you'll spend all of your total return on your portfolio. You may want to only spend 75 percent of it so that it keeps growing. If so, use a 9 percent rate of return (.75 × 12 percent).

6. Estimate yearly and monthly TSGs.

Your yearly TSG is calculated by dividing your TPG by the Future Value Factor, which appears in the future value table in this chapter:

_____ ÷ _____ = _____

(Target Portfolio Goal) ÷ (Future Value Factor) = Yearly TSG

Find your monthly TSG calculation by dividing your yearly TSG by 12:

_____ ÷ 12 = _____

(Yearly TSG) ÷ 12 = Monthly TSG

Using the 19.6546 factor from the "Future Value of Annuity" chart (see Table 4.4) that corresponds to 12 percent and 10 years, your yearly TSG would be (169,292 ÷ 19.6546 = 8,613) $8,613 and your monthly TSG would be (8,613 ÷ 12 = 717.75) $717.75.

7. Now that you know your TSG, it's time to make it happen.

8. Once you've made it happen and you've achieved Wealth Stage 1, do all you can to maintain your savings amount.

43

# Step 1: Measure and Maximize Your Current Income

Write down on a piece of paper your current yearly salary or income before tax. Under that amount, write this question: What can I do to increase my income now and in the future? Find a peaceful place of solitude and complete 20 answers to this question. If you can't come up with 20 answers, ask a friend to help you. Here are a few ideas to get you started:

➤ Ask the boss for a raise; prepare a proposal that illustrates what you would do for the raise.

➤ Offer to take on more responsibility for more pay.

➤ Start a small income-generating business on the side.

➤ Consider a second job.

➤ Present an idea at work that will make the company more profitable.

➤ Find another job that will pay you what you're worth.

Afterwards, select the best answers and make an effort to implement them. If building wealth is really important to you, you'll take the time to complete this step. As I've mentioned in Chapter 1, "Are You Going to Be Rich?" your journey toward wealth doesn't require a huge salary. However, if you at least attempt to maximize your income, you might shorten the distance you have to travel. There are so many different ways to do this. If you're creative and proactive by nature, you'll have no problem. In Chapter 6, "An Employee's Guide to Building Wealth," I discuss several techniques you can use to maximize your salary if you work for others. In Part 3, "Building Wealth with Your Own Business," I discuss ways to maximize your net income if you're self-employed.

The ultimate goal in this step is to calculate the amount of yearly income you want to make before taxes and 401(k) contributions. What amount of income do you need to be happy? Before you answer this question, you might want to complete Step 2 regarding expenses.

**Treasure Tip**

In 1993, census reports claimed that 205,623 households in the U.S. had incomes of more than $500,000. Of the 2.7 million people making more than $100,000, 89 percent are men, 81 percent are married, 49 percent had postgraduate or professional degrees, and 31 percent had only bachelor's degrees.

# Step 2: Measure and Maximize Your Current Expenses

What are your current yearly expenses? How much money do you spend each month? If you're married, how much do both of you spend? The best way to keep track of this is by keeping pen and paper with you for a month. This sounds like a lot of trouble, but remember, we're talking about building your wealth. I always find that whatever is measured seems to improve. If you take the time to do this, you will learn a lot about yourself and quickly see where your money is going. Do this for one month and calculate your actual monthly expenditures. Then, multiply the result by 12. This should give you an approximate idea of your yearly expenses. You could also perform a quick analysis of your checkbook and credit card statements for the last month to get an idea of how most of your money is being spent. You could estimate your cash expenditures by calculating how much cash you've taken out of your account for the month.

If you prefer a more structured approach, the Weekly Expense Worksheet is designed for you to copy four times, one for each week of the month. (Make five copies if the current month spans five weeks.) You might want to enlarge it to fit a full page. Take a sheet with you and begin recording now. If possible, record every penny you spend for one month. This includes all cash, credit, and checkbook expenditures.

**Treasure Tip**

All work and no play makes Jack a dull boy. Don't forget to record the money you spend for entertainment as a regular expense.

## Table 4.1   Weekly Expense Worksheet

| Expense Items | Mon | Tues | Wed | Thurs | Fri | Sat | Sun | Total |
|---|---|---|---|---|---|---|---|---|
| Auto: Gas | | | | | | | | |
| Auto: Maintenance | | | | | | | | |
| Children: Tuition/Child Care | | | | | | | | |
| Food: Dining Out/Credit Card | | | | | | | | |
| Food: Grocery | | | | | | | | |
| Fun: | | | | | | | | |
| Fun: | | | | | | | | |
| Fun: Vacation/ Entertainment | | | | | | | | |
| Home: Furniture | | | | | | | | |
| Home: Housekeeper | | | | | | | | |
| Home: Pest Control | | | | | | | | |
| Home: Rent | | | | | | | | |
| Home: Repair/Maintenance | | | | | | | | |
| Home: Security Monitoring | | | | | | | | |
| Home: Yard Maintenance | | | | | | | | |
| Insurance: Auto & Liability | | | | | | | | |

*continues*

## Table 4.1    Continued

| Expense Items | Mon | Tues | Wed | Thurs | Fri | Sat | Sun | Total |
|---|---|---|---|---|---|---|---|---|
| Insurance: | | | | | | | | |
| Insurance: Disability | | | | | | | | |
| Insurance: Health | | | | | | | | |
| Insurance: Life | | | | | | | | |
| Loan: | | | | | | | | |
| Loan: Home Mortgage | | | | | | | | |
| Membership: Athletic Club | | | | | | | | |
| Membership: | | | | | | | | |
| Membership Dues: | | | | | | | | |
| Misc: | | | | | | | | |
| Misc: | | | | | | | | |
| Misc: Clothing | | | | | | | | |
| Misc: Contributions/Gifts | | | | | | | | |
| Misc: Laundry/Dry Cleaning | | | | | | | | |
| Misc: Medical/Dental | | | | | | | | |
| Misc: Parking | | | | | | | | |
| Misc: Personal Care | | | | | | | | |
| Misc: Transportation | | | | | | | | |
| Taxes: Property | | | | | | | | |
| Taxes: Income (out of paycheck) | | | | | | | | |
| Taxes: Quarterly Federal | | | | | | | | |
| Taxes: Tax Account to Pay April | | | | | | | | |
| Utility: Electric | | | | | | | | |
| Utility: Gas | | | | | | | | |
| Utility: Phone | | | | | | | | |
| Utility: Water | | | | | | | | |
| Retirement Account (SEP, 401(k)) | | | | | | | | |
| Other | | | | | | | | |
| Other | | | | | | | | |
| Other | | | | | | | | |
| Other | | | | | | | | |

At the end of each week, total each row. Once you have all four sheets, total the corresponding row entries for your weekly total. Do this for four weeks to get a monthly total. For example, total your four weeks' worth of expense for Misc: Personal Care. Using a copy of the Weekly Expense Worksheet, record the sum of the four weekly totals for each expense item to get a full month's total expenses. If you don't want to complete the Weekly Expense Worksheet now, you might want to just estimate your monthly expenses for each category so that you can get started. That's okay, but don't completely disregard the idea of accurately measuring your expenses using the Weekly Expense Worksheet. If you do, you may be basing your entire financial future on incorrect data.

Once you get each monthly total, take a look at where you're spending money. Find the expenses that are unnecessary. What could you do without? Record what you think your expenses should be. This will be your budget. If you want, do the same exercise again next month: Record your actual expenses again and see how close you came. Make this process easy so that it won't seem overwhelming. It's easy to do if you take the time. You might learn more about yourself (and your spouse) than you knew before. This process also may give you more control over your life. I have found that simply by measuring expenses, I tend to be more in control of my spending habits. The goal is to find additional money that you can save.

Using your monthly expense total, calculate a yearly total by multiplying by 12. You need this yearly total for the next step. If you want more exact numbers, look back over the past year's expenses using your checkbook register and credit card statements. You'll want to add yearly expenses such as insurance and property taxes that might not have shown up in your monthly analysis. Set up these numbers on a computer spreadsheet and see what your actual yearly expenses have been. The most effective way to do this is by using one of the personal financial software packages that are available, such as Quicken. This program will help you perform an expense analysis in great detail. For those who don't have a computer, old-fashioned notebook paper works just as well; it just takes longer.

You're not finished yet. Do you foresee any change in these spending habits? Some common spending-habit changes occur after marrying, buying a home, having a child, or sending a child to college. Ask yourself what changes you expect to make in the next five years. Estimate the costs and project how much your monthly spending will increase or decrease. Multiply this estimate by 12 to get a yearly figure. The result is the amount of money you will need per year for the added expense, and you should add it into the expense total you've just calculated. Make sure that this result is a conservative figure with some room for error. Pad the amount if you want, just to be sure you've covered all your expenses. Your goal is to establish the lowest amount of expenses you'd be happy to live with now. If you are not satisfied with your current standard of living and you feel you need additional money, then add it. Just remember that if you do so, your target savings goal will be higher and more difficult to achieve.

**Treasure Tip**

So you want to be a doctor or the CEO of a major corporation? The average income for physicians in private practice in 1994 was $218,000. In 1994, the average total compensation of America's 100 highest paid CEOs was $3,554,000, which included bonuses and stock options. This is 190 times the average American worker's income.

# Step 3: Calculate Your Pretax Income Needs

Step 3 is easy. Estimate your total federal, state, and local income tax rate. You might want to use the income tax rate you calculated in Chapter 2, "Eleven Tools for Building Wealth." Your income tax rate is just a shortcut. If you want to get serious, you could calculate your actual taxes using the current tax tables. You might want to call your CPA if you have one or get a federal and state tax table from the Internal Revenue Service and your state tax agency. Once you have your estimated tax rate, subtract the percentage from 1 to calculate the *inverse* of your tax rate. For example, if your income tax rate is 35 percent, then the equation looks like this:

$1 - .35 = .65$                     .65 is the inverse of your tax rate.

**Words of the Wealthy**

The **inverse** of a percentage number is easily calculated by subtracting the number from 1. The inverse of 40 percent is 1 − .4, which is .6 or 60%.

Take your projected yearly expenses that you calculated in the preceding section and divide your expenses by this number. For example, if your estimated yearly expenses add up to $40,000, the equation looks like this:

$\$40,000 \div .65 = \$61,538$

Therefore, you are going to need $61,538 in income per year before tax in order to maintain your spending habits. In other words, if you had $61,538 in taxable income, you would have approximately $40,000 after you paid your income tax. This may not be an exact figure, but for our purposes here, it's close enough.

**Words of the Wealthy**

Most people think that **inflation** is the simple rise in prices. The technical definition is an increase in the volume of money and credit relative to available goods, which results in a substantial and continuing rise in the general price level. The rate of inflation is measured by the month-to-month percentage change of the Consumer Price Index (CPI).

# Step 4: Consider the Inflation Factor

The next step is to calculate the effect of *inflation* on your expenses in later years. If we continue the example from the last section, we know you need $61,538 each year in today's dollars to cover your expenses, but what about when you retire? What will inflation do to prices by that time?

The only way to answer that question is to make an estimate of future inflation and calculate its effect on your yearly expense needs. This process involves a simple calculation. To calculate the one-year effect of inflation, take the yearly expense total and multiply it by 1 plus your estimate of inflation:

(Yearly expenses before tax) × (1 + estimate of inflation) = Next year's expense estimate

If we use a 3 percent estimate of the annual inflation rate, here is what the calculation looks like:

$$\$61,538 \times (1 + .03) = \$63,384$$

This calculation shows you that you will need $63,384 in income next year to cover the same amount of expenses if the inflation rate is 3 percent.

Now that you understand the calculation, you can project further into the future. First, you have to decide how many years you are willing to wait to achieve Stage 3 wealth when your portfolio is producing enough income for you to retire. Let's say you're willing to wait 25 years. Continue the calculation 24 more times. Using the same example, Table 4.2 shows what the result should look like.

## Table 4.2 Estimating Future Income Needs Based on Inflation

| No. of Years | Year | Pretax Income Needed for Expenses (Base of $61,538) | Estimated Inflation |
|---|---|---|---|
| 1 | 1997 | $63,384 | 3% |
| 2 | 1998 | $65,286 | 3% |
| 3 | 1999 | $67,244 | 3% |
| 4 | 2000 | $69,262 | 3% |
| 5 | 2001 | $71,339 | 3% |
| 6 | 2002 | $73,480 | 3% |
| 7 | 2003 | $75,684 | 3% |
| 8 | 2004 | $77,954 | 3% |
| 9 | 2005 | $80,293 | 3% |
| 10 | 2006 | $82,702 | 3% |
| 11 | 2007 | $85,183 | 3% |
| 12 | 2008 | $87,738 | 3% |
| 13 | 2009 | $90,371 | 3% |
| 14 | 2010 | $93,082 | 3% |
| 15 | 2011 | $95,874 | 3% |
| 16 | 2012 | $98,750 | 3% |
| 17 | 2013 | $101,713 | 3% |
| 18 | 2014 | $104,764 | 3% |
| 19 | 2015 | $107,907 | 3% |
| 20 | 2016 | $111,144 | 3% |
| 21 | 2017 | $114,479 | 3% |
| 22 | 2018 | $117,913 | 3% |
| 23 | 2019 | $121,451 | 3% |
| 24 | 2020 | $125,094 | 3% |
| 25 | 2021 | $128,847 | 3% |

As you can see from Table 4.2 in 25 years, you will need approximately $128,847 in income to cover your yearly expense needs. Isn't it scary what inflation of only 3 percent can do to your standard of living? If you have a computer, this calculation is much easier to do on a spreadsheet.

# Step 5: Estimate Your Target Portfolio Amount

You have to assume several variables before you can estimate how much money you'll need. You have to estimate your rate of return. Depending upon whom you ask,

### Wealth Warning

Social Security was never intended to fully fund retirement. It's a U.S. Government program established in 1935 for old-age, survivor, and unemployment insurance. It was meant to supplement income, not replace it.

estimates of rate of return can vary widely. If you ask a conservative investor, the answer could be as low as 5 percent. On the other hand, an aggressive investor might say 15 percent. Your return obviously depends upon the level of risk you take and how your investments perform. The stock market was incredible during the years of 1995 through 1997 when it produced a yearly average return of 28.46 percent. This average is certainly not normal. However, many people new to the market got accustomed to these returns and expected them to continue. This assumption is a grave mistake. Don't get too ambitious with your estimated return factor. For now, let's continue to assume a 10 percent rate of return, which is a little below the average return on the S&P 500 (the major New York Stock Exchange performance index) over the last 40 years.

### That Reminds Me...

To achieve real wealth, you must be open minded enough to recognize and break down the self-imposed barriers that keep you in your present financial condition. These barriers are usually mindsets that need a little adjustment. Normally, the adjustment requires a catalyst or disruption to get it started. The most common catalysts and disruptions come from reading and discussing ideas with others. Take some time to understand your own barriers about building wealth. Then, discuss them with others who have achieved the level of wealth you desire. How do these people think? How did they overcome their barriers? Did they have similar barriers or different ones? This meeting might be just the catalyst you need.

Divide your yearly before-tax income, adjusted for inflation, by your estimated net rate of return.

$$\frac{\text{Yearly before-tax income adjusted for inflation}}{\text{Estimated net rate of return}} = \text{Target portfolio goal}$$

For example, here is the calculation using the preceding assumptions:

$128,847 ÷ .10 = $1,288,470

Therefore, to retire comfortably and begin living off the return from your portfolio, you'll need a portfolio of assets totaling $1,288,470, producing a rate of return of 10 percent per year.

Isn't this easy? Now, you can measure exactly what you will need in assets to achieve Wealth Stage 3. Don't be overwhelmed by the result. You're about to learn how to build this pool of assets.

# Step 6: How to Reach Your Target Portfolio Amount

Using Table 4.2, you can find what your yearly target savings goal should be. Let's review the assumptions before we calculate:

| | |
|---|---|
| Target portfolio goal | $1,288,470 |
| Yearly before-tax income needed at retirement | $128,847 |
| Estimated rate of return | 10 percent |
| Number of years until retirement | 25 |

In Tables 4.3 through 4.5, find the future value of annuity due factor that corresponds to your assumptions. Look at the top row and find your estimated rate of return of 10 percent. (If you want to use a different rate of return, select it from the table.) Look down the column until you find the factor for the number of years until you retire—in this scenario, 25 years.

## Table 4.3 Future Value of Annuity Factors (Annuity Due), Part 1

| Years Until You Retire | 1% | 2% | 3% | 4% | 5% | 6% | 7% |
|---|---|---|---|---|---|---|---|
| *Rate of Return* | | | | | | | |
| 5 | 5.1520 | 5.3081 | 5.4684 | 5.6330 | 5.8019 | 5.9753 | 6.1533 |
| 6 | 6.2135 | 6.4343 | 6.6625 | 6.8983 | 7.1420 | 7.3938 | 7.6540 |
| 7 | 7.2857 | 7.5830 | 7.8923 | 8.2142 | 8.5491 | 8.8975 | 9.2598 |
| 8 | 8.3685 | 8.7546 | 9.1591 | 9.5828 | 10.0266 | 10.4913 | 10.9780 |
| 9 | 9.4622 | 9.9497 | 10.4639 | 11.0061 | 11.5779 | 12.1808 | 12.8164 |
| 10 | 10.5668 | 11.1687 | 11.8078 | 12.4864 | 13.2068 | 13.9716 | 14.7836 |
| 11 | 11.6825 | 12.4121 | 13.1920 | 14.0258 | 14.9171 | 15.8699 | 16.8885 |
| 12 | 12.8093 | 13.6803 | 14.6178 | 15.6268 | 16.7130 | 17.8821 | 19.1406 |
| 13 | 13.9474 | 14.9739 | 16.0863 | 17.2919 | 18.5986 | 20.0151 | 21.5505 |
| 14 | 15.0969 | 16.2934 | 17.5989 | 19.0236 | 20.5786 | 22.2760 | 24.1290 |
| 15 | 16.2579 | 17.6393 | 19.1569 | 20.8245 | 22.6575 | 24.6725 | 26.8881 |
| 16 | 17.4304 | 19.0121 | 20.7616 | 22.6975 | 24.8404 | 27.2129 | 29.8402 |
| 17 | 18.6147 | 20.4123 | 22.4144 | 24.6454 | 27.1324 | 29.9057 | 32.9990 |
| 18 | 19.8109 | 21.8406 | 24.1169 | 26.6712 | 29.5390 | 32.7600 | 36.3790 |
| 19 | 21.0190 | 23.2974 | 25.8704 | 28.7781 | 32.0660 | 35.7856 | 39.9955 |
| 20 | 22.2392 | 24.7833 | 27.6765 | 30.9692 | 34.7193 | 38.9927 | 43.8652 |
| 21 | 23.4716 | 26.2990 | 29.5368 | 33.2480 | 37.5052 | 42.3923 | 48.0057 |
| 22 | 24.7163 | 27.8450 | 31.4529 | 35.6179 | 40.4305 | 45.9958 | 52.4361 |
| 23 | 25.9735 | 29.4219 | 33.4265 | 38.0826 | 43.5020 | 49.8156 | 57.1767 |
| 24 | 27.2432 | 31.0303 | 35.4593 | 40.6459 | 46.7271 | 53.8645 | 62.2490 |
| 25 | 28.5256 | 32.6709 | 37.5530 | 43.3117 | 50.1135 | 58.1564 | 67.6765 |
| 26 | 29.8209 | 34.3443 | 39.7096 | 46.0842 | 53.6691 | 62.7058 | 73.4838 |
| 27 | 31.1291 | 36.0512 | 41.9309 | 48.9676 | 57.4026 | 67.5281 | 79.6977 |
| 28 | 32.4504 | 37.7922 | 44.2189 | 51.9663 | 61.3227 | 72.6398 | 86.3465 |
| 29 | 33.7849 | 39.5681 | 46.5754 | 55.0849 | 65.4388 | 78.0582 | 93.4608 |
| 30 | 35.1327 | 41.3794 | 49.0027 | 58.3283 | 69.7608 | 83.8017 | 101.0730 |
| 35 | 42.0769 | 50.9944 | 62.2759 | 76.5983 | 94.8363 | 118.1209 | 147.9135 |
| 40 | 49.3752 | 61.6100 | 77.6633 | 98.8265 | 126.8398 | 164.0477 | 213.6096 |
| 45 | 57.0459 | 73.3306 | 95.5015 | 125.8706 | 167.6852 | 225.5081 | 305.7518 |
| 50 | 65.1078 | 86.2710 | 116.1808 | 158.7738 | 219.8154 | 307.7561 | 434.9860 |

## Table 4.4 Future Value of Annuity Factors (Annuity Due), Part 2

| Years Until You Retire | 8% | 9% | 10% | 11% | 12% | 13% | 14% |
|---|---|---|---|---|---|---|---|
| *Rate of Return* | | | | | | | |
| 5 | 6.3359 | 6.5233 | 6.7156 | 6.9129 | 7.1152 | 7.3227 | 7.5355 |
| 6 | 7.9228 | 8.2004 | 8.4872 | 8.7833 | 9.0890 | 9.4047 | 9.7305 |
| 7 | 9.6366 | 10.0285 | 10.4359 | 10.8594 | 11.2997 | 11.7573 | 12.2328 |
| 8 | 11.4876 | 12.0210 | 12.5795 | 13.1640 | 13.7757 | 14.4157 | 15.0853 |
| 9 | 13.4866 | 14.1929 | 14.3974 | 15.7220 | 16.5487 | 17.4197 | 18.3373 |
| 10 | 15.6455 | 16.5603 | 17.5312 | 18.5614 | 19.6546 | 20.8143 | 22.0445 |
| 11 | 17.9771 | 19.1407 | 20.3843 | 21.7132 | 23.1331 | 24.6502 | 26.2707 |
| 12 | 20.4953 | 21.9534 | 23.5227 | 25.2116 | 27.0291 | 28.9847 | 31.0887 |
| 13 | 23.2149 | 25.0192 | 26.9750 | 29.0949 | 31.3926 | 33.8827 | 36.5811 |
| 14 | 26.1521 | 28.3609 | 30.7725 | 33.4054 | 36.2797 | 39.4175 | 42.8424 |
| 15 | 29.3243 | 32.0034 | 34.9497 | 38.1899 | 41.7533 | 45.6717 | 49.9804 |
| 16 | 32.7502 | 35.9737 | 39.5447 | 43.5008 | 47.8837 | 52.7391 | 58.1176 |
| 17 | 36.4502 | 40.3013 | 44.5992 | 49.3959 | 54.7497 | 60.7251 | 67.3941 |
| 18 | 40.4463 | 45.0185 | 50.1591 | 55.9395 | 62.4397 | 69.7494 | 77.9692 |
| 19 | 44.7620 | 50.1601 | 56.2750 | 63.2028 | 71.0524 | 79.9468 | 90.0249 |
| 20 | 49.4229 | 55.7645 | 63.0025 | 71.2651 | 80.6987 | 91.4699 | 103.7684 |
| 21 | 54.4568 | 61.8733 | 70.4027 | 80.2143 | 91.5026 | 104.4910 | 119.4360 |
| 22 | 59.8933 | 68.5319 | 78.5430 | 90.1479 | 103.6029 | 119.2048 | 137.2970 |
| 23 | 65.7648 | 75.7898 | 87.4973 | 101.1741 | 117.1552 | 135.8315 | 157.6586 |
| 24 | 72.1059 | 83.7009 | 97.3471 | 113.4133 | 132.3339 | 154.6196 | 180.8708 |
| 25 | 78.9544 | 92.3240 | 108.1818 | 126.9988 | 149.3339 | 175.8501 | 207.3327 |
| 26 | 86.3508 | 101.7231 | 120.0999 | 142.0786 | 168.3740 | 199.8406 | 237.4993 |
| 27 | 94.3388 | 111.9682 | 133.2099 | 158.8173 | 189.6989 | 226.9499 | 271.8892 |
| 28 | 102.9659 | 123.1354 | 147.6309 | 177.3972 | 213.5828 | 257.5834 | 311.0937 |
| 29 | 112.2832 | 135.3075 | 163.4940 | 198.0209 | 240.3327 | 292.1992 | 355.7868 |
| 30 | 122.3459 | 148.5752 | 180.9434 | 220.9132 | 270.2926 | 331.3151 | 406.7370 |
| 35 | 186.1021 | 235.1247 | 298.1268 | 379.1644 | 483.4631 | 617.7493 | 790.6729 |
| 40 | 279.7810 | 368.2919 | 486.8518 | 645.8269 | 859.1424 | 1145.4858 | 1529.9086 |
| 45 | 417.4261 | 573.1860 | 790.7953 | 1095.1688 | 1521.2176 | 2117.8060 | 2953.2439 |
| 50 | 619.6718 | 888.4411 | 1280.2994 | 1852.3359 | 2688.0204 | 3909.2430 | 5693.7543 |

### Table 4.5 Future Value of Annuity Factors (Annuity Due), Part 3

| Years Until You Retire | 15% | 16% | 17% | 18% | 19% |
|---|---|---|---|---|---|
| *Rate of Return* | | | | | |
| 5 | 7.7537 | 7.9775 | 8.2068 | 8.4420 | 8.6830 |
| 6 | 10.0668 | 10.4139 | 10.7720 | 11.1415 | 11.5227 |
| 7 | 12.7268 | 13.2401 | 13.7733 | 14.3270 | 14.9020 |
| 8 | 15.7858 | 16.5185 | 17.2847 | 18.0859 | 18.9234 |
| 9 | 19.3037 | 20.3215 | 21.3931 | 22.5213 | 23.7089 |
| 10 | 23.3493 | 24.7329 | 26.1999 | 27.7551 | 29.4035 |
| 11 | 28.0017 | 29.8502 | 31.8239 | 33.9311 | 36.1802 |
| 12 | 33.3519 | 35.7862 | 38.4040 | 41.2187 | 44.2445 |
| 13 | 39.5047 | 42.6720 | 46.1027 | 49.8180 | 53.8409 |
| 14 | 46.5804 | 50.6595 | 55.1101 | 59.9653 | 65.2607 |
| 15 | 54.7175 | 59.9250 | 65.6488 | 71.9390 | 78.8502 |
| 16 | 64.0751 | 70.6730 | 77.9792 | 86.0680 | 95.0218 |
| 17 | 74.8364 | 83.1407 | 92.4056 | 102.7403 | 114.2659 |
| 18 | 87.2118 | 97.6032 | 109.2846 | 122.4135 | 137.1664 |
| 19 | 101.4436 | 114.3739 | 129.0329 | 145.6280 | 164.4180 |
| 20 | 117.8101 | 133.8405 | 152.1385 | 173.0210 | 196.8474 |
| 21 | 136.6316 | 156.4150 | 179.1721 | 205.3448 | 235.4385 |
| 22 | 158.2764 | 182.6014 | 210.8013 | 243.4868 | 281.3618 |
| 23 | 183.1678 | 212.9776 | 247.8076 | 288.4945 | 336.0105 |
| 24 | 211.7930 | 248.2140 | 291.1049 | 341.6035 | 401.0425 |
| 25 | 244.7120 | 289.0883 | 341.7627 | 404.2721 | 478.4306 |
| 26 | 282.5688 | 336.5024 | 401.0323 | 478.2211 | 570.5224 |
| 27 | 326.1041 | 391.5028 | 470.3778 | 565.4809 | 680.1116 |
| 28 | 376.1697 | 455.3032 | 551.5121 | 668.4475 | 810.5228 |
| 29 | 433.7451 | 529.3117 | 646.4391 | 789.9480 | 965.7122 |
| 30 | 499.9569 | 615.1616 | 757.5038 | 933.3186 | 1150.3875 |
| 35 | 1013.3757 | 1300.0270 | 1668.9945 | 2143.6489 | 2753.9143 |
| 40 | 2045.9539 | 2738.4784 | 3667.3906 | 4912.5914 | 6580.4965 |
| 45 | 4122.8977 | 5759.7178 | 8048.7701 | 11247.2610 | 15712.0750 |
| 50 | 8300.3737 | 1210.5353 | 17654.7170 | 25739.4510 | 37503.2500 |

Your factor for this example should be 108.1818, which we'll call the future value factor. Thus, the calculation to find your yearly TSG looks like this:

Target portfolio goal ÷ Future value factor = Yearly TSG

Here are the actual numbers for the example:

$1,288,470 ÷ 108.1818 = $11,910

To calculate your monthly TSG, divide this number by 12:

$11,910 ÷ 12 = $992.50

Understand that this simple calculation does not consider the effect of taxes on the total return of your investments. If this amount of money were saved in a tax-deferred qualified retirement plan such as a 401(k) or SEP, the math is almost perfect. However, if you are saving in a taxable account (such as a savings account, certificate of deposit, or taxable mutual fund) or the combination of a taxable account and a tax-deferred qualified plan, then you must consider the effect of taxes each year on your total return accumulation.

Let's assume your net tax liability on dividends, interest, and capital gains is 30 percent. If you make an average total return of 10 percent, then you could subtract 30 percent of the 10 percent return to get a net total return of 7 percent. This 7 percent can then be used to estimate your target portfolio return. (That is, you should choose a 7 percent rate of return factor from Table 4.2 rather than the 10 percent rate of return factor from Table 4.3 before making your calculation.) However, remember this is still only an estimate. Your capital gains may not all accrue each year, which means that there will be irregular capital gains taxes to pay each year, depending upon when your investment transactions result in a capital gain.

**Wealth Warning**

This process of finding your target savings goal is not difficult to complete, but it is easy to make a mistake. Once you complete all the necessary steps and calculations, be sure to go back and check your math.

# Step 7: Strategies for Achieving Your Target Savings Goal

If you are overwhelmed by your target portfolio size, don't be concerned. Don't forget that this amount is based upon some assumptions you made that can be adjusted. First, you could decrease the assumed inflation rate used to project your future living expenses. Second, you could accept some more risk and increase your estimated total return assumption. Third, you could extend the number of

**Treasure Tip**

Many wealthy people I know built part of their fortune using residual income, which is income derived over time from previous efforts or past accomplishments that continue to produce cash flow. This includes rental income and income from books, tapes, or other media that continue to sell with little additional effort.

years you are willing to wait before you reach Wealth Stage 3. Fourth, when you retire, you could move to some developing country and live on less money!

If you want to achieve your target savings goal, you have to ask yourself what factors you have the most control over. You have the least control over things like inflation and total return. You have the most control over expenses and the amount of money you save. You have some control over income, but reducing your expenses is usually easier than increasing income. It may not be as glamorous, but it is effective in achieving a larger savings goal. The less you spend, the more you have available for savings. The following list of ideas is designed to reduce your expenses. This is a small list—the rest of the book presents more tips and ideas—but it's a start:

➤ **Lower expenses.** Find expenses you can do without. Don't eat out as much. Turn down your heat or air conditioning at night or when you're gone. Use the phone book instead of information when you can. Stop smoking and you'll not only save the money you spend on cigarettes, you'll also save on your health insurance, not to mention medical bills later.

➤ **Avoid buying lottery tickets.** If you understand the odds of winning the lottery, you will never buy a ticket.

➤ **Home and auto maintenance actually lower expenses.** I just replaced my 15-year-old air-conditioning system with a new one. My electric bills are less, and my home is much cooler when it's hot outside.

➤ **Don't use life insurance for investment purposes.** This is one of the most common mistakes investors make. The cost of the insurance and commissions drain your investment, which decreases the total return you get. A friend who is an insurance agent says, "But the investment grows tax deferred." My reply is, "I don't care! It costs too much, and the policy holder is limited to only a handful of investment choices that usually are mediocre at best." My suggestion is to separate your investment money from your life insurance. Consider a less expensive term policy and depositing the savings in a no-load mutual fund.

*Warning:* Do not drop your existing life insurance first. If you plan to change to the term policy, do it first. Once it is set up, then cancel your past insurance. You don't want to be uncovered. If you can't get a term policy because of a preexisting condition, you will have your existing policy to fall back on.

➤ **Shop by phone for life insurance.** You can get quality life insurance by phone. Here are three companies that will shop the term life insurance market for you and show you the best deal:

| | |
|---|---|
| Select Quote | 800-343-1985 |
| Quotesmith | 800-431-1147 |
| Master Quote | 800-337-5433 |

These companies will contract with a medical technician who will come to your office to draw blood and fill out medical forms.

➤ **Save money when you travel.** Smart travelers know that airlines want to charge business travelers more money than vacationers. They assume that business travelers can write off the travel and therefore are more willing to pay higher prices. By simply staying at your destination over a Saturday night, you can sometimes save 75 percent on your airline ticket. You can also book hotel rooms cheaper in large cities by using services that offer more inexpensive lodging by purchasing rooms in bulk. Here are a few companies that offer this service:

| | |
|---|---|
| Hotel Reservations | 800-964-6835 |
| Express Reservations | 800-356-1123 |
| Quickbook | 800-789-9887 |

➤ **Consider increasing your insurance deductible.** If you increase your deductible, your insurance premiums should drop considerably. Insurance was designed to protect you from big, catastrophic losses. However, many people today have their windshields replaced with insurance money. A broken windshield is far from a catastrophic loss. People who make insurance claims on such items don't realize they are actually paying more for the windshield in the long run than they would if they had a larger deductible. Call your agent and ask him or her how much you would save by boosting your deductible.

# Step 8: Stay on Track

The last step is to maintain your plan. Each year, you should redo all the calculations for the Wealth Builder Worksheet and the Weekly Expense Worksheet in this chapter. You should measure your monthly expenses each month, if not quarterly. If you continue to measure your expenses, you will be better able to meet your goal. I guarantee that your plan will change over time. Some of the changes will be small and some will be large. Your success in maintaining your plan depends a great deal upon several things:

➤ **Your flexibility and creativity.** You must be willing to respond to the inevitable changes that life brings. You must be able to handle adversity.

➤ **Your organizational skills.** You must keep current, at least yearly, with all the elements of your plan.

**Wealth Warning**

Associate with other people who share your ambitions and aspirations and who are willing to share ideas and support you in your efforts. Look for win/win relationships. Avoid those people who pull you down and drain your enthusiasm.

➤ **Your willingness to work on your plan.** Your journey toward wealth will take some time, so make certain you enjoy the journey; the payoff will be worth it.

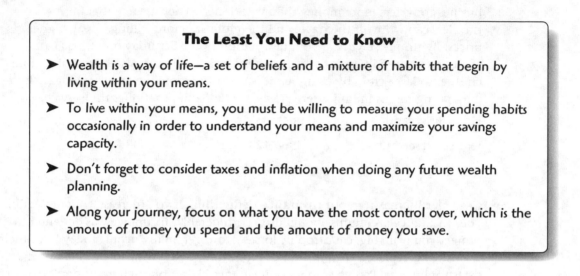

### The Least You Need to Know

➤ Wealth is a way of life—a set of beliefs and a mixture of habits that begin by living within your means.

➤ To live within your means, you must be willing to measure your spending habits occasionally in order to understand your means and maximize your savings capacity.

➤ Don't forget to consider taxes and inflation when doing any future wealth planning.

➤ Along your journey, focus on what you have the most control over, which is the amount of money you spend and the amount of money you save.

# Chapter 5

# The Secrets of Millionaires

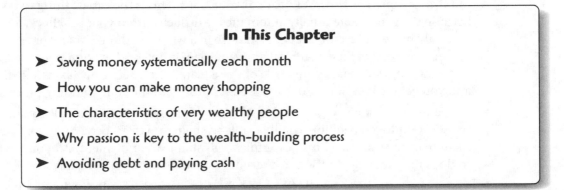

**In This Chapter**

➤ Saving money systematically each month

➤ How you can make money shopping

➤ The characteristics of very wealthy people

➤ Why passion is key to the wealth-building process

➤ Avoiding debt and paying cash

I realized long ago that if you want to achieve anything great in life, find the people who are already the best at what you want to do and imitate them. First, identify their habits. What are they doing on a consistent basis that enables them to achieve their results? Second, what are the key characteristics that enable them to achieve their results? This is what I've done for more than 13 years in business and for more than 30 years in my life. I am fascinated by what enables some people to build great wealth and why others never seem to get there no matter how hard they try.

Remember the couple I mentioned in Chapter 1, "Are You Going to Be Rich?" Mr. and Mrs. Post, who never made more than $30,000 per year, yet their portfolio was worth more than $800,000? Not to mention the $240,000 in homes they had paid cash for as gifts for their two daughters and the fully funded $100,000 college education account! How could this couple have so much money with so little income? Well, that is exactly what I asked, and they said, "We saved it and invested it in no-load funds." I said, "Please tell me your story. There's got to be more to this, right?" They sat back and shared some simple truths that every investor should follow. I call them the seven habits of very wealthy people, and I detail them in this chapter.

# The Seven Habits of Very Wealthy People

The seven habits for building wealth include saving every month, staying out of debt, shopping before you buy, buying used when you can, taking care of your stuff, investing in stocks, and taking time to plan your future.

## 1. Be a Consistent Saver

The Posts said that each month, no matter what they made in salary, they put money in savings and invested in no-load mutual funds. They said, "No matter what happens, pay yourself first and make it a habit." The combination of systematic savings and compound growth is incredible. Here are several ways you can start saving money now:

➤ **Maximize your 401(k) or SEP-IRA contributions.** This is the easiest thing to do because the deposits are usually automatically deducted from your paycheck, and you only make an investment decision once in a while. If your company or employer offers one of these plans, take advantage of it now and maximize your contributions. Millionaires are made of these plans. The assets grow tax deferred, and you get the benefit of using Uncle Sam's money in the compounding process.

➤ **If you are self-employed, consider starting your own SEP-IRA (an IRA plan for self-employed people).** You'll be able to shelter up to 15 percent of your income until you retire. This powerful step is simple to implement. All you have to do is fill out an application, make a deposit, and you're on your way.

➤ **Maximize your IRA or Roth IRA contribution.** An IRA is an Individual Retirement Account into which you can deposit a maximum of $2,000 of earned income each year. The true benefit of the IRA is that all interest, dividends, and capital gains are tax deferred until they are withdrawn. The second benefit is the flexibility of investment alternatives that are available. You can invest in CDs, stocks, bonds, and mutual funds. Because there are more than 5,000 different mutual funds, your alternatives are almost endless. The third benefit is convenience. An IRA is simple to start. All you have to do is fill out an application and make a deposit. The regular IRA is deductible from your income, which lessens your tax burden. You can withdraw money from this IRA after you are 59 $1/2$ years old, but it's taxable as ordinary income. The Roth IRA is different because it's not deductible from your income, but it can be withdrawn after you are 59 $1/2$ years old tax-free. The power of the IRA is in the compounding, not the deduction from your taxes. Just because you can't deduct the Roth IRA doesn't mean it's not attractive.

The tax deductibility of your deposit depends upon your income and involvement in a qualified plan. If you are not enrolled in a qualified retirement plan, you may be able to deduct your deposit from your total taxable income. Be sure to check with the IRS, your CPA, or a financial planner to find out more about your situation.

➤ **Write yourself a check.** Before you start paying your bills each week or each payday, write yourself a check and deposit the check in a separate account. The whole idea is to pay yourself before anyone else. Your 401(k) works the same way; it comes out of the check before you get it. Your goal should be to save your target savings goal and then use the remainder to budget your spending. Act as if the target savings goal amount doesn't even exist and budget accordingly.

➤ **Let a mutual fund direct-debit your account.** Most mutual funds offer a direct-debit feature that automatically withdraws a predetermined amount from your checking account each month. This is one of the easiest ways to save money. Each month at bill-paying time, just record the withdrawal in your check register. Don't be afraid of this feature. Try it for a year and cancel if you don't like it.

➤ **Save your pennies, nickels, dimes, and quarters.** I spend only whole dollar bills and save my change every day in a bowl. When the bowl is full, I deposit it in my investment account. The bank's not too excited about counting all those coins, but they get over it!

➤ **Save your raises.** Another trick is to ignore any raises in income when budgeting for expenses. When you get a raise, save the entire raise. Instead of increasing your spending habits, increase your saving habits. Let the raise boost your saving percentage.

I can't guarantee you'll be rich if you use all these strategies, but I can promise you that they certainly increase your chances.

**Treasure Tip**

If you can't deduct your IRA deposit, you might want to make a Roth IRA deposit anyway. The assets grow tax deferred (you don't pay tax on any interest or other income), and you get to make tax-free withdrawals. With the freedom to invest in almost any liquid security, the Roth IRA *is* a powerful tool.

## 2. Pay Cash When You Can

Debt is a tool, and it works just like a lever. The word *leverage* is often used when people refer to debt, and that's exactly how debt can operate. The more debt you have, the more buying power you control. However, many people in today's world have gone crazy with debt, and the result is a record number of bankruptcies. Debt is okay if you know how to use it. I have few simple rules that I live by when it comes to debt. It's okay to leverage your home, and it's okay to leverage a business venture as long as you can afford to cover the payments. However, it's not okay to leverage your self-image. Using debt to live in a lifestyle you can't afford is wrong.

Many rich individuals pay cash for everything and avoid debt (except for their home mortgage). Instead of borrowing money to purchase an item, they wait until they save enough money to buy the item with cash. Save money for the things you want and pay cash.

Here are four ideas that will help you eliminate debt:

1. **Refinance your mortgage.** Shop around when mortgage rates drop to see if you can get a better fixed rate. If you plan to stay in your home for more than two years, and if you can improve your mortgage rate by as much as 2 percent, you should consider refinancing. This may reduce your mortgage payments and reduce the amount of money you spend each year on interest payments. Reduce or avoid points and origination fees. These are often negotiable. Offer to refinance if the mortgage company will reduce their fees.

2. **Use only low-interest credit cards.** Do some research to find the credit card with the lowest possible rate. You must understand the tactics of credit card companies. Don't be fooled by the introductory rate they tease you with in order to get you as a cardholder. Ask the company whether the rate they quote is an introductory rate. Also, you might want to consider getting a debit card. These cards look like a standard credit card but directly debit your checking account for purchases. Because you are not financing your purchase, there is no finance charge. Check your local bank for this option.

3. **Home equity loans can help.** If you have a great deal of credit card debt and you own your own home, you might consider applying for a home equity loan and using the loan money to pay off your credit card debt. Avoid origination fees and points, which tend to counteract your overall interest savings. Check with your tax preparer to find out whether this interest is deductible. Getting a home equity loan to pay another debt is one way to convert a non–tax-deductible expense to a tax-deductible one. If you have any equity in your home and you anticipate having to borrow money to buy a car, consider a home equity loan. You'll more than likely get a lower interest rate and, at the same time, you'll be able to deduct the interest on the loan from your taxable income. BE SURE THAT YOU DON'T BORROW MORE MONEY THAN YOUR HOME IS WORTH! There are commercials on TV telling you that you can borrow up to 125 percent of your home's value. This is an easy way to get into trouble.

**Treasure Tip**

Debt used to build a business or increase cash flow is acceptable. Consumer and credit card debt used to build your image in society is not acceptable and will reverse the wealth-building process.

4. **Pay more each month on your mortgage.** If you can afford to add money to your mortgage payment each month, you will reduce the overall interest costs on your mortgage and speed up the time it takes to retire your mortgage. If you can double your payments, your home will be paid off more quickly. You might also want to consider a 15-year mortgage versus the typical 30-year mortgage. You'll pay a little more each month, but you'll save an enormous amount of money in interest later. Be sure to check with your mortgage holder about how your extra payments can apply to your loan.

**Treasure Tip**

Don't be seduced by the low introductory rates on credit cards. If you read the fine print on most of these cards, you'll see that much higher rates kick in after the first year.

## 3. Shopping Saves You Money

Our society today is known for its impatience. Our attitude has become, "We want it right now, and we get what we want!" This attitude doesn't help motivate anyone to shop. I'm not talking about going shopping. I'm talking about doing your homework before you buy anything of significance.

The Posts also said that they shopped extensively before they bought anything. This is a simple concept, but few people take the time. It is my belief that women by nature are shoppers and men are not. My personal habit is to get into the store, buy exactly what I need, and get out of there. I've learned my lesson. Now I ask everyone I know where I can get the best price. This saves me a great deal of time. If you hate to shop, get some help from others who enjoy it. Take a moment and think about your own habits. Do you take the time to shop around? Are you an impulsive buyer?

➤ **Shop at warehouse clubs.** I learned many years ago that I could save a lot of money by shopping at warehouse clubs. It was difficult to store the large quantities when I lived in my tiny, 500-square-foot apartment, but it is much easier now in my house. As you can imagine, I spend a lot of money at Sam's Club.

➤ **Buy seasonal items out of season.** When you do shop, think opposite of the crowd's thinking. When do most people buy the item you want? If you want to buy a boat, start shopping at the end of the summer. Owners will accept a lower price, knowing the expense of keeping it another winter in storage. Most people buy their boats in the early spring. Avoid the buying pressure, and get it cheap later in the summer. You can say the same thing about lawn mowers, convertible automobiles, and landscaping materials. If snow is a problem in the winter, buy a snow blower in the late spring. If you time your purchases right and negotiate properly, you might pay only a fraction of the normal in-season price. Many times, I put off buying an item just so I can wait until the off season to buy it cheaper. Have you ever been to the Disney World in Orlando during the month of September? It's great! All the kids are back in school, and the place isn't crowded. I've also been there between Christmas and New Years...big mistake!

➤ **Learn to haggle.** The United States is the only country I know where people accept paying the full price on merchandise without negotiation. I'm guilty of this, too. However, I've learned to always ask, "Is there any way I can get a better price on this?" And it works. Contrary to popular belief, this is not rude. A few months ago, I offered to purchase $8,000 worth of antiques from a large antique warehouse. I asked whether it would give me a discount for the amount of money I wanted to spend. They gave me more than 10 percent off, which added up to $800. What a great reward for asking such an easy question. The next time you buy a big-ticket item, negotiate.

➤ **Delay purchases of items you don't need.** Before you rush out to the store or pick up the telephone to buy that widget you just have to have, write it down, and think about it for a week. Then, ask yourself whether you still want it as much. How many things do you have in your closet, storage room, or drawers that you used only a few times? I've practiced this tactic over the past five years and even built a file of things I've wanted to buy. Would you believe that I've bought only maybe 10 percent of them? This habit really cuts down on the amount of stuff you'll be selling in your next garage sale. Remember that the more stuff you have, the more responsibility you take on.

### Words of the Wealthy

The word **haggle** comes from the Old English term *heawan*, which means to beat or cut. Haggling is the process of negotiating the lowest price possible in a purchase transaction. The U.S. is one of the few countries where haggling is not a normal part of everyday shopping.

Don't confuse shopping with buying. My associate Linda shared this story with me: "One of the ongoing jokes in our family is about the time when my sister-and-law and I went shopping and found a huge sale. She returned from the store with her car full of bags. As she went through each bag, she kept referring to the sale prices and how much money she had saved. My brother, who was about to bust a blood vessel, wasn't too happy about all the money she had saved. I don't know if it was just coincidence, but they got divorced a short time later. Anyway, any time we find a sale, we show it to the family with the introduction of 'Look how much money I saved!'" The moral of this story is that just because it's a good price doesn't mean you are saving money if you're buying something you don't need.

# 4. Consider Previously Owned Merchandise

The Posts often bought previously owned merchandise, especially if they could find good quality at lower prices. They spent a lot of time shopping for used items in the local want ads. They said they saved a lot of money over the years by focusing on used instead of new cars. They bought quality used cars from previous owners and eliminated the commission paid to the salesperson, along with the heavy depreciation incurred in the first year. Don't be a fanatic about buying everything new. Consider a used car before you purchase a new one. Consider antique furniture instead of new. Check the want ads before you buy. Sometimes I use last week's ads, because if the seller still has the item, he is usually more motivated to sell it at a cheaper price.

Used cars seem more attractive than ever before. New car prices have risen approximately 29 percent since 1990, and consequently, buyers are not as eager to buy more. We have also seen a huge supply of program cars or previously leased cars hit the market. This large supply of two- and three-year old cars has resulted in more competitive prices.

If you have to buy a new car, call eight of the surrounding dealers within four hours driving distance and ask for the best price on the automobile of your choice. Be sure to be specific with your model and desired options.

I tried to buy a used Chevy Suburban two years ago but could not find one available at a reasonable price. They were in such high demand that the used prices actually exceeded the new prices. Therefore, I had to look at new models. I did some homework and found a company in California called IntelliChoice (800-227-2665) that offers a service called Just the Facts, which gives you dealer's cost and discounts available on most cars available here in the U.S. The service is $14.95 by mail and $17.99 by fax. I called IntelliChoice to find the dealer's cost on the model I wanted. I then called eight dealers around the state and actually negotiated a price $200 above the dealer's cost. If you have to buy new, IntelliChoice can help you.

When you buy a used automobile, focus on quality and resale value. In the mid 1980s, I purchased a used, one-year-old Jeep Cherokee with no frills or extras. I paid $7,000 for it, drove it 20,000 miles, and sold it 18 months later for $6,800.

If you want to know approximately what an automobile is worth, call your bank and ask for

**Treasure Tip**

If possible, sell your own car instead of trading it in. You have a better chance of getting a higher price than a dealer will offer you on trade.

**Wealth Warning**

Before you buy a used car, take it to an independent car repair service for a check-up. If you unknowingly buy a poor-quality, unreliable car, you may end up with big problems later. There's nothing worse than sinking your hard-earned money into something that's not reliable—except having to sell it later.

blue book values. There are three prices to notice. First is the loan value, which is the amount of money a bank is willing to loan a customer to buy the car. Second is the trade-in value or wholesale price, which is what a car dealer might be willing to pay for the car on a trade. Third is the retail price, which you might pay if you were buying it from a used car dealer. Your goal as a buyer is to buy the car at or below the loan value. Your goal as a seller is to sell it at or above retail. Either way, if you don't get the price you want, you have to be willing to walk away.

If you do get a loan to buy a car, be sure to shop several banks for the best rate. If you do this before you look for a car, you'll be better prepared to negotiate.

## That Reminds Me...

If at all possible, don't lease a car. The commission and financing charges are all disguised in the payment, which makes it difficult to make an intelligent decision. Most of the time, the lease is much more expensive in the long run. If you purchase a used vehicle, take care of it with regular maintenance, and sell it later, your total out-of-pocket expense should be much less than the cost of a lease agreement.

Consider antique furniture. A few years ago, a dear friend taught me an invaluable lesson. I was looking for furniture for my office, and he said, "Larry, don't waste your money on new furniture. Buy functional antiques." He explained that, "You can depreciate them on your balance sheet as they appreciate in value." This man is a genius. My office is full of these antiques. Not only are they beautiful, but they have also appreciated since I bought them. You can certainly find some good deals at local antique stores, but the best deals happen at estate auctions where you can cut out the middleman. Where do you think the antique stores get their inventory?

Don't misunderstand my point about buying used merchandise. You should focus on quality. Whether you buy new or used, you must focus on quality and resale value. Always research the big-ticket items in the classified ads before you buy, and look at how they fall in price relative to their original retail price. How do they fall in price each year? Are there any consumer reports out on the product? Go to the library and look in the periodical index for the particular item you want to buy. See whether any studies exist. *Consumer Reports* is a magazine that can save you a lot of money. It does studies on different products regarding quality, maintenance, and resale value. Why not subscribe?

## 5. Be a Great Steward

Another pearl of wisdom the Posts shared with me involved stewardship, which in their case was simple maintenance. They said they took care of what they owned. They said that it is amazing how long things will last if you take good care of them. They bought great quality items and took great care of them. For example, I have a tree farm, and I needed a tractor. I bought a John Deere because of its track record of holding its resale value and the local service dealer's dedication to servicing the tractor after the sale. I bought a top-quality machine and paid a lot of money for it, but the dealership actually helps me be a great steward.

More than likely, the largest "machine" you have is your automobile. If you want it to last a long time and hold its resale value, you must conduct regular maintenance. The Posts had both of their automobiles serviced every 4,000 miles, which included an oil and filter change. They also waxed their cars every six months. These simple steps helped keep their cars running better and helped maintain the resale value.

Home maintenance is also important. Have your heating and air-conditioning system checked once a year to prolong the life of your equipment. Pay for a good pest control service now so you don't have to pay later for termite damage. Prevent exterior damage of your home by regularly cleaning out your gutters and replacing the old ones. If you have to, get someone to help you.

## 6. Learn the Basics of Investing

The next habit this couple taught me was to develop a basic understanding of the stock and bond markets. They studied the basics, knew the benefit of owning *stocks*, invested in stocks through no-load funds, and learned on their own the hard way. They learned a great deal from the mistakes they made and understood that investing money in the stock market involves occasionally making mistakes. In spite of all that, they kept learning more each day and stayed the course.

If you feel uncomfortable with your investment knowledge, get proactive and do something about it now. There is no excuse for ignorance. Books and classes available can teach you everything you need to know. Part 2, "Becoming an Investor—Wealth Stages 3 and 4," is a great start. Do yourself a favor and learn all you can now.

The best way to learn is to start investing. You'll want to learn because your money is at stake. The next best way to learn is to join an organization dedicated to educating investors. One of the best organizations I've found is the American Association of Individual Investors (800-428-2244). Call and ask for an information packet. You might also read some books on stock investing. Here are some of my favorites:

**Words of the Wealthy**

When you buy shares of **stock** directly or through a mutual fund, you become part owner of a company. These shares can build your wealth by paying you dividends and by rising in price.

*Beating the Street*, Peter Lynch, retired manager of Fidelity Magellan

*One Up on Wall Street*, Peter Lynch

*Value Investing*, Ben Graham (This may get a little technical, but Ben is the father of value investing.)

*Bogle on Funds*, John Bogle, the past chairman of Vanguard Funds

### That Reminds Me...

When you purchase a bond or mutual fund, you are essentially buying IOUs of companies or the government. The total interest paid each year is your reward for loaning the money. Additional reward comes when interest rates fall and the price of the bond increases. The reverse is also true. If rates go up, the price of the bond will fall. A bond is simply a source of future cash flow that can be bought and sold at different prices until maturity. However, at the bond's maturity, the bondholder is paid only the face amount or maturity value of the bond along with the appropriate interest amount.

## 7. Do Your Homework

Finally, Mr. and Mrs. Post also did their homework. They took time to research their options before they made an investment, and they understood that quick decisions get you hurt in the market. Rumors get started and before you know it, a "hot tip" turns out to be a cold nightmare. They recognized and avoided the traps.

Don't forget to measure the results of your portfolio. Not measuring results is one of the most common mistakes made by individual investors. They invest for years, never actually knowing their portfolio's true performance on a monthly or yearly basis. They might estimate it, but they rarely do it accurately, and they almost never compare it to the proper benchmark indexes. I talk more about this in Part 2.

Each year, you should reevaluate your progress toward your wealth goal. Do the calculations in Chapter 4, "How to Become a Saver," again if you need to. This will help you stay on track. Did you know that planes that

### Treasure Tip

Time is money and requires just as much management as your money. If you don't have a day planner, get one. If you do have one, shop around and make sure yours is the best for your needs. I've used a day planner since I was 13 years old. They just make my life so much easier.

fly on autopilot from the U.S. to Hawaii are off track almost 95 percent of the time? It's because of wind. The autopilot resets the plane's course every few minutes because the wind keeps knocking it off course. The plane makes it because the autopilot mechanism continues to repeatedly reset the compass bearing. Your journey toward wealth is similar. You'll experience wind along the way that will blow you off course. Don't forget to reset your compass bearing at least once a year.

## Do You Have What It Takes to Be Wealthy?

What does it take to be wealthy? Is there a trick? If you want to improve your odds of achieving your desired level of wealth, you have to think like a wealthy person. Over the last 10 years in the investment business, I have spoken to thousands of wealthy individuals like Mr. and Mrs. Post. I've learned a great deal from these people. Mr. and Mrs. Post taught me the seven habits in this chapter, but they and other wealthy individuals also taught me things that went unspoken. These unspoken lessons were characteristics they portrayed. Most of these people were happy and enthusiastic about life, and I have a lot of admiration for them. I tried to avoid the people who were consistently unhappy. I had so much admiration for the ones with great attitudes about life that I began to make notes about them. It was fascinating because they all seem to have several mental characteristics in common. The rest of this section presents the four most common characteristics. If you incorporate them into your life, you will have little difficulty getting to Wealth Stage 2.

**Treasure Tip**

According to the Census Bureau, the number of poor people making less than the poverty threshold of $15,000 per year in the U.S. fell by more than 1 million in 1993—the first decline in five years.

## Follow Your Passion

Most of my friends know me and the amount of passion I have for life. I do what I love to do, and somehow little miracles happen almost every day. I have come to realize that the more I focus on my dreams and passions, the more I get accomplished. When you focus on your dreams and passions, you live from your soul. Unfortunately, not many people do this. Most of those who do understand the power in this. When you live from your soul, you become like a magnet, drawing everything you need into your life that will help you accomplish your goal. That might sound like a little hocus-pocus, but I speak from experience.

The great irony today in society is that most people are really afraid of following their dreams. If people would let themselves focus on what they are passionate about in life, they not only would live a happier life, but they would also be able to accomplish more. They would naturally be more competitive. They would achieve greater accomplishments than they thought possible.

The world is so competitive now that markets around the world have opened up their doors to outside consumers. To compete in any business today, you have to work harder and be smarter than your competition. In the long run, the winners in any industry will be those companies and individuals who were passionate enough about their work to spend the time and effort it takes to produce outstanding products and services. Without this passion, a company or individual will be less likely to make the effort or spend all night to meet a deadline. During the first four years of building my company, I spent at least one full night a month in my office working. Sometimes I would work 32 hours straight. I've fallen asleep right in the middle of a conversation with a client.

It's not that I'm an advocate of working this many hours. (It's unhealthy.) My point is that I was excited enough about my company to want to. The question I'm asking here is this: In your present position, are you willing to work all night on a project if you have to? If the answer is no, then you need to seriously consider making a job change or starting your own business doing what you enjoy.

The happiest wealthy people I know have a passion for what they do, which seems to naturally create a certain level of tenacity and perseverance toward achieving their goals. They have a vision, and they are enthusiastic about life. Their enthusiasm is sincere, and it comes from deep inside. They don't necessarily have a passion for building wealth. Wealth, for them, is a result of their passion and effort for the work they do.

A student asked me recently, "If you could change anything in the business world, what would it be?" I told her that if everyone loved what he were doing in his life today, or if everyone at least had a plan to achieve this, the world would be a better place. There would be less frustration, anger, and unhappiness. People would feel more gratification.

**Treasure Tip**

"Great dancers are not great because of their technique; they are great because of their passion."
—Martha Graham

When you love what you do, your chances of great achievement improve dramatically. If you are unsure about where your passion lies, the following five questions will give you some ideas to consider. These questions could change your life for the better. It all depends upon how honest you are with yourself when you answer each question. There are no right or wrong answers, so relax and enjoy yourself. Write down exactly what comes to mind. Do not judge any answer! Let your mind go and list anything that comes to mind, no matter how impossible it might seem. Write each question at the top of a separate page, go to a quiet place where you will not be interrupted, and spend some quality time with yourself answering these questions:

1. Your doctor calls and tells you that in exactly six months, you will die a peaceful death due to a weird, unknown virus. What would you do during this six-month

period? Whom would you spend time with? What activities would you spend time doing? What would be important to you? (List at least 20 answers.)

2. An unknown relative dies and leaves you a portfolio of cash totaling $2,000,000. What would you do? Whom would you spend time with? What activities would you spend time doing? What would be important to you? Would you quit work? How would you spend your money? (List at least 20 answers.)

3. What three great endeavors would you dare to attempt if you were guaranteed you could not fail?

4. What do you want more of in your life? (List at least 20 answers.)

5. What do you want less of in your life? (List at least 20 answers.)

The answers to these questions give you insight into your most important values in life. They illustrate what's really important to you and, in the case of number 5, what you want less of in your life. They should act as a guide in your search for what you really want in life. Use these answers not only to find your passion, but also use them as parameters against which you compare any major endeavor in life.

If you really take the time to list 20 or more answers, you might find some things you enjoy doing that you haven't participated in for a long time. One of your answers could be something you're passionate about that you can use as a business idea. It might be another position within a company or your own company.

If you can't figure it out now, put the pages away and try this exercise again in a week. Be sure to change your surroundings next time. Sit in a comfortable spot with no interruptions. Try it a third time if you have to.

# Be a Decision Maker

The wealthiest people I know are good decision makers. They don't procrastinate or live in denial. They take the time to identify all the issues, research the alternatives, and select the best answer. They don't waste too much time worrying about things they have little control over. They also look carefully at all the possible consequences of each decision. They list the pros and cons, take time to think about all the options, and finally ask themselves, "What is the worst thing that can happen?" If they can accept the worst possible outcome, they press forward. If not, they hold back. They understand zero-based thinking, which I cover in Chapter 11, "Building the Perfect Portfolio," in more detail.

**Wealth Warning**

Remember that no matter what you do in life, you will always reap what you sow. In your journey toward wealth, make sure your work helps others or improves the world in some way. If not, your efforts will eventually backfire and reverse the wealth-building process.

# Develop Discipline

Discipline is simply sticking to a decision. If you make decisions based on your passions, the discipline should come naturally. The clients I have who built their wealth from the ground up have a certain discipline that helps them adhere to the simple habits necessary to build wealth. Climbing the social ladder is unimportant to them. They focus instead on what they are passionate about.

Discipline is simply a subconscious habit that is established by repetition. It's difficult to start a habit, but I'm told that after 21 days, it becomes part of your life. Here's an idea. For 21 days, take 15 minutes in the afternoon to plan tomorrow. This will give your brain time to think about what you have to do, which will help you get closer to your vision.

# Be Patient

Wealthy people are patient and maintain a long-term outlook. They plan for the future and do what it takes to build wealth, and over time, they naturally know they will succeed. When they're faced with failure, they get right back on track again and go for it. They understand that wealth building is a journey, not a destination. It's a practice of patient habits that naturally produces riches.

# Have Faith

Having faith may be the most powerful tool in this book. All great accomplishments require faith. I'm talking about faith in yourself, faith in your dreams, faith in others, and spiritual faith. You must have faith in yourself and your abilities. The wealthy people I know look at life with an open mind. What they don't know or understand, they do what it takes to learn. Faith in yourself is something that can be learned. Numerous books, classes, and counselors can help you develop more faith in yourself.

**Treasure Tip**

Along with faith in yourself, faith in others is almost as important. One of the most common characteristics among wealthy people is their belief in the inherent good in others. I don't know how I could have achieved anything significant in my life without my belief and faith in the people who helped me.

Most wealthy people I know also have a strong spiritual faith. Regardless of your beliefs or religion, it is difficult to imagine that we are not all connected in some way. All that you do in life affects the world in some little way. Like the ripples from a rain drop in a pool of water, what you do in life has some effect on the world. You matter, and your life is important. If everyone lived his or her life with this belief, the world would have much more faith to work with. My hope is that this book, in some way, gives you faith and that you are able to make a greater difference in this world.

# Be Willing to Sacrifice

Every great accomplishment involves a sacrifice. To achieve any great endeavor, you must first decide exactly what you want. Then, you must be willing to make the sacrifices necessary. You can only focus on one thing at a time, and that means that you have to sacrifice your focus on other endeavors. If you have several passions in life, you know how difficult it is to choose one passion to focus on. I have several passions in life, and it's not easy making the sacrifices. I've learned that the bigger the endeavor, the bigger the sacrifices. Most people aren't willing to make the sacrifices. Don't be like most people!

---

### The Least You Need to Know

➤ The basis of all the habits of wealthy people involves maximizing income, minimizing expenses, and making your savings work for you.

➤ If you want to achieve anything great in life, find the people who are already the best at what you want to do and imitate them.

➤ If you will delay most major purchases by writing them down, filing them away, and not thinking about them for a month or more, you may save a lot of money and prevent a lot of mistakes.

➤ Buying used cars and antique furniture can save you a fortune in commission and depreciation expenses.

➤ To be really wealthy in life, you must have enough passion for what you do that you lose yourself in your work.

➤ Building wealth requires certain habits that are easy to implement and maintain.

# Chapter 6

---

# An Employee's Guide to Building Wealth

> **In This Chapter**
>
> ➤ How to get the job you've always wanted
>
> ➤ How to design a job proposal that really works
>
> ➤ Do you need a role model?
>
> ➤ Designing the automatic savings plan as an employee

Passion produces enthusiasm, which is a powerful tool. It's all about living your life on purpose—doing what you enjoy doing. If you have a enthusiasm for what you do, you have a better chance of being the best at it and people will want to hire you. Every employer in your field will want to have you around, and they might be willing to pay you a lot of money to get you on their team. Enthusiasm is contagious, and employers look for it. They know that's the one thing they can't teach. If they can find sincere enthusiasm, they can teach everything else. Some people are naturally enthusiastic and that's great.

However, if you put a naturally enthusiastic person in a job she hates, you kill the enthusiasm. Therefore, to maintain your enthusiasm and get paid what you're worth, you must enjoy your work. It may take some time to figure it out, but to maximize your salary, you have to be good at what you do. As I said in the last chapter, to be good—I mean really good—at what you do, you have to be passionate about it. To be passionate, you have to love what you're doing.

**Wealth Warning**

Wealth is never worth sacrificing your happiness, family, or integrity.

# Design Your Own Dream Job

How many people do you know who are enthusiastic about their work? Many people live their lives in frustration and unhappiness working at jobs they despise and for people they don't respect. They stay in this self-imposed prison, locked in by their own fear of change, their inflexible standard of living, or procrastination. Often, it takes something dramatic or life threatening to break them out. What they don't realize is that this situation eats away at their self-confidence and self-worth. Don't let this happen to you.

## Five Questions Revisited

If you don't know what you like to do, or if you lack the vision or ability to see yourself advancing from your current position, don't get discouraged. That's a common problem that you can solve, and here's how to solve it. Return to the five questions in Chapter 5, "The Secrets of Millionaires," in the section titled "Follow Your Passion." Follow the instructions and list your answers. If you have already done this, try it again if you need to. Your answers will give you insight into your values and passions. Find something you can focus on that will make you money. It doesn't have to involve owning your own company.

If you think you can't make money doing what you love, you might be right. If nothing else, you could write a book about it. As I said, if you are passionate enough about your work, you will be the best at it and people will want to be a part of your world. If you are passionate about painting, then focus your time and energy on being the best painter you can be.

**That Reminds Me...**

A high school student asked me recently whether I thought he should get a real job or continue pursuing his real love, which was painting in oils. I said both, but I also said that he should focus most of his attention on painting. He was hesitant because he wondered whether he could make any money if he painted. I reminded him that people love art and are often willing to pay big money for it.

Several friends of mine are now professional artists. They took the hobby they were the most passionate about and made it into a business. One of them travels the world and sells his paintings to people in many different countries. One of his paintings recently sold in an auction for more than $5,000. His wife manages his business affairs and schedules his appearances. What a great idea. No matter what your passion is, find a way to make money doing it.

## What Are You Doing Now

Take a look at what you are doing now, and ask yourself these questions:

➤ Do you find yourself stressed out on Sunday night before work on Monday?

➤ Do you have a vision of what you want in life?

➤ Is your current job part of that vision? Do you feel as if you are wasting time in your current position?

➤ Do you see yourself working at your present job for a long time?

➤ Does your employer treat you with respect?

➤ Is your job a stepping stone for what you really want to do?

➤ Do you have a plan for the next step?

Your answers should tell you whether you are in the right job now. If you're not, why waste your time, your life, or the money you could be making? Develop a plan and move on.

**Treasure Tip**

One of the most common characteristics of happy wealthy people concerns their attitudes every Sunday night before work. Most of them enjoy their work so much that they don't know the difference between a weekday or weekend night.

## Design the Perfect Day

Next, find an hour of peace and quiet where you can think clearly. Take a piece of paper, and write a vision of you at work doing what you love to do. Title it, "The Perfect Day at Work." Make sure you have no interruptions, and let your imagination run. Don't worry about grammar, spelling, or order. Just write whatever comes to your mind. Get as specific as you can. Imagine yourself in your dream job doing exactly what you love to do. Where are you? Describe your surroundings, the people you work with, your boss, and the company. Fill at least one page, if not several.

Once you complete this exercise, take some more time to brainstorm how you can make this dream a reality. Believe it or not, you can make your perfect day a reality if you believe it's possible. Your disbelief may be the only obstacle between you and your dream day. Don't accept defeat immediately by saying, "This is only a dream. I can't really do this." That's what most people would say, and it's a self-imposed limiting thought. If you can think it and believe in it, it's possible. But if you don't believe in your vision, you'll never get there. Brainstorm for a minute on how you can make this dream a reality. Remember the words of Vincent Van Gogh who said, "If you hear a voice within you saying 'You are not a painter,' then by all means paint...and that voice will be silenced." Once you finish brainstorming, design a plan to get there. If the dream is really worthwhile, it may take some time to accomplish it. If it's what you really want, you won't mind the effort it takes to get there.

## What Are Your Options

Now that you have a better idea of what's important to you, think about all your options. They are unlimited. I can think of four basic directions you can go:

1. Stay with your present employer, and design a job proposal to move into the position you want or a new position that might not even exist.

2. Look into other companies or employers within your industry who might have more appreciation for your work and give you more opportunity. Find the best firm in the industry and submit a job proposal, which is outlined later in this chapter.

3. Study other fields of interest. Find the best companies or employers in that industry and submit a job proposal.

4. Start your own company. I discuss this in Part 3, "Building Wealth with Your Own Business."

Each option involves some homework on your part. For now, focus on role models and job proposals.

### Treasure Tip

I can't emphasize enough the power of having a role model in your life. A good role model can change your life and give you hope for your passion. In almost every facet of my business, I have a role model. Each has helped me add more life to my business, which has in turn helped me get more life out of my business.

## You Need a Role Model

Spend some time identifying the people who do what you want to do. Then, find the best in the business. Ask everyone you know in that field, "Who's the best at this?" Find at least three people who are successful at what you want to do. If you can, find out in advance what makes them different or special. Call these people, or write them a letter. First, compliment them by saying, "I've been told that you are one of the best in the country at what you do." Compliment them further by mentioning what you think makes them so special and unique. They will be impressed with what you know.

Second, tell them that you are enthusiastic about learning more about their industry and business. Third, ask them if you can talk with them about their success for a few minutes. Just say, "I'd like to hear your story. Would you have a minute to meet with me now or next week (over the phone or in person) for a few minutes?" If you compliment these people (without overdoing it) and ask them about their story, most of them will meet with you. If you have to travel to meet them, go for it. Do what it takes. When you do meet with them, ask them specific questions and let them talk. Here are some questions to choose from. Don't forget to take notes; you might want to ask them whether you can record the conversation:

➤ Tell me the story of your company.

➤ What are the five most important things that have contributed to your success?

➤ What do you love about your work?

➤ What do you dislike about your work?

➤ What are your biggest concerns each day?

➤ What do you focus most of your time on?

➤ Describe a typical day.

➤ If you had to do it all over again, what path would you take?

➤ Where would you start?

➤ Would you share with me your 5- or 10-year vision?

Take some time and review their answers. Did you find what you expected? Are you still as excited as you were? After the appointment, be sure to write them a thank-you note. Often, I call their secretary to find something they really like that I can have delivered from a local store in the area. You might even mention in the thank-you letter the one thing that excited you the most. They will appreciate your attention to detail and welcome another contact from you, which could prove to be valuable later.

# The Job Proposal

If you've designed your dream job, why not put it into the form of a proposal? Put all the pieces into the form of a job proposal. This simple tool is one of the most powerful job search tools you'll ever find. This is an idea I came up with years ago to help my brother get the job he wanted. It's a simple idea that can get you the job you want. The first step in building the job proposal is to know what you really want to do. The job for which you are making the proposal must be your dream job or a stepping stone toward your dream job. Otherwise, you will not have the enthusiasm needed to get the job.

Second, you must find a company that can offer you the opportunity you are looking for. Give your

**Wealth Warning**

The job proposal is a unique and powerful tool. If you use this just to get a job, with no attention to your values or interests, you may get a job you eventually dislike. Before using this technique, make sure you have an idea about what you enjoy doing.

current employer a chance if possible. If your present employer is out of the question, then look elsewhere. There are several ways to find company candidates for your proposal. First, checking the Yellow Pages is the easiest way because it categorizes listings by industry and service. Second, you should find a corporate directory, which is normally produced by the local Chamber of Commerce. I've seen both state and city directories.

Third, try the Internet. You must make certain that your vision matches the vision of the company or the duties of the position you want. To ensure this, interview the companies you've selected. Just ask whether you can talk to someone about his company. If the company is small, ask whether you can see the owner. If the company is larger, ask to see the person in charge of hiring. If all else fails, ask to speak to someone in sales about their services. Tell them you may need their service.

Fourth, conduct interviews with the companies you've selected. Study everything you can, and make sure this is where you want to be. Use the same questions from the "Role Model" section to find out all you can about the company. Don't ask them whether they need anyone! They might not even know they need anyone yet. It's your job later to convince them they do. Your goal here is gathering information. You want to know all about the company so you can decide whether this is where you want to work.

Finally, design the employment (job) proposal. In this proposal, describe the position you want on paper and be as specific as you can. What are you willing to do? What are you willing to be responsible for? What are you willing to accept in salary and benefits? Focus on the information you found in the interview. Match your strengths with their weaknesses. Match your talent with their needs.

I have included a copy of a proposal that I helped my brother design. He is an electrical engineer who wanted to work for a small software company. He interviewed for the job first and was told they were going to hire someone else. He was discouraged but still wanted the job. We wrote a job proposal that he submitted later that week. A week later, he got the job.

### Treasure Tip

If the company shows no interest in your job proposal, go to the company's competitor and offer the same proposal. Don't waste your efforts on someone who doesn't appreciate your enthusiasm and talent.

There are no rules here, and your proposal will be completely different from his, but I thought that an example might help you design yours.

The proposal should be done on a word processor and printed on bond paper. It doesn't have to be fancy; it just has to look good and use correct grammar and spelling. Be sure to present this proposal in person and go over it if you can. Bring several copies in case you must present it to several people. If you cannot get a face-to-face meeting, send it registered mail. Then, call within two days of receipt. Don't ask what your contact thinks of your proposal. Instead say, "I'd like to stop by next week on Wednesday to discuss the proposal. Would 10 in the morning be good, or would 2 in the afternoon be better for you?"

**Employment Proposal For XYZ Company**

I. Why I want to work for XYZ Company.

   A. I want to work for a small, growing company.

   B. More opportunity for growth and experience.

   C. Opportunity to work in a team-oriented atmosphere.

   D. I admire the management's philosophy and vision.

II. What am I able to offer XYZ Company?

   A. Sales assistance in the marketing department as you acquire new clients.

   B. Project assistance.

   C. Hardware design, development, and installation.

   D. Programming assistance in producing the best software available.

   E. Troubleshooting and maintaining the highest-quality service in the industry.

III. What I expect to be paid initially.

   A. Hourly pay of $X per hour.

   B. $X per hour after forty hours in a one week period.

IV. Available working hours.

   A. Regular working hours (8:00 A.M. to 5:00 P.M.).

   B. After hours.

   C. Weekends.

   D. Moment's notice.

V. Future compensation expected.

   A. To be negotiated in two months.

   B. Subject to the value you think I can add to your business. (You could be more specific here if you want.)

   C. Bonuses based upon a percentage of net profits.

   D. Full benefits including health insurance and retirement plan.

VI. Trial period.

   A. Two months.

   B. If things do not work out, I will walk away with no questions asked.

VII. Vision for the future: My goal is to be the chief engineer for XYZ Company and, if possible, stockholder/partner in the firm. I would like to develop new product services that compliment existing ones and participate in strategic planning and development for XYZ.

Proposal conclusion: The best thing that can happen is that you get a good engineer with education and experience that adds more value to your company than you pay him. The worst thing that can happen is that you get a good electrical engineer at an annualized salary of $XX,000 ($X per hour) for two months.

# Getting More Life Out of Your Job

The one thing I learned while working for others is that salary is always negotiable. The second thing I learned was that if I am good at what I do, there is always another company out there willing to pay me what I am worth. At least I had to convince my current employer of this fact. If I was successful, I was paid what I was worth. Therefore, you should always make it a habit to do some research into the salary range of your current job. What are other people in your field getting paid? How do these salaries compare to yours? Be sure to take into account the living expenses of the cities where these people live. For example, everything else being equal, someone in New York City will naturally be paid a higher salary than someone in Little Rock, Arkansas.

If you think you are worth more than what you are currently paid, but you think that getting a raise is impossible, I have an idea for you. Don't ask for a raise. Raises are the traditional means to higher pay, but they are limiting and often obscure in nature. Most companies don't even have a written policy on how raises are given. Many employers don't realize that this can lead to disenchantment among the employees.

The better alternative is what I call performance-based bonuses, which are bonuses usually based upon a percentage of a company's net income. The benchmark that measures the bonus must be a net result of income and expenses. If bonuses are based solely on gross income, employees pay little attention to expenses. If bonuses are based on net income after expenses, something magical happens. Employees begin to consider the cost of everything. Your employer may not understand this concept.

I know this from experience. Until recently, I based bonuses for my employees on gross income. The day I changed the benchmark to net income, the entire atmosphere changed. My employees began to act like shareholders and started paying much more attention to the costs of everything. I get into more detail about performance-based bonus programs in Part 3, but my point is that if your company does not have a performance-based bonus program, ask for it. Convince your boss that if you and the other employees are paid a bonus based upon net profits of the company, you will all pay more attention to reducing expenses and increasing gross income. This means that the company will make more money, which more than pays for the bonuses. If your company does not start one, put together a proposal. Include in that proposal all the benefits, which include

➤ Employees will be more motivated to produce.

➤ Employees will pay more attention to the cost of everything.

➤ Employees will be more efficient.

➤ The company's capacity for work will increase.

➤ Employees will be willing to do more.

➤ Expenses will decrease.

➤ Income will increase.

Note, however, that proposing such a plan might be difficult to do if you work for a large company with policies already in place.

# Four Ways to Automatically Build Wealth While Working for Others

Can you get to Wealth Stage 3 or 4 without starting your own company? Absolutely! I've met hundreds of people who've done it. If you want to build serious wealth, whether you work for yourself or someone else, the key is to live well within your means so you can save money systematically each month. At each pay period, a certain percentage of your income must go to your investment account, retirement plan, and savings account. It's even better if this takes place automatically at the time you get your paycheck.

If you are not doing this now, or if you haven't made the decision to do this, then stop right now and make the decision. Read this out loud: "I am a saver and a good steward of my money and financial future. I save a significant percentage of my income each month, which I invest for my future." If you don't make this a habit now, you may never reach Wealth Stage 3 or 4. It's only a decision; the rest is easy if you set it up to happen automatically. You might have an excuse now to wait, but you may always have some excuse.

## *Maximize Your Contributions to a 401(k), SEP, or Simple Plan—the Last Tax Shelters*

A *401(k)* and Simplified Employee Pension (*SEP* or SEP-IRA), or Simple plans, are excellent ways to save money automatically. They are both accounts into which your employer automatically deposits a percentage of your salary before tax. Your money can then be invested in stocks and mutual funds within the accounts. The taxes you normally pay on the income are deferred until you withdraw the money after you retire. Plus, the capital gains taxes you normally pay on the growth are deferred until you start making withdrawals. The combined effect of compound growth and tax deferral can be powerful in building your portfolio.

### Words of the Wealthy

**401(k)s** and **SEPs** are some of the types of qualified plans that allow employees to deposit part of their own salaries into the plan. The deposit is made pretax, and the account grows tax deferred. Each employee has her own individual account in which she can select from a number of different investment alternatives.

A qualified plan such as a profit-sharing plan, 401(k), or SEP-IRA is one of the last true tax shelters. The term *qualified* means that they meet the IRS rules for tax deferral, both on the deposits as well as the earnings. These retirement plans or investment accounts are qualified under IRS law to be sheltered from any taxes until withdrawal at retirement age, which begins at 59 ½. They could have chosen 60 or even 59, but for some unknown reason, 59 ½ is the established age after which you can begin withdrawing money from a qualified plan. The plan grows tax deferred until the money is withdrawn, which means that all capital gains, interest, and dividends can be reinvested.

**Treasure Tip**

Most of my clients have a net worth that exceeds $1 million. How did they do it? Did they sell a business? Did they inherit money? No! The most common characteristic among all these clients is that they all systematically contributed to a 401(k), SEP, or similar plan.

**Treasure Tip**

Visit with your human relations department or employer and maximize your 401(k) or SEP plan contributions. You not only get a tax deduction for the deposit, but you also get the benefit of tax-deferred growth.

There is a 10 percent penalty for early withdrawal of funds, which is levied on top of the taxes that also have to be paid. Therefore, it is usually smarter to borrow money rather than make an early withdrawal. Almost all qualified plans allow you to roll over your account tax-free into an IRA once you retire or terminate your employment. This allows your money to continue growing tax deferred until withdrawal. Partial withdraws become mandatory once you become 70 ½ and are based upon life-expectancy tables. Examples of qualified plans include SEP, 401(k), profit sharing, money purchase, and defined benefit plans.

If you do have a 401(k) or SEP, make sure it offers a large number of investment alternatives. For example, the most common missing alternative in a 401(k) plan is a foreign investment fund. If you want additional alternatives such as this added to your plan, ask for them. If you are put off, do your own homework and find out what it would take to get the alternative added.

If your employer doesn't offer either an SEP or 401(k), encourage the employer to start one. Most employers think that a retirement plan costs too much money or that it involves putting extra money in for everyone. The 401(k) is much more expensive than the SEP. Visit a discount brokerage firm and get the paperwork you need. Learn all you can about these two plans and show your employer how inexpensive it is to start these plans. Focus on the benefit of having a retirement plan for the employees, and at the same time, a way for the employer to save money tax deferred.

## Investigate Additional Retirement Plans

Other types of retirement plans that are different from the 401(k) are designed to put an extra contribution into a tax-deferred account on your behalf. These plans are known as defined-contribution and defined-benefit plans. These plans can be somewhat complicated, but they are a great company benefit. If your company doesn't offer these, you might want to suggest it.

## Maximize Savings in Your Investment Account

Even though you might have maximized your 401(k) or SEP contributions, you should continue to maintain your own investment account deposits. Look back at Chapter 5, where I discussed several different ways to save money so you can invest it. You should always continue saving in as many ways as you can. Most mutual funds offer an automatic debit feature from your checking account. This can be an addition to your 401(k) type plans or a substitution. We'll talk more about this feature in Part 2, "Becoming an Investor—Wealth Stages 3 and 4."

You need a place to put that money you save. Where should it be invested? If you work for someone else and you want to get to Wealth Stage 3 or 4, you have to invest in stocks (also known as equities). This includes the money in your retirement plans and investment accounts. It may also include privately held stock of your own company or your employer's company. The stock market is one of the most powerful tools you can use to truly grow your portfolio and beat inflation. Don't overlook ownership of your employer's stock as an investment alternative. My research has convinced me that in the last century, more fortunes have been built with stocks, both private and publicly traded, than with real estate or any other asset.

In the next chapter, I cover more on the benefits of owning equities of publicly traded companies. For now, take a look at the company you currently work for. Would you ever want to be a shareholder?

**Wealth Warning**

The real risk in maximizing 401(k) or SEP plan deposits is higher tax rates at the time of withdrawal. If your heart believes that tax rates will be higher tomorrow, then investing after-tax dollars outside of the plan may be the best alternative.

**Treasure Tip**

If you want to build wealth, you must consider investing in something that can produce a double-digit return. The most common investment with this potential is stock in a fast-growing company. There is risk, but your exposure can be reduced by spreading your investment among many different companies.

## Buying Your Company's Stock

First, before you even consider owning your own company's stock, look back at the answers to the questions in the earlier section titled "What Are You Doing Now?" If you answered favorably and you plan on staying with this company for a long time, then buying their stock might not be a bad idea. You also need to consider your employer's earnings growth potential. Is your company making any money? If the company's earnings aren't growing, you may want to avoid their stock.

Second, you have to consider the size of the company and the availability of the stock itself. If the company is small and owned by a few people (that is, if it's owned privately rather than traded on a stock exchange), then it may be difficult if not impossible to become a shareholder. You might have to convince the owners to let you buy shares or take shares instead of a part of your salary or bonus. Your employer might say "no," but it won't hurt to ask. Remember, if your company is small and experiencing normal cash-flow problems, your employer might welcome the idea. The company may prefer to pay part of your salary or bonus in stock.

It's much easier to own your company's stock if you work for a large company that has stock publicly traded on an exchange. Whether your company is small or large, or has closely held or publicly traded stock, it might be available through an employee stock ownership plan or ESOP. ESOPs are becoming popular as employers begin to see the benefits of employees being shareholders. The plan issues shares to its employees each month or year based upon their salary or profits of the company. ESOPs can also be part of a retirement plan, which means the gains and dividends can be tax deferred until retirement. It's a great idea if you want to own your company's stock. If not, don't participate. One of the most successful ESOP plans ever was Wal-Mart's employee stock-purchasing plan. This plan made hundreds of their employees millionaires who might otherwise have retired with a little pension and a small Social Security check.

## The Least You Need to Know

➤ Design your own job using your values, goals, and perfect day description.

➤ You can get your dream job if you have enough enthusiasm and a good enough job proposal.

➤ One single role model could save you years of experience, shorten your learning curve, and make your life much easier.

➤ Set up an automatic savings plan that requires little to no effort to maintain using 401(k), SEP, and other retirement plans.

## Part 2

# Becoming an Investor— Wealth Stages 3 and 4

*Your focus in Stages 1 and 2 was saving money. This focus is now second in importance to your rate of return and, therefore, your risk as well. In Wealth Stage 3, your portfolio produces a compound growth rate strong enough to cover your desired lifestyle and inflation. According to my research, only about 5 percent of the population achieve this stage of wealth by retirement age.*

*During your climb toward Wealth Stage 3, as well as toward Wealth Stage 4, you focus on how to properly manage an investment portfolio. First, recognize the investment tools to avoid. Second, understand the investment tools that will help you achieve your objectives. Third, learn how to hire professional help. Fourth, know what to look for when you're ready to take your first step into the investment world. Fifth, to be your own successful portfolio manager, you must have six key fundamentals. Sixth, know how the investment cycle works. Seventh, there are 10 investment tactics you should know. Eighth, know how to keep your investment-related expenses and mistakes to a minimum. Ninth, certain laws of investing that might come in handy. Tenth, it is helpful to know the most common mistakes made by investors. I discuss all of these topics in this part.*

# Chapter 7

# Stay Away from This Stuff

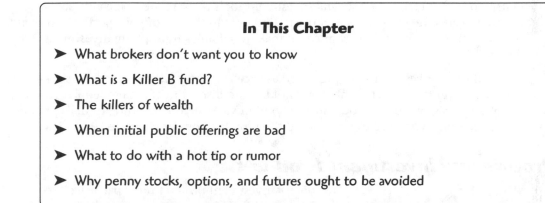

## In This Chapter

➤ What brokers don't want you to know

➤ What is a Killer B fund?

➤ The killers of wealth

➤ When initial public offerings are bad

➤ What to do with a hot tip or rumor

➤ Why penny stocks, options, and futures ought to be avoided

I almost titled the chapter, "It's what you don't know that will kill you." This is what I've found as an investment advisor. There are so many ways to make mistakes even with the right investments, let alone the bad ones. That's what this chapter is all about—the bad investment choices. I discuss the ones you should avoid.

Have you ever noticed that every nice neighborhood has one house that just doesn't fit? Maybe the builder used poor-quality materials or the wrong tools or just did a poor job altogether. Whatever the case, you know the end result is a money pit, and every homeowner's nightmare is to own one of these. I look at portfolios the same way. I meet these wonderful people who have built their portfolio neighborhood from scratch. Many of them have been built correctly and only need an adjustment or two. But a good number of them are just waiting to cave in. I call these "investment pits." The investor usually doesn't have a clue about the risks and costs they're incurring.

Before you can build anything, you need to know the proper tools to use. Whether it's a house, building, or investment portfolio, if you use the wrong tools and materials, eventually you're going to have problems. Unfortunately, you might not know you've made a mistake until it's too late. The tools I discuss in this chapter are all financial tools, most of which are investment vehicles used to maximize a portfolio's total return. I've met thousands of unhappy investors over the last 13 years, and a great many of them were using the wrong tools to accomplish their goal. These tools were either too expensive, mediocre in quality, unsuitable, or all of the above. Why is this the case? I explain the answer in this chapter and show you how to avoid the same mistake.

Don't be surprised if someone disagrees with the points in this chapter. Do your own homework and make your own decisions.

# What You Should Avoid in Your Portfolio

Outlined in this chapter are several investment tools that are mediocre at best. Avoiding them can save you money and frustration later in the life of your portfolio and, at the same time, improve your chances of making suitable, appropriate investment decisions.

Many of these investments are presented as excellent investment choices by salespeople all over the U.S. This chapter is not built to discredit these salespeople. This chapter is designed to give you another point of view. If you are going to make investment decisions, you need to understand the pros and cons of every decision.

## *Proprietary Investment Products*

**Wealth Warning**

The biggest investment nightmares I've observed in the last 10 years seem to be the result of complicated tax shelters, limited partnerships, bad stock tips, life insurance products, or futures contracts. As long as there are unsuspecting investors and commission-based sales people, the nightmares will continue. The best defense is knowledge.

Proprietary investment products are "packaged" securities that are sold by brokerage firms, usually in the form of unit investment trusts, limited partnerships, and mutual funds. They are underwritten or managed by the brokerage firm that offers them, and they are often your enemy. They will slowly squeeze your portfolio to death through unnecessary fees or bad investment performance. There are so many different possible conflicts of interest involved with these securities. For example, the manager might feed all his trades to one firm. In this case, there are two big possible conflicts of interest. First, the manager might not get you the best commission rate available on the securities he's buying for you. Second, the brokerage firm could fill the orders for the manager and add on points to the spread that makes the stocks purchased more expensive. This is especially true with over-the-counter stocks. Run away from these blood-sucking investments.

## Heavily Loaded Mutual Funds

A mutual fund is an investment company that raises money by offering shares of the company to investors. The money is then invested into a diversified portfolio of securities for the benefit of the shareholder. Shares can be purchased directly from the mutual fund or through brokerage firms. The money from the purchase or redemption goes directly in or out of the portfolio. If a *full-service brokerage firm* offers a mutual fund to its clients, a load or commission is involved. It may be hard to find without a *prospectus* (the fund's disclosure document), but it's there. This commission, or load, pays the salesperson and brokerage firm offering the fund. You can always find the commission charges of a fund in the first few pages of the prospectus. Mutual funds can be categorized according to the commission they charge to purchase or own the fund:

➤ Heavily loaded mutual funds—over 6 percent

➤ Medium loaded funds—4 to 6 percent

➤ Low load funds—2 to 4 percent

➤ No-load funds—0 percent

All mutual funds have a management fee that is paid to the manager of the fund. However, not all funds have commission charges. Legally, a mutual fund can charge up to 8.5 percent in commissions at the date of purchase. If you paid an 8.5 percent commission on a $1,000 mutual fund purchase, the end result would be an investment worth $915 ($1,000 × .085 = $85). To break even with your original investment, you will first have to make a 9.29 percent return. I can't think of any investment worth that much commission.

### Words of the Wealthy

A **full-service brokerage firm** offers its clients securities as well as advice. The firm is compensated by commissions that are paid at the time transactions are made. A discount brokerage firm offers the same selection of securities, but because they do not offer advice, their commissions are usually lower than the full service firm's rates.

### Words of the Wealthy

All mutual funds have a **prospectus**, which is the fund's disclosure document. This multi-page document explains in great detail all the aspects of the mutual fund, such as fees, commission charges, fund manager restrictions, and the objective of the fund. Newly issued stocks and bonds also have prospectuses.

## Killer B Funds

The most misunderstood concept in the mutual fund industry is the Killer B fund. It's so misunderstood that people actually read this book and then go out and buy these funds! It happens all the time. The problem here is that the load or commission is almost invisible, which is not unusual in the investment world.

Often, the load or commission is hidden from the investor, and unless he carefully reads the prospectus and understands it, he may never know how much he's really paying to own the fund each year. This practice of hiding the load has become the newest and biggest investment trap in the investment industry. Back in the 1980s when no-load funds began to get popular, brokerage firms around the country came up with a defense mechanism using part of the investment company regulation code called 12(b)1. This regulation allows mutual funds to charge a fee in addition to the management fee for such things as "marketing expenses, distribution expenses, or sales expenses." In reality, these expenses disguise the commission, which is paid to the salesperson either in advance, each quarter, or a combination of both. Table 7.1 provides an example of fees for a municipal bond fund I found.

## Table 7.1    The Killer B Fund Expense Chart

| Year | Back Load | 12(b)1 Fee | Management Fee |
|------|-----------|------------|----------------|
| 1 | 6% | 1% | .35% |
| 2 | 5% | 1% | .35% |
| 3 | 4% | 1% | .35% |
| 4 | 3% | 1% | .35% |
| 5 | 2% | 1% | .35% |
| 6 | 1% | 1% | .35% |
| 7 | 0% | 1% | .35% |

As you can see in Table 7.1, the original 12(b)1 funds had a declining back load that disappeared after a six-year period. If the investor sold the shares during the first year, there would be a six percent commission or back-end load due at the time of sale. If the investor sold the shares during the second year, there would be a five percent commission, and so on. After six years, there was no commission to sell the shares. It seemed that after six years, the fund became somewhat of a no-load fund. Many times, this is how these Killer Bs are portrayed. Salespeople have been known to say, "After 6 years, the fund is no-load," which is misleading to say the least. The only expense to pay seemed to be the management fee, which in this case is .35 percent. However, each year there is an additional 12(b)1 charge of 1 percent. This 12(b)1 fee can be higher or lower, but the average is 1 percent. Therefore, it didn't matter when you sold the fund; you were going to pay a six percent commission whether you waited six years or two months. If you waited six years, you still pay six years of 12(b)1 expenses. The fund becomes a killer because the 12(b)1 fees continue after the sixth year. This concept is only offered by brokerage firms and mutual funds that have little empathy for their clients and shareholders. It's bad enough to disguise the commission in the 12(b)1 fee, but it should be a crime to charge it beyond a six-year period. Fortunately, some funds have stopped charging the 12(b)1 fee after the sixth year.

**That Reminds Me...**

A gentleman who had read my book asked my opinion of his portfolio. While listening, I realized his entire portfolio consisted of Killer B funds. I kindly asked him whether he read Chapter 7 regarding Killer B funds. He said he had and was sure he didn't own any. I said modestly that maybe other people also had trouble understanding Chapter 7 and that I'd work harder on improving it. Well, he was convinced I insulted his intelligence. I was really trying to save him money on the high 12(b)1 fees he was paying. Only when the pupil is ready will the teacher appear.

## UITs

Unit Investment Trusts, or UITs, include municipal (bond) investment trusts, equity (stock) investment trusts, and corporate (bond) investment trusts. They are sold in $1,000 units just like a bond. These investments are similar to traditional mutual funds in that money is raised initially by selling units to investors and is then invested according to the prospectus of the UIT for the benefit of the unit holder. What makes UITs different from traditional mutual funds is the method of investment management. UITs are passively managed, as opposed to traditional mutual funds, which are actively managed. Passive management means that once the securities are purchased, they are not traded or sold until the maturing or end date of the trust. At the time of the end date of the trusts, all the securities are sold and the proceeds are dispersed to the unit holders.

If you examine them carefully, UITs don't offer a lot of advantages to the unit holder. They might offer diversification for small amounts of money and enable the unit holder to buy securities that might be difficult to buy, but that's about it. Because they are passively managed, the portfolio remains static and cannot be maneuvered to take advantage of changing market trends. The fees are usually extensive and are not discussed except in the prospectus. Normally, UITs have an up-front commission plus a management fee. Why would you pay a management fee for a passive (unmanaged) portfolio? The better choice is usually an actively managed fund with no sales commission.

# Limited Partnerships

Over the past several decades, limited partnerships have caused more trouble than any other investment vehicle. These are the real killers of wealth. They're not as popular as they were in the 70s, but they are still around. I personally have met hundreds of investors who have lost their entire fortunes in limited partnerships. The chain of events usually unfolds like this. The investor buys a limited partnership from a broker or advisor. The first problem that's encountered is a commission charge of unknown proportion. Unfortunately, the commission is not indicated on the confirmation slip you get in the mail, and it might not be clearly stated in the disclosure document. You can't see it, but believe me, it's ugly.

### Wealth Warning

I remember the last limited partnership I was pushed to sell. It took me nearly five hours of reading the prospectus to find all the fees and expenses involved. I estimated them to be a total of 19 percent. The deal was eventually pulled and never sold. I wonder why?

### Words of the Wealthy

A **secondary market** is any market where previously issued securities are traded. The New York Stock Exchange (NYSE) is the best known example. Investors can buy and sell stocks from each other through the designated traders on the floor of the exchange.

The second problem encountered is the pricing of the limited partnership on the brokerage statement each month or quarter. This price is usually held at the original purchase price, which is total garbage. After you purchase the partnership, you never know what your units are actually worth because there is no *secondary market*. You might not ever know the true value of your units. If you did, it would make you sick.

The third problem occurs when you decide to sell the limited partnership. That's when you find there is no place to sell it and no one to sell to. The only way you can sell is to accept the price a scrap yard will offer you. A scrap yard is a company that researches limited partnerships around the country. They make their living by offering limited partners 20 to 50 cents on the dollar for their units. They are scavengers. They will buy the units and attempt to sell them at a higher price later or dismantle the whole partnership and sell off the partnership's individual securities, land, and so on. There are certainly exceptions to this rule. Not all limited partnerships are bad. The most common exception is a private venture that just so happens to benefit all parties. If you are considering a limited partnership and are well aware of all aspects of the venture, then by all means explore this as an investment. However, if you are approached by someone offering you a limited partnership in a venture you do not understand, chances are you'll be better off by running away immediately.

With most every rule, there are certainly exceptions. Some limited partnerships available today are legitimate investments with profits as the chief objective. However, there's still the problem of little to no secondary market. Be sure to do your homework and get an unbiased opinion from someone you trust before you invest.

# Initial Public Offerings of Closed-End Funds

A closed-end investment company or mutual fund issues a set number of shares, after which no additional shares can be sold. The fund theoretically "closes" the door and manages the money. If you purchase closed-end shares when they are initially offered to the public, your money goes directly into the fund to be managed. If you want to sell your shares later, you must do so in a secondary market. Most closed-end funds can be sold on the New York Stock Exchange (NYSE).

Closed-end funds by their nature and function can be attractive with one big exception: when they are offered initially to the public. Just like stock, closed-end funds are underwritten by a brokerage firm. That firm is paid by marking up the shares of the fund above their *net asset value.* This mark-up is normally about 8.5 percent and is not felt until a few weeks after the underwriting is completed. Why a few weeks? The firm underwriting the issue holds back some shares for its own account and attempts to keep the price of the issue at least as high as the initial public offering price. Because the firm only buys so many shares, they can keep this up only so long. After the initial public offering, the shares become available on the secondary market, and their price usually falls back to approximately what the shares are actually worth, which is the net asset value. Therefore, there is usually little reason to buy a closed-end fund until it hits the secondary market.

Please understand that this arrangement does not apply to initial public offerings of stocks. They are completely different, and my warning regarding closed-end funds does not apply to stocks.

**Words of the Wealthy**

The **net asset value** of a fund is the actual true value of each share of a mutual fund. This is calculated by dividing the total value of the fund by the number of shares outstanding.

**That Reminds Me...**

An initial public offering or stock underwriting is the process by which a brokerage firm or investment banker promises a company a certain amount of money for the securities they issue. The brokerage firm hires people to sell the securities and takes the risk of not being able to raise all the money promised. The brokerage firm is paid by marking up the shares before selling them. This is important to understand because many brokers explain this by saying, "The shares are offered net commission," which implies no commission. You better believe that if a broker is selling it, you're paying a commission.

# Options

Options are marketable securities that give their owners the right but not the obligation to buy or sell a stated number of shares (usually 100) of a particular security, at a fixed price, within a predetermined time period. Many different books published on this subject go into great detail. Fortunately for both of us, this is not one of them! The one thing you need to understand is that options are complicated, involve a lot of risk, and are not worth any attention. What kind of risk am I talking about? You can quickly lose 100 percent of your investment. I can tell you that I don't know anyone who made any significant money in the long run by buying options. I'm sure such people exist, but they are the exception, not the rule.

One of my first investment experiences involved a $1,500 option on gold. I lost every penny of it, but I learned two great lessons: Avoid options and don't always listen to investment advice from friends. No matter what your friends tell you, the risk in options is not worth the reward. The only possible exception is a strategy called selling covered calls. If you want to learn more, many other books available can teach you about this technique. It is a conservative way to add income to your portfolio.

# Futures

A futures contract is a legal agreement in which a buyer promises to pay a seller some fixed price for a specified quantity of a particular good at some future date. The goods can be commodities or financial instruments such as Treasury bills or market indexes. These contracts are negotiable financial instruments that are bought and sold like stocks in a secondary market called commodity exchanges. Futures contracts are usually referred to as futures or contracts. They are similar to options, and the risk is not worth the reward. You can even lose more than 100 percent of your investment. Avoid futures like the plague.

# Penny Stocks

**Words of the Wealthy**

An **over-the-counter market** is a secondary market where securities are traded by phone and computer. The NASDAQ market is the largest and most popular over-the-counter market.

Penny stocks are stocks that are initially offered to the public at a price of $1 or less and are traded primarily in the *over-the-counter markets* of Vancouver, Denver, and Salt Lake City. Some penny stocks trade for as much as $10 or more, but they are the exception and not the rule. Penny stocks are the bastards of the investment industry. The brokerage houses that specialize in penny stocks are notorious for using fraudulent sales pitches. It is estimated that penny stock fraud costs U.S. investors $2 billion each year. I guess the sales people are just too convincing for investors to "just say no." The Securities and Exchange Commission issued three primary warning signs of penny stock fraud:

1. Unsolicited phone calls from brokers offering penny stocks.

2. High-pressure sales tactics.

3. The inability to sell the penny stock and receive cash.

## Rumors and Hot Tips

It seems like every investor in the world has fallen victim to a rumor or hot tip. I certainly have. I get one almost every day. Rumors and hot tips are normally intended to show others at parties and meetings the brilliance of the person sharing them. The person might mean well by sharing the information, hoping that others can profit too. However, what people don't realize is that these rumors and hot tips usually result in exactly the opposite of what is intended. First, they can show the ignorance of the person sharing them. Second, if the information is garbage, the person receiving it may act on it and lose money. Avoid hot tips in your wealth-building program. Avoid listening to them and avoid starting them.

## Insurance Products as Investments

Insurance products are not bad for what they are intended to be, but they are horrible if used for investment purposes alone. They became popular in the 1980s when tax laws tightened and limited partnerships in real estate lost their tax savings appeal. Brokerage firms lost one of their most profitable sources of income. They could no longer make the big commissions they were paid by selling the partnerships. Therefore, they had to find alternatives. They decided to focus on insurance products. Every major full-service brokerage firm bought or established an insurance company or at least an agreement with one. Soon brokers all over the country added insurance products to their quiver of investment arrows. Because the tax laws tightened, brokers and commission-based financial planners began selling insurance products such as *fixed* and *variable annuities,* as well as variable life insurance policies. Most often, the variable life policy is positioned as an investment.

A variable life insurance policy can be a whole life or universal life insurance policy with a cash value and death benefit that varies in value, according to the performance of a portfolio of mutual funds from which the policy holder can select. Typically, these policies offer a stock fund, a bond fund, and a money market fund.

Variable life insurance policies are described as mutual funds covered by a tax umbrella that allows them to grow tax deferred. The variable life insurance policy even allows the withdrawals to be

**Words of the Wealthy**

A **fixed annuity** is a policy with a life insurance company whereby you give them a sum of money, and based on your age, life expectancy, and current interest rates, they calculate how much they'll send you each month for as long as you live. You decide when you want to receive payments, and until then, the money grows tax deferred.

completely tax-free as long as the withdrawal is considered a loan against the policy. However, there are three primary problems with these investment products.

First, they are extremely expensive. You have to pay both the money management fees as well as the costs of the insurance. Second, the selection of mutual funds within these policies is usually limited and mediocre. Third, these investments can become a ball and chain later in life. If you want your money back, you might have to pay an early withdrawal penalty to the insurance company. You might also have to pay the IRS a 10 percent penalty if you withdraw money from an annuity before you become 59 ¹/₂ years of age. Plus, if you ever terminate your policy, you have to pay ordinary income taxes on all your gains from day one of the policy. The variable life policy might offer tax-free loans, but you have to keep the policy intact for the rest of your life to keep them tax deferred.

Now that the long-term capital gains tax rate is 20 percent, these policies have lost even more of their luster as investment vehicles.

If you really like the variable annuity idea, Fidelity, Vanguard, and Charles Schwab all have no-load variable annuities with relatively low annual expenses compared to the other traditional loaded policies.

Variable life policies might be an excellent vehicle for estate planning, but not for investment purposes alone. I talk more about that later in Part 4, "The Advanced Strategies for Building Wealth."

### Words of the Wealthy

A **variable annuity** works the same way a fixed annuity does, but its value and pay-out amount varies according to the performance of a portfolio of mutual funds from which the contract holder can select. Typically, these policies offer a stock fund, a bond fund, and a money market fund.

## Wrap Accounts

During the first five years in the investment business, I learned something very important. Out of all the wealthy people I had met, the best stewards of money were those who understood the importance of using other people's talents to manage their money. Most of them hired several individual money managers, which seemed logical. Hiring several money managers provides more diversification than one single manager can provide. However, the problem with directly hiring several managers is that they can be expensive and time-consuming to fire.

Soon, I saw that almost every full-service brokerage firm was coming out with a concept called the "wrap account." The wrap account concept works like this: A client fills out a questionnaire that measures risk tolerance, experience, and performance expectations. According to this measurement, the client is shown two or three managers that match the client's measurement of risk tolerance and so on. Most firms in the industry used a list of approximately 17 money management firms. The minimum investment was $100,000, and once the client chose from the three managers in his or her corresponding risk level, the money was allocated among individual stocks and bonds within the client's own account. Each month, the client received a statement showing the securities the management firm had purchased as well as all the transactions. The annual fee for this was 3 percent per year, which was based upon the value of the assets in the portfolio. What I couldn't help but notice in these accounts was the high level of trading volume. These accounts typically had 10 to 30 individual trades per month. My experience and intuition told me that something was wrong. Why did these guys trade so much?

**Treasure Tip**

Real wealth is built by owning equity in a company—if not your own, then someone else's.

I studied further and found out why. The full-service brokerage firm makes money trading. The money management firm makes money by charging a management fee. If a brokerage firm hires a money manager and feeds him millions of dollars of new accounts, what do you think the brokerage firm hopes to get in return? That's right— trades. Trades equal commissions. Commission equals profit. But they also equal conflict of interest and slow death for the client. The media had a field day with this and found even further conflicts of interest.

Without the conflicts of interest, the concept was great, but the limitations on invest-ment alternatives were horrible. How could you select from only 17 firms and expect to maintain a portfolio of the best minds in the world? I wanted more variety and convenience. That's when I began researching mutual funds, more specifically, no-load funds. At that time, there were more than 1,500 no-load funds available. Not only did I find variety, but I also found a way to switch from one manager to another quickly and cost efficiently.

In the following chapters, I show you how to combine these concepts to build and maintain a superior portfolio of no-load mutual funds.

# Why Do People Use the Wrong Tools?

One of the first keys to building wealth is knowing the correct investment tools, which means you also need to know the tools to avoid. It might be appropriate to start with what you should avoid. Improper tools are the most common killers of wealth. If that's true, then why don't people do something about it? Well, as I said before, most of them have no idea there's a problem. Here are some of the reasons people get them-selves into the wrong investment tool.

## *People Skip Their Homework*

The first reason is that most investors simply do not do enough homework before they invest their money. I've met hundreds of investors who spend more time planning a vacation each year than they do planning or researching their own investment portfo-lio. This is scary. Maybe they know the basics, but they justify quick investment decisions with their limited knowledge.

## *People Are Persuaded by Commission-Based Salespeople*

The second most common reason investors use the wrong investment tools is that they buy their investments from commission-based sales people. Not all commission-based brokers are bad, but there is a conflict of interest. If you are an experienced investor, understand the details of the market, and how brokers charge for their services, then you probably know how to work with a broker. You use their research, you both come up with ideas, and then you make a decision. You also know how these folks are paid, and you know commissions are negotiable.

If you do not fully understand the details of the market, why would you buy from someone who gets paid a commission every time you buy or sell an investment? Because their paycheck depends upon your making transactions, their natural motivation is to promote transactions and not performance. If they are paid a commission on each trade, can you really count on the investment to be in your best interest most of the time? You have to ask yourself this question: What motivates the commission-based broker?

Toward the end of each month, brokers all across the country have to make their commission quota. What do you think is going through their minds during the last week of every month? I've been there. I was a broker for almost five years. If you deal with a commission-based broker, take a look at all your trades for the last year. Are most of them made during the last half of the month? Before you make another investment decision with a commission-based broker, read Chapter 8, "Investments That Do Work," on how to select an investment advisor. One thing I can almost guarantee is that a commission-based salesperson will ignore non–commission-based alternatives that may benefit you.

### That Reminds Me...

The biggest problem I see with commission-based brokers is the hidden fees they charge. These are fees you might never find or know about. Before you buy any investment from a commission-based broker, have them describe in detail every expense that is involved in the investment. Then, read the prospectus. If the broker left anything out, stay away from the investment. If the broker says there is no commission or the commission is built in, ask exactly how much it is. Demand an answer. If you can't understand all the fees and commissions, leave it alone.

## People Don't Recognize Conflicts of Interest

Many people use the wrong investment tool because they don't check for bias before they make a decision. They mistake marketing information for good advice. I believe that approximately 95 percent of what you read and hear about investing in your lifetime is marketing related. Most of the investment information available today is biased and does not portray the whole story. Your job as an investor is to uncover the truth to help your portfolio. If you can't find substantial unbiased evidence to support your investment choice, I suggest you keep looking, be patient, or move on to something else.

Why is bias so important? If the person is paid by a company to promote its investment products, he might have a one-track mind and focus only on the product. The end result is that bias tends to ignore the alternatives and drive investors into decisions based on limited thinking.

Unfortunately, most investment decisions are made with bias, and knowledge of the mistake may go unrecognized for years. Often, undoing the mistake involves a penalty or exit commission, which in itself tends to prolong the mistake. Investors don't like paying penalties. They would rather wait and keep the mistake alive until there's no penalty. It seems ironic, but I've seen this happen hundreds of times. If it's not a penalty, it's the absence of a secondary market that keeps the mistake alive. A secondary market enables you to sell the investment at a later date. If there is no secondary market and you have no buyers, you end up with a worthless investment, which is an even worse mistake. Therefore, recognizing the bias before taking advice can reduce your chances of making a mistake.

**Wealth Warning**

I hosted a radio show called "Arkansas' MoneyTalk" for three years and was never paid a penny by any fund or investment product I suggested on the show. Beware of the TV and radio talk shows on investing with hosts who get paid to promote mutual funds, insurance products, or any investment. Most listeners don't understand the conflict of interest inherent in these programs.

# What Are Consequences of Owning the Wrong Investments?

The end result of using bad tools is an investor with an unsuitable, expensive, or mediocre investment. The first problem seems like the most common.

## Unsuitability of the Investment

Investors sit in front of me every day with portfolios filled with unsuitable investments. Usually, one stock represents a huge chunk of their net worth. In Arkansas, it's

**101**

Wal-Mart. In Michigan, it's Ford or GM. This is a big risk, and to some degree, the investor is really a speculator. If something went wrong with that one company, the portfolio's net worth would take a big hit. If they really understood the risks, they would immediately sell at least most of it. There are certainly exceptions such as huge capital gains tax liabilities or restricted stock regulations, but for the most part, you still have a problem.

Even after I explain the risks, do you know how they justify hanging on? They often say, "Well, I'll wait until the price comes back up to my original purchase price." This is crazy. My next question is always, "If you had the value of this investment today in cash, would you buy this investment?" Their answer is almost always, "No" or "No way." I then tell them they ought to consider selling the investment because their subconscious is telling them something. This is referred to later in the book as zero-based thinking. The reality of the risk, unfortunately, sets in too late.

**Wealth Warning**

People may say they can handle risk, but they don't know their true feelings until the market takes a big fall.

## Unknown Expenses

The second end result is a portfolio filled with unknown expenses that eat away at the profits, if any are even made. This result is what I call slow portfolio death. I personally believe that more than 50 percent of the individual portfolios in the U.S. are experiencing slow death. This percentage is beginning to decrease because investors are finally learning more about all the charges investment companies levy on their clients and shareholders. Publications such as *The Wall Street Journal* and *Barron's* do teach investors most of the traps out there, but most novice investors don't read these publications.

## Mediocrity

The third end result of using the wrong investment tool is mediocrity. Again, most investors don't know their portfolio performance is mediocre. Often, they don't even know how their own portfolio is performing. They get a monthly statement showing the dollar amount of change from last month, but that's it. Brokerage firms normally do not illustrate portfolio performance for their clients. I've always wondered why. It would be so easy to do. If my company can do it, why can't theirs? Instead of waiting for your brokerage firm to measure your percentage performance, learn how to do it yourself or get someone to do it for you. Your CPA might help.

## The Least You Need to Know

➤ Avoid complicated investments such as proprietary investment products, options, and futures contracts.

➤ Avoid investments that have little or no secondary markets such as limited partnerships, penny stocks, and proprietary products.

➤ Avoid the most expensive investments such as loaded mutual funds, UITs, insurance products, and Killer B funds.

➤ Beware of the rumors and hot stock tips you hear at parties; they don't usually work out.

➤ Do your homework, don't be persuaded by a slick salesperson, and watch out for conflicts of interest.

# Chapter 8

# Investments That Do Work

---

### In This Chapter

➤ Exactly what you need to know before making an investment

➤ The tricks of the trade that most brokers aren't willing to share with you

➤ What to look for when selecting bonds and fixed income funds

➤ The power of stocks in the wealth-building process

➤ How mutual funds can help the smallest and the biggest investors

---

Don't assume that the investment tools used to build wealth are too complicated to understand and use. That is a big mistake. They might seem complicated at first, but once you get the basics, it's relatively easy. However, you need to know the right tools to use. I have presented them in reverse order of importance and power. The first is the least important and least powerful tool, whereas the last is the most important and most powerful tool.

You can certainly buy illiquid securities, but as I said in Chapter 2, "Eleven Tools for Building Wealth," you'd better understand what you're getting into. This chapter deals with liquid securities—ones you can sell and convert to cash quickly.

## Before You Invest

Before you buy any investment, you need to fully understand what you are buying. There are many hidden traps you could fall into. It's what you don't know that will hurt you. That's why you need these five questions answered. They will help you make better investment decisions:

1. **In one sentence, what exactly am I investing in?** Keep things simple. If you or the person selling you the investment can't explain in one sentence what you are investing in, then the investment might be too complicated. If so, don't buy it.

2. **Does this investment fit into my plan?** Make sure the investment meets your own personal goals. If you want no risk of fluctuation, you'll focus on money-market funds, short-term CDs, and Treasury bills. If you have a long-term horizon and can withstand higher levels of fluctuation, then stocks may be what you need. Make sure the investment accomplishes your mission and fits into your portfolio goals. Don't worry; you might not know the details of your portfolio goals now. The next several chapters will help you narrow them down.

3. **What are the risks involved in owning this security?** Risk is always a confusing subject because there are so many different types. There's inflation risk, fluctuation risk, and company risk, all of which are discussed in a later chapter. For now, you need to remember to ask this question before buying an investment.

4. **Is there a secondary market for this investment?** This question is important and yet so few investors ask. A secondary market is simply a place where you can sell your investment whenever you want. Once you purchase a security, you must have a secondary market that will allow you to sell the security later. If the security is a stock listed on the NYSE, then you know there is a real secondary market. If it is a packaged product such as the ones mentioned in the previous chapter, then you need to stay away. Markets do change, and you need to know whether you can sell the investment later. If there is no established secondary market, the security is illiquid, and you should avoid it. Most investors don't appreciate the need for a secondary market until they suddenly need one.

   Without a secondary market for your investment, another problem is getting daily and monthly pricing data. No one is making regular transactions, so there is no source for current prices. If there is no way to get an accurate price each month, you'll rarely know what your investment is worth. Therefore, the price on your statement each month is an estimate. If you have owned limited partnerships before, you understand what this is like. It's not fun. Full-service brokerage firms that sell limited partnerships are known for using the original purchase price on the monthly statement. Many of them have stopped this practice, but in the past, I've seen firms leave limited partnerships for years on a statement with the original purchase price, knowing full well that they were worth about half that price. This is bad business.

5. **What will this investment cost me?** Investment costs are easy to hide. If you buy a stock from a brokerage firm, you are charged a commission on top of the purchase price of the stock. What can be hidden from you is an additional commission, which is part of the spread. The spread is the difference between the price the brokerage firm paid for the security and the price at which it sold the

security to you. Brokers are only able to do this with over-the-counter (OTC) stocks because the NYSE no longer allows this practice. Bonds are different in that the commission is part of the price you pay for the bond. You may never know the commission. It is usually measured in percentage points. (One percent equals $1,000 commission.) Short-term bonds are easier to sell, and therefore, the commission can be a fraction of a point or a point. Long-term bonds can have as much as 5 percentage points in commission. Even if you ask the broker, "How many points did this bond pay you?" you might not get a straight answer. However, the broker may be amazed that you even knew to ask.

Commissions are hidden from the investor in more ways than even I know after almost 11 years in the business. You can always look in a prospectus when buying a mutual fund. You can also ask this question: "If I sell this investment tomorrow and the price of the security remains unchanged from today, what will it cost me?" This is a great question. If your proceeds are significantly lower than your original purchase price, don't buy the security. It's probably a commission trap.

I selected the tools in this chapter based upon certain attributes that correspond to these questions. Almost all of the tools can be easily researched and understood. They all have certain types of risk that are somewhat measurable, and each has a secondary market that is easily accessible. These securities will cost you less than most other types of securities cost. However, each tool is still used to indirectly hide commissions and fees. If you are aware of this possible practice and you learn more about how to prevent it, you shouldn't encounter many hidden fees.

# The Bond Tools

*Bonds* or fixed income securities are basically IOUs issued by companies or the government that pay a certain amount of interest each year and the full principal amount at a certain known date in the future. By their very nature, fixed income securities pay a fixed rate of interest that today, depending upon maturity and quality, is only a few points above the inflation rate. Because your goal of building wealth involves beating the rate of inflation by a significant amount, fixed income securities are not powerful tools. However, if your goal is to reduce risk and maintain your principal instead of maximizing its growth, then fixed income securities may be just the thing for you.

### Words of the Wealthy

**Bonds** represent the debt of a company, whereas stocks represent equity ownership. If a company files for bankruptcy, a bondholder is paid off before the stockholder. The equity holder's claim to the company's assets is subordinated to the bondholder's claim.

Many investors think that the price of a bond stays constant while it pays its interest. This is not the case. In fact, bond prices fluctuate more than people know. Most bondholders only get a chance once a month (on their brokerage statements) to see the prices of their bonds, as opposed to the prices of stocks and mutual funds, which are printed daily in the paper. What makes a bond fluctuate? Interest rates. When interest rates rise, bond prices fall, and when interest rates fall, bond prices rise. When is the best time to own a bond? When interest rates go down. I discuss this in more detail later in the book, but for now, understand that in order to get an above-average return from bonds, interest rates must fall. Otherwise, bonds are not powerful wealth-building tools because they don't produce enough of a return in the long run, relative to stocks.

One prevalent conventional theory is important to understand. If you haven't heard it yet or read it somewhere, you will. Some people believe that an investor should have a percentage of his portfolio that is equal to his age invested in bonds. If the investor is 20 years old, then 20 percent of the portfolio should be in bonds. If the investor is 80, then 80 percent of the portfolio should be in bonds. What a bunch of garbage! The percentage of bonds in a portfolio shouldn't have anything to do with the age of the investor.

Everyone has her own individual goal and risk tolerance. If my 80-year-old clients had 80 percent of their portfolios in bonds in 1994 when the bond market fell 15 plus percent, they would have all called me on the phone and said, "Uh, have you lost your mind? You manage every penny of our retirement money, and we just lost 15 percent of it. What happened? We're extremely concerned." A portfolio's bond allocation should be based upon an individual's risk tolerance and interest rate forecast, not the age of the investor.

### Words of the Wealthy

An **automated account** at a brokerage firm offers an automatic money-sweep feature that deposits all deposits, interest payments, dividends, and proceeds of sales into a money market account. When purchases are made within the account, or when checks are written against the account, money is automatically withdrawn from the account. Most full-service brokerage firms charge a custodial fee, but almost all discount brokerage firms waive their fee.

## Money Market Funds

A money market fund is actually a mutual fund of short-term, fixed income securities that all have maturities of less than one year. Most investment accounts are *automated*, which means that all deposits, dividends, interest, and proceeds from sales are automatically deposited into a money market account. These funds are primarily used as parking places for cash. When the market seems overvalued, money market funds come in handy. Parking a small percentage of your portfolio in a money market fund might be a smart thing to do when you feel nervous about the market being too high. The perfect scenario is to use the funds later when the market falls.

Money market funds offer certain advantages that no other security can offer. The biggest advantage is the price, which is designed not to fluctuate. It stays constant at $1 per share, which means that there is little risk of loss. These funds have a next-day settlement, which means they can be sold one day and the proceeds will be available the next day. You can also write checks on most money market funds. The only real disadvantage is that they don't pay a whole lot of interest.

## Certificates of Deposit

Certificates of deposit, or CDs, are useful when you have short-term goals. If you have a sum of money that you know you'll need within three years, CDs might be a perfect idea. The advantages include that they are insured up to $100,000 and pay higher rates than money market funds.

The main disadvantage with CDs is the penalty for early withdrawal. This can be eliminated if you purchase marketable CDs from a brokerage firm. Many brokerage firms offer CDs from banks all over the U.S. If you want to sell before maturity, the brokerage firm will offer you a price based upon current interest rates. As with a bond, if interest rates go up, the CD's price will fall. If rates have fallen, then you might get a capital gain on your CD when you sell. However, if you plan to hold the CD until maturity, it really doesn't matter if the price fluctuates because you are guaranteed to receive the face value of the CD at maturity.

The primary benchmark to use when comparing your CD's yield is the yield on a money market account. If a money market account offers higher interest, you might want to reconsider the CD.

## Treasury Bonds, Bills, and Notes

Treasury securities are IOUs offered by the U.S. Government. They have maturities extending from one day to 30 years, and their interest payments on *notes* and *bonds* are semiannual and exempt from state taxes. The Fed has weekly auctions of 3-month and 6-month *bills*. Other auctions include 1-, 3-, 5-, 10-, and 30-year bonds. You can find all types of maturities in the secondary markets, which will allow you to use bond strategies such as laddering maturities. Laddering is a strategy where you buy an equal amount of bonds that mature each year for a period of years:

| Year 1 | $1,000 bond matures |
| Year 2 | $1,000 bond matures |
| Year 3 | $1,000 bond matures |
| Year 4 | $1,000 bond matures |
| Year 5 | $1,000 bond matures |

**Words of the Wealthy**

**Treasury bonds** are similar to notes, but their maturities extend from 10 to 30 years. Their prices fluctuate the most because of the longer maturities. This is explained further in later chapters.

### Words of the Wealthy

**Treasury bills** are issued with 1-month, 6-month, and 52-week maturities. They are normally sold at a discount to the face value, which is $1,000 per bond. The difference between their face value and their discounted value is the interest you will receive at maturity. Until maturity, their price fluctuates daily according to short-term interest rates.

### Words of the Wealthy

A **Treasury note** is also an IOU offered by the U.S. Government, but they have maturities of 1 to 10 years. They are issued at face value and pay fixed interest payments every six months. Their price also fluctuates with interest rates, and the fluctuation is greater than that of Treasury bills.

This strategy is used to reduce the risk of interest rate fluctuation. If rates are going up, you can use a bond that is maturing to reinvest at the higher rates. If interest rates are going down, you have existing bonds that are paying the higher rates.

Traditionally, the longer-term maturities pay higher interest rates than the shorter term. Because they all pay so little in interest, however, don't waste much time here looking for big gains in the long run. Treasury bonds can be purchased in increments of $1,000. Bills can be purchased in increments of $10,000 in face value (and in some cases $5,000), whereas notes come in increments of $5,000.

Investors use short-term Treasury securities for temporary parking places. The longer maturing notes and bonds can be used strategically to take advantage of falling interest rates. Treasury securities offer one great advantage: They are guaranteed by the U.S. Government. The disadvantage is that they don't pay a lot of interest, but they are definitely safe investments if you hold them until maturity.

One possibly helpful wealth-building tool is the long-term zero coupon Treasury bond. This can be an outstanding tool for exploiting falling interest rates. A zero coupon bond is a bond that pays no coupon interest but is instead issued at a discount from its face or maturity value to yield income from capital appreciation. They are wildly volatile but tend to do extremely well when interest rates fall.

Because Treasury securities are often used as benchmarks, it's hard to compare them to other securities. Before I've purchased any for clients, which is seldom, I check current CD rates. If CDs are paying more than the Treasury security, I'll buy the CD. If I'm investing more than the $100,000 insured amount, I'll stick with the Treasury.

## Municipal Bonds

Municipal bonds are IOUs issued by state and local municipalities, and the interest they pay is exempt from federal taxes, as well as state taxes within the state that issues the bond. They are rated according to their estimated ability to pay their interest and principal payments on a timely basis. The two rating services are Moody's and Standard & Poor's (S&P), both of which have ratings that are similar:

| Moody's | S&P |
|---|---|
| Aaa | AAA |
| Aa | AA |
| A | A |
| Baa | BBB |
| Ba | BB |
| B | B |
| C | CCC |
| | CC |
| | C |
| NR | NR |

Below Baa and BBB is considered non-investment grade, which was referred to years ago as junk or junk bonds. The lower the rating, the higher the interest rate (and the risk). The more risk you are willing to take, the more the bond will pay.

Municipal bonds are only useful when they produce a tax equivalent yield that exceeds what you can get from high-quality corporate or Treasury issues. To calculate the tax equivalent yield, simply divide the interest rate of the bond by the inverse of your tax rate:

(Interest rate paid by the bond) ÷ 1 – (Your tax rate) = Tax equivalent yield

**Words of the Wealthy**

The **risk/reward ratio** is a term used to describe a security's return relative to its risk. If a security has the potential for a 10 percent return on the upside, you should only be willing to accept an equal or lesser degree of risk on the downside. For example, why risk a 20 percent loss for a possible 10 percent return?

Most people buy municipal bonds only because they are tax free. They focus on this first before they focus on total return, which is a big mistake. The total return should always be the first priority. If you are in the highest tax brackets, by all means consider municipal bonds. However, if you are not in the higher tax brackets, you should avoid them. One more thing to consider is that municipal bonds should only be part of your portfolio. Given that you are a moderate to aggressive investor, stocks should make up the majority of your portfolio until you reach Stage 4, where protection of principal is more important.

The primary advantage of owning municipal bonds is the tax free income feature they provide the bond holder. This feature is especially attractive to investors who are in the highest tax brackets. The disadvantage is that currently they pay relatively low interest rates, and the only way an investor can achieve a better return after purchasing the bond is if interest rates fall. This would cause the bond price to rise and therefore increase your "paper profit," which is the price appreciation on the bond while you hold it during times of falling interest rates. You would only see an actual profit if you sold the bond while it had a higher price.

*The Wall Street Journal* prints several municipal bond indexes on a daily basis on the front page of the third section.

## Corporate Bonds

Corporate bonds do offer higher yields than Treasury bonds, but they involve a little more risk. They are also rated according to the issuing company's estimated ability to pay their interest and principal payments on a timely basis. High-quality corporate bonds are designed to give a portfolio stability. They are not designed to produce double-digit total returns.

The real advantage in corporate bonds is in the lower non-investment grade issues called junk bonds. A *junk bond* represents an IOU issued by a company whose ability to repay its interest and principal in a timely manner depends upon the economy and its ability to sell its products or services.

### Words of the Wealthy

A **junk bond** is any corporate bond rated below Standard & Poor's BBB rating or Moody's Baa rating. They are also known as **non-investment grade bonds** or **high-yield bonds**.

If you consider buying these bonds individually, you are asking for trouble. If you purchase a fund, however, you get a manager who knows the junk market better than you ever will because this is all he handles on a daily basis.

## Hybrid Fixed Income Securities

You can also use convertible bonds and preferred stocks, which I call hybrid fixed income securities. I call them hybrids because they act like both a stock and a bond. Both the convertible stock and bond have a fixed conversion ratio that gives the holder the right to convert to a fixed number of shares.

Convertible bonds are bonds that can be converted into stocks. This feature is put in place just in case the stock of the company rises considerably during the lifetime of the bond. The bondholder can convert his bond at any time. At that time, you convert your bond to so many shares of stocks, which you hope will be worth more than the bond.

A convertible stock is usually a preferred stock with a convertible feature. Preferred stocks are normally issued without voting rights, but with higher dividends. Often, these stocks move with the dividends rather than earnings, which limits their upside potential. Therefore, some companies issue these preferred stocks with a conversion feature that allows the shareholder to convert the preferred stock into so many shares of common stock. This gives the shareholder the opportunity to take advantage of the common stock price appreciation if something spectacular takes place later at the company.

Like a bond, hybrid securities do well when interest rates go down, and like a stock, they go up when the underlying company's earnings grow substantially. When you need to stabilize the value of your portfolio, these types of securities can help. They pay higher income than traditional stocks but don't fluctuate as much in price. These hybrids are great for the more conservative part of your portfolio.

## A Little Secret About Bond Funds

Bond funds, just like funds, do give the shareholder diversification with many different individual bond issues, which is a great benefit. However, if you are going to build a portfolio and you need to allocate money to bonds, you should first consider buying individual bonds. The only exception might be if you want to buy a few individual junk bonds or if your portfolio is too small to diversify your money into at least 10 investment-grade bonds. What's wrong with a bond fund? Individual bonds are primarily purchased for their interest payments that are usually fixed at a given rate. Given today's current interest rates, these bonds don't pay a lot of money, and if they're purchased within a mutual fund, you're going to receive even less money in interest payments. Bond funds, just like all other mutual funds, have management fees. I've seen 1.35 percent management fees on a bond fund that only paid about 6 percent interest. The net interest payment to the shareholder was only 4.65 percent. That means that 22.5 percent of the interest payment went to management fees, which is crazy. People actually buy these things every day! Be aware of the details before you buy a bond fund. The least expensive bond funds I've seen are at Vanguard Funds where the management fees can be as little as a quarter of a percent.

## The Equity Tools: Stocks and Such

You can invest your money in a conventional savings account or CDs, but your net return after inflation and taxes will not be strong enough (at least at today's rates) to compound the portfolio growth at a sufficient pace. However, equities, or stocks, will provide sufficient growth. Whether they are publicly traded or privately held, they can compound much faster because their value or price is directly related to the earnings growth of the company. That's what makes stocks the wealth tool of choice. They are the key to building wealth because they represent equity ownership in a company and their value will grow relative to the growth in net earnings. If a company is expected to have continued earnings growth of 30 percent or more, its stock price may have the same growth potential. Few opportunities in the investment world offer this much growth potential. Investing in stocks is the single biggest and most popular wealth builder in the world, but ironically, most people don't take the time to understand the concept or its power.

The market value of a stock is based upon what people perceive the value to be. This perception of value is normally based upon the amount of net cash the company produces (or is perceived to produce) on a per-share level after expenses. This cash is referred to as earnings or earnings per share. The majority of these earnings are usually retained by the company and are used to finance further growth with the remainder distributed as dividends to shareholders. Small or fast growing companies usually do not distribute any earnings as dividends because they need the money to continue their fast-paced growth. On the other hand, larger or slower growing companies usually distribute a great deal of their earnings as dividends. If you want to maximize the growth of your portfolio, your goal should be to focus on the smaller companies whose growth is compounding with the reinvestment of dividends.

One advantage stocks offer is protection from the risk of inflation, which bonds don't seem to provide. The only real disadvantage is the performance risk that stocks carry. If the underlying company goes bankrupt, the stock could become worthless.

The relative comparison of a company's stock price to its earnings is commonly referred to as the price/earnings ratio (or *P/E ratio*). For example, according to *Investor's Business Daily*, the stocks on the New York Stock Exchange (NYSE) are trading now at an average P/E ratio of 29. This means little unless you can look back over time and see what it has been. Looking back over the past five years, the lowest average P/E of the NYSE was 11 and the highest level was 40. If you know historical P/E averages, you can maintain a better idea of how underpriced or overpriced the market is on a daily basis. *Barron's*, another investment publication, prints the average P/E ratio on the Dow Jones industrial averages, as well as the S&P 500 index. When a stock's P/E ratio is much higher than comparable companies in the same industry, the stock might be considered overpriced. What I focus on is the opposite situation. I look for stocks that have P/E ratios below the industry average. That makes me a *value investor*.

### Words of the Wealthy

The **P/E ratio** is a stock's price per share divided by its earnings per share. It is used to estimate the true value of a stock and is often used in comparison with other stocks. If Wal-Mart's market price closed at $25 per share today and its current quarterly earnings equaled $.25 (or $1 on an annualized basis), its P/E ratio is 25.

### Words of the Wealthy

A **value investor** is someone who looks for good value in the market. A stock selling at an unusually low P/E ratio is a great example. Occasionally, stocks drop in price well below what they should. Value investors search for opportunities such as this and try to take advantage of the stock's price returning to more normal (higher) levels.

## Domestic Stocks

Domestic stocks are equities of companies that are headquartered in the U.S. Domestic stocks can be purchased individually through a broker or through a mutual fund. They should make up a good bit of your investment portfolio, but not the whole thing. Such an imbalance is a common mistake made by investors here in the U.S. Domestic stocks tie you to the overall U.S. market, which can correct unexpectedly. Therefore, domestic stock prices can be volatile. I talk more about this in the next section.

Successful investors use certain stock indexes as relative benchmarks for their own portfolios. Therefore, it is important to understand the most common indexes and what makes them unique. The Dow Jones industrial average is the most popular benchmark used in the U.S., but it represents a basket of only 30 different stocks. A better index to use is the S&P 500 index, which represents 500 different stocks. There are many other narrowly gauged indexes, but it's difficult to list them all. These indexes all act as broad-based windows into the stock market. For investors who are really interested in healthcare-related stocks, there are several healthcare-related indexes of stocks and mutual funds available. If you knew the healthcare-related stock index took a dramatic dive over the past year, you might consider it an over-reaction by the market and decide to buy a mutual fund specializing in this area.

If investing is your hobby and passion, it's okay to build a portfolio of individual domestic stocks. If it's not your hobby and you're picking your own stocks, you may be setting yourself up for future losses. If you don't enjoy investing, you will not do a good job. Consider mutual funds or hiring a fee-only investment advisor.

## Foreign Stocks

Only in the last few years have investors understood the value of foreign stocks. If your portfolio is invested only in U.S. companies, you are actually taking more risk than someone with a portfolio diversified all over the world. Allocating approximately 35 percent of your portfolio into a diversified mix of foreign stocks will actually reduce your risk and, at the same time, increase your performance potential. I firmly believe that all stock portfolios should have a certain percentage allocated into foreign stocks.

The most popular benchmark that represents a portfolio invested all over the world is the Morgan Stanley World Market Index, which is printed daily in *The Wall Street Journal*.

# The Mutual Fund Tools

A mutual fund, also known as an investment company, is a corporation, trust, or partnership into which investors combine their money in order to benefit primarily from professional management, diversification, and liquidity. Each fund has a manager or management team responsible for making the investment decisions of the fund and for purchasing securities with the money invested by the shareholders. The securities can include stocks, bonds, options, CDs, and real estate, depending upon the fund's stated objective.

What makes each mutual fund different is the fund's *objective* that is explained in the prospectus. The objective of the fund outlines the intentions of the manager, including the type of investments he will use as well as the different philosophies or strategies he will employ. The objective is the most important item in the prospectus to understand. The second most important item to look for is the list of restrictions. These guidelines are set up to keep the fund manager focused.

## Mutual Funds Aren't Just for Small Accounts Anymore

Conventional wisdom might have you believe that mutual funds are designed to help investors diversify small amounts of money. It's certainly true that mutual funds offer a great deal of diversification, but they offer many other benefits that most investors completely overlook. Here is a list of what a portfolio of mutual funds offers the shareholder:

➤ Because you are able to virtually hire several money managers at one time, you benefit from combining all their unique investment styles into your portfolio.

➤ Services such as automated checking account debit purchasing make it easier to invest on a monthly basis.

➤ Because the management fees are so inexpensive compared to the expenses of hiring a private individual money manager, mutual funds offer an inexpensive way to hire a group of investment managers.

➤ Mutual funds provide a cost-efficient method of investing all over the world, considering the high cost of foreign security commissions that are charged to individuals.

➤ You have the ability to diversify among hundreds of securities all over the world—which is almost impossible for an individual investor to do with a small amount of money and a limited amount of time to research.

➤ If you build a portfolio of several different funds, each manager may have a different investment philosophy, which gives you even greater diversification in your portfolio.

➤ Because you can sell your mutual fund as quickly as a stock, funds offer a great deal of portfolio liquidity.

➤ Investing in mutual funds gives you peace of mind that someone is watching the portfolio.

Mutual funds are not perfect. They do have their limitations and disadvantages. Here is a list of possible disadvantages. I'm sure you'll agree that the advantages certainly outweigh the disadvantages:

➤ High portfolio turnover can result in higher management fees.

➤ Some people think mutual funds are too limited because they can only invest in marketable securities.

➤ Investors may experience a loss of control over when taxable gains are taken.

➤ Mutual funds can see poor performance during bear markets.

➤ Legal limitations of the fund manager could affect performance.

Mutual funds aren't just for small accounts any more. As investors learn more about what it takes to build wealth, they quickly realize the advantages mutual funds have to offer.

## Open-End Funds

An open-end fund is a mutual fund that continually offers new shares to investors. When an investor purchases shares, money is directly deposited into the fund. When the shareholder eventually redeems his shares (he hopes at a higher price than he paid), money is withdrawn directly from the fund.

You need to understand the costs involved before you purchase a mutual fund. There are two types of open-end funds: load and no-load. The term *load* refers to a commission. No-load means there is no commission to buy the fund. Therefore, the price you pay is the net asset value.

### That Reminds Me...

My parents taught me, "If something sounds too good to be true, it probably is," and this is the reaction most investors have when they first hear about no-load mutual funds. The first question that pops into their minds is, "What's the catch? How can these mutual funds make money when they don't charge anything?"

All funds have a management fee paid by the mutual fund shareholders. This fee can range from .01 percent to 3.00 percent per year. This fee goes directly to the fund manager and fund company for operating expenses.

However, some funds charge a load or commission, which is an additional charge levied at the time of purchase, at the time of redemption, or each year the fund is held. This commission is paid to the salesperson or broker who sold the fund and the brokerage firm that hired the salesperson.

Many people think that the management fee on a no-load fund is higher than that of a loaded fund to compensate for the absence of commission. This is not always true. Many loaded funds have higher management fees than no-load funds. Buying no-load funds is like buying directly from the manufacturer. This secret can save an investor up to 9.29 percent on every net invested dollar.

Why do people still buy loaded mutual funds? The two most common reasons are that the investor is unaware of what a no-load fund can offer or the investor does not know how to find a no-load alternative to the loaded fund he has selected.

If you want to learn more about no-load funds, visit your local library. It should have several publications, such as *Money, Kiplinger's Personal Finance, Fortune,* and *Forbes.* They regularly feature articles on subjects such as no-load funds. You can also call Morningstar ($395 per year, 800-876-5005). They offer a $55 trial subscription, which is a small price to pay if you are serious about your research. You will get the entire past year's worth of information. This publication has updated information on most mutual funds and is presented in a format that enables you to easily compare one fund to another.

There are two ways to buy a no-load mutual fund: directly from the company or through a discount brokerage firm. If you want to buy direct, *Morningstar* can provide you with each fund company's phone number. If you want to buy the fund, request a prospectus and new account application. If you decide to buy the fund, fill out the application and send it back with a check made out to the name of the mutual fund company.

If you want to buy several different funds, it may be much easier to consolidate everything into one account at a discount brokerage firm. Charles Schwab and Co., the discount brokerage firm (800-435-4000), offers a unique service that allows investors to purchase more than 300 different no-load mutual funds within the same account without any transaction fee. You may want to call and get more information on this service.

Open-end funds are normally divided by their objectives or investments of choice. Here are a few different types:

| | |
|---|---|
| Aggressive growth funds | Equity income funds |
| Growth funds | Balanced funds |
| International | Flexible portfolio funds |
| Global equity funds | Index funds |
| Growth and income funds | Specialized industry funds |

I could define each of these categories, but it would be futile. Because every magazine, every mutual fund service, and every author has different definitions, it makes no sense to include one here.

Several different services provide an extensive list of mutual fund indexes. Lipper Analytical and Morningstar are the two most popular. You can find many of their indexes listed in *The Wall Street Journal* and *Barron's*. Be sure to compare apples to apples when you measure a fund's performance in an index.

## Closed-End Funds

One of the most overlooked investment vehicles is the closed-end fund. You know from the previous chapter not to buy these during an initial public offering because they are too expensive. However, once these funds make it to the secondary market, they can trade at a discount to their actual net asset value. Because they trade like stock, their market price has little to do with the actual net asset value. I've seen some funds trade for as little as 65 cents on the dollar. This may be hard to believe, but it's true.

Just like open-end funds, closed-end funds can focus on many different sectors. Most of the closed-end equity funds focus on one individual country or geographic region. Therefore, closed-end funds can be a perfect way to invest in a specific country or region that you might be excited about.

Closed-end funds offer two unique advantages. It is certainly an advantage to buy a mutual fund at a discount to its net asset value. However, the most important advantage is rarely ever discussed. What makes a closed-end fund so attractive is the fact that the manager doesn't have to worry about shareholders withdrawing money on a daily basis. If there is a market correction, most open-end fund managers must sell securities to cover daily redemptions. Closed-end fund managers do not have to worry about withdrawals, which means they are rarely ever forced to sell the stocks in their fund. They can focus single-mindedly on managing the portfolio. Open-end fund managers have to worry about redemptions every day.

Few closed-end fund indexes are available for comparison. Therefore, most of the time, you will have to compare performance to other similar closed-end funds. You might find other open-end funds that are also similar.

**Treasure Tip**

The bottom line is that the commission, or load, pays for the broker. With a little homework, you can do it yourself: Buy a no-load fund and save an enormous amount of money.

# Real Estate

If you decide you want to invest in real estate, that's also fine. Be sure to learn all you can before buying your first rental property. Property management can be a nightmare. Waking up to a tenant's call at 3 a.m. because the toilet broke is not my idea of fun.

Real estate is just like any other industry or business. I don't believe real estate is a particularly better industry than any other. It has its good and bad years just like other industries. In the late 70s, for example, we had double-digit property appreciation

**Wealth Warning**

If you want to speculate on undeveloped land, remember it is one of the riskiest investments available. Therefore, you'd better make real estate your business before you make a purchase. For example, if you are a licensed real estate appraiser, then by all means focus your attention on real estate as an investment. You'll see deals before anyone else does.

almost nationwide. Banks would loan money on almost any property. Those days are long gone, and we don't have that environment any more. Real estate is simply another industry now—one that happens to be filled with con men on TV offering "no money down" books, cassettes, and videos that lead to little actual success. However, many fortunes have been made in the real estate market, and if you expect to make your fortune this way, go for it. Just remember one thing: No matter what industry you decide to use to build your wealth, you better have a passion to be the best. Otherwise, you won't have the desire to learn all you can.

# The Best Tools for Building Wealth

I have found that most wealthy people use the same wealth-building tools. The following sections serve as a list of the most lucrative tools.

## Your Own Business Is the Best Tool

Equity in a fast company, preferably your own, is the best tool to use when attempting to achieve Wealth Stages 3, 4, and 5. Your own business may be the only way to get potential returns in excess of 10 percent. The value of the stock is tied to the earnings growth of the underlying company. If earnings are growing at 50 percent, then the stock is likely to be growing at 50 percent. This is truly the only way to achieve consistent returns that exceed the stock market. You might be able to accomplish above-average returns in the stock market, but you don't have the same control over that return unless it's your own company. I discuss starting your own business in Part 3, "Building Wealth with Your Own Business."

## Stocks Are the Second Best Tool

There are two ways to buy stocks. You can buy them individually or through mutual funds. If you have the time and passion, you might consider individual stocks. If not, try mutual funds. The point is that you need to invest in stocks somehow.

Would you rather invest in a stock representing a particular company in Mexico or invest in a mutual fund of Mexican stocks managed by an advisor who actually lives in Mexico and knows the country better than you ever will? Do the basics yourself, but delegate the most difficult and time-consuming task of investment management to the people who do it professionally. For an average management fee of one percent, they will follow industry trends, keep up with geopolitical events, visit the actual companies in person, and buy the individual securities for you. Can you do all this and spend less than one percent of your portfolio? The real question is this: Can you beat their portfolio performance?

### That Reminds Me...

After studying money management for almost 11 years, I've come to realize my own personal limitations and recognize the power of tapping into the greatest money management minds in the world. Sir Isaac Newton once said, "If I have seen further, it's because I stood on the shoulders of giants." When I heard this humble statement, I realized just how important it is to get help from others. By delegating the monumental task of following certain segments of the market, you stand a better chance of maintaining not only your own personal life, but also your financial future.

## The Perfect Portfolio

The optimal wealth-building portfolio has these characteristics:

➤ The portfolio is built primarily of stocks and maybe some bonds in an automated account. The aggressive investor may not own any bonds, whereas the conservative investor may have as much as 60 percent bonds.

➤ The stocks are globally diversified among the U.S., foreign developed countries, and foreign emerging market countries. The ideal percentage of foreign securities for a moderate risk investor is approximately 30 percent.

➤ When an opportunity presents itself, it must be easy to skew the portfolio toward the best opportunities in different sectors such as countries and industries.

➤ The portfolio must be able to employ the greatest specialists in the world to manage each sector that results in a level of synergy and diversification of thought that is impossible to achieve alone.

➤ When your portfolio needs more diversification, you must be able to switch from sector focus to a more broad-based focus.

➤ The portfolio can be quickly, easily, and cost-efficiently adjusted to take advantage of better opportunities.

# The Perfect Specialist When You Need One

If you want to manage own portfolio, that's great. However, why not be a manager of fund managers? Why not build a portfolio of mutual funds that give you a team of specialists who all work for you? What do you look for when you hire all these specialists? Following is a list of the most important requirements:

➤ These specialists must focus on the micro-economic picture, allowing you to focus on the macro-economic picture.

➤ The specialists must be inexpensive, held accountable, and easily measured against each other on a daily if not weekly basis.

➤ You must be able to find and understand what makes each specialist unique or better than the others. What is their idiosyncratic advantage (unique characteristics that make them superior managers)?

➤ The specialist must be independent of a brokerage firm.

➤ The specialists hired can be fired and re-hired with little or no emotion involved.

Finding such a specialist is almost impossible with individual stocks. However, no-load mutual funds enable the investor to achieve all of these goals. They are the only investment vehicle that gives me all of the characteristics along with the type of specialists I need. While I focus on what is happening in the world, I need other specialists to focus on what is happening in each individual country and industry. I realize I can't follow all the stocks in the world, but a team of specialists can for me.

No-load mutual funds give me the ability to combine the power of equity growth along with what I call the multiple manager concept, which can result in an efficiently managed portfolio with potential returns exceeding 10 percent.

---

## The Least You Need to Know

➤ Whatever the investment, make sure you ask the right questions and keep everything simple.

➤ Bonds are great for a portion of your portfolio and should be considered the more conservative portion.

➤ If your goal is to maximize the growth of your portfolio, you have to use stocks.

➤ The best portfolio is one that is diversified all over the world through no-load mutual funds managed by the greatest money managers in the world.

➤ Consider learning all you can about closed-end funds because they are unique and offer substantial advantages over regular open-end mutual funds.

# Chapter 9

# How to Find Help

One of these days, you may decide you need some help with your portfolio. If you like doing all your own investing and financial planning, that's great. You may still want a second opinion. The larger your portfolio and the greater your net worth, the more sense it makes to consider getting help. This chapter will help you focus on how to find the right help for you.

Every investor has different needs, and every professional offers somewhat different services. This chapter will help you match your needs with the best professional available: a financial planner, full-service broker, or other professional.

Whatever professional you need, one thing they all can do for you is eliminate procrastination in your financial plan. They can keep you accountable and even make decisions for you. The key question is whether you are better off financially with an advisor helping you. If you think you can do a better job, then try it yourself. Don't be a complete island. Even the greatest do-it-yourselfers get second opinions.

# Where to Find a Great Advisor

The best place to start looking for an investment advisor is with friends. Find friends whose investment knowledge you respect the most, and ask whom those friends recommend. You can also talk to your CPA or tax preparer, if you use either; these folks see brokerage statements every year and know firsthand which advisors make money for clients. Watch your local newspaper for investment seminars and workshops in your area. Otherwise, you might have to resort to the Yellow Pages.

### That Reminds Me...

If you are just starting out with your portfolio and have less than $20,000 to invest, you are in what I call the "gray zone." You'll find few quality investment brokers or advisors willing to spend any significant time with you. Why? Because the commission or fee income from $20,000 isn't usually enough to get most brokers or advisors excited. If you're in the gray zone, don't let an unscrupulous advisor steer you into a commission trap to make up for your lower portfolio size. The commission trap is any investment that charges above-average commissions. If you don't understand the possible hidden commissions and fees, the next chapter will help you through the gray zone.

The most difficult question an investor will ever have to answer is, "What kind of professional should I trust?" This decision is usually the first one to make and often the least researched. Many people in my workshops ask me to explain the difference between fee-only investment advisors, investment advisors, money managers, brokers, and certified financial planners. Therefore, I thought it might be useful to discuss the various titles that accompany these professionals in the investment industry. The primary differences to be aware of include the services offered, source of compensation, how are they influenced, and who regulates them.

## Full-Service Investment Brokers

The first and most widely known investment professional is the full-service investment broker (broker). Other titles that describe a broker include registered representative, financial consultant, investment banker, and even vice president (usually awarded once certain levels of commission are achieved). Investment brokers are security salespeople who help investors buy and sell securities for a commission. Brokers seldom have *fiduciary responsibility* for client's accounts, so the clients must be contacted prior to and must agree to any investment transaction. Some brokers may also offer financial planning, estate planning, and retirement planning services.

Brokers are regulated by the Securities and Exchange Commission (SEC), your state's securities department, and the National Association of Securities Dealers. The primary advantage of using a full-service broker is the extensive research about investment decisions they can provide. However, many discount brokerage firms now offer similar research information. The full-service brokerage firm might have a team of security analysts, but they make mistakes, too. When selecting stocks and other securities, pay attention to facts, not the opinions of security analysts. With a little experience, your instincts may produce better results.

The primary disadvantage of working with a full-service broker involves the way they are compensated—via commission for each investment purchase or sale you make. Commissions usually range from 1.5 percent charges on stock trades to 8.5 percent charges on mutual funds and other packaged products. Many investors feel commission-based investment advice is a conflict of interest. When you have any investment planning done by a broker, make sure you know the full extent of the commissions involved in every recommendation.

**Words of the Wealthy**

A fiduciary is a person legally appointed and authorized to hold assets in trust for another person and manage those assets for the benefit of that person. An advisor has **fiduciary responsibility** when he is responsible for buying and selling securities for the client.

## Registered Investment Advisors

The second most popular type of investment professional is the registered investment advisor (RIA). Investment advisors are typically independent and have fiduciary responsibility for their clients' portfolios, meaning they make the investment decisions on behalf of the client based upon the individual client's objectives. Advisors are paid in one of three ways: fee-only (flat rate based on assets managed or time), commission (based on the amount of your purchase), and fee-based (a combination of fees and commissions).

What is a fee rate? Fees charged by RIAs usually range from 1 to 4 percent, depending upon the size of the account. The average fee rate is about 1 percent. If your portfolio is less than $250,000, expect to pay a higher rate of 1.6 percent, and if your portfolio exceeds $1 million, your fee should be 1 percent or lower. Remember, all fees are somewhat negotiable.

## Fee-Only Advisors

There are three types of fee-only RIAs: money managers, financial planners, and advisors who do both. Fee-only managers make investment decisions for clients based on the risk tolerances and goals of the client. They are paid a percentage fee that is usually based upon the value of the account. No income is derived from commissions. Fee-only financial planners assist investors with budgeting, retirement planning, estate planning, taxes, investments, life insurance, and real estate. On smaller estates, they are paid a fee usually based on the amount of time it takes to complete the plan. These fees usually run about $200 per hour. Once you have achieved Wealth Stage 3, you might want to pay a yearly retainer based upon the size of your estate or net worth. Retainers are negotiable but usually range from .5 to 1 percent. Most importantly, they do not receive any commission from any investment or life insurance product they recommend. The advisors who do both money management and financial planning normally charge a percentage fee based upon assets. However, some charge a percentage fee for the money management and an hourly fee for financial planning. My firm does both, but we currently charge only the percentage fee.

**Words of the Wealthy**

A **fee-only** advisor is a money manager or financial planner who receives a fee for service that is usually based upon a percentage of assets under management or time. Fee-only advisors do not receive any commissions for any investment they recommend. Money manager is simply another name for a fee-only investment advisor.

The primary advantage offered by *fee-only* advisors is the way they are compensated. Advice and commissions are separated. The only way a fee-only money manager can increase his or her own income is to increase the performance and therefore the size of the client's portfolio. This produces a win/win relationship for both the client and advisor. If the fee-only advisor is independent, there is no management influence or commissions quota. The only disadvantage might be the experience of the advisor. The new Investment Advisor Act recently divided the regulation of investment advisors between the SEC and the state securities department. Firms with assets under $25 million are regulated by the state securities department, and firms with assets over $25 million are regulated by the SEC.

## Commission-Based or Fee-Based Investment Advisors

Don't be confused by the two terms fee-only and fee-based. They are not the same. Fee-based RIAs manage portfolios for clients but receive commissions and fees. Some offset their fees by the amount of the commissions charged to each account. The commissions can be somewhat disguised using a technique known as soft dollars. The broker used by the advisor for trading purposes will charge additional commission (a few cents per share) to each trade made in each client's account. The brokerage firm will pass along the additional commission to the advisor by paying for certain services that are normally part of the advisor's own overhead expenses, such as research, software, and market quotation services. Some fee-based RIAs offer financial planning.

The advantage of using an independent fee-based RIA is the absence of influence from management normally experienced at full-service brokerage firms. The primary disadvantage involves how they are compensated. As is the case in dealing with investment brokers, many investors feel commission-based investment advice from a non–fee-only RIA is a conflict of interest. When you have any investment planning done by a non–fee-only RIA, make sure you know the full extent of commissions that will be involved in all the suggested investments. Fee-based RIAs are regulated by the SEC, your state's securities department, and the National Association of Securities Dealers.

## Certified Financial Planners

*Certified financial planner (CFP)* is the most confusing term you'll encounter. It is a title often used to disguise a commission-based broker. CFPs are people who have passed a set of comprehensive exams offered by the Foundation for Financial Education in Colorado. This is a great program; however, many investment professionals take advantage of the title. CFPs can be insurance agents, brokers, mutual fund salespeople, fee-only advisors, and non–fee-only advisors. Most of these professionals want to sell you something for a commission, except for the fee-only CFP. The true fee-only CFP will profile your financial situation and goals and develop a comprehensive financial plan. Some will even implement this plan for you. The plan usually includes how much to save, how much to spend (budgeting), how much insurance you need, how you can save on income taxes, how to save for college expenses, and how you can protect your heirs from estate taxes. The fee for a plan is usually based upon the time spent preparing the plan and normally ranges from $100 to $200 per hour. A large comprehensive plan may even run up to $10,000. This might seem high, but the commission-based CFP could easily get $10,000 in commissions if you were to invest $120,000 in heavily loaded mutual funds or insurance policies. Fee-only CFPs are rare because the commissions offered by loaded mutual funds and insurance products seem to dwarf the average $200-per-hour fee.

**Words of the Wealthy**

A **certified financial planner (CFP)** is someone who has passed the comprehensive CFP exams administered by a company in Denver, Colorado, called the Foundation for Financial Education (303–220–1200). CFPs can be brokers, CPAs, insurance agents, salespeople, or fee–only advisors.

**That Reminds Me...**

If you hire a CFP who is also an insurance agent, be careful. You may find yourself investing in insurance products with huge commissions. This is not conducive to the wealth–building process. If you want to build wealth, you can't do it with insurance products. You might protect your wealth with them, but you won't build it. I believe in insurance products for insurance and estate-planning reasons, but not for investment purposes.

If you want to check for any past complaints regarding the CFP you are considering, or if you have a complaint regarding your existing CFP, call the CFP Board of Standards Incorporated at 800-647-0526.

The advantages and disadvantages of using a CFP are similar to the RIA. If the CFP is fee-only, then there is no conflict of interest from commissions. However, some CFPs are fee-based, charging both fees and commissions, so be aware of their charges and motives.

# Finding an Advisor Who Is Perfect for You

To make it easier, I use the term advisor to refer to all of the different types of professionals I've mentioned in this chapter. If you decide to hire an advisor to help you in your journey toward your next Wealth Stage, you need to know what to look for and the right questions to ask. What you should envision is a relationship between you and your advisor that is based upon trust and compatibility. You need to focus on finding someone who will keep *your* best interest in mind and be rewarded for doing so. Your goal is not only to find the best advisor for you, but it is also to gain a certain degree of respect from that advisor. Often, the amount of attention and service you get from the advisor is directly related to the amount of respect he has for you.

How do you gain that respect? First, you ask the right questions. The four Cs of advisor-client compatibility are credentials, compensation, characteristics, and customer service. Your questions should at least cover these four areas. The rest of this section covers each area, including the key questions that you need to ask before you hire an advisor.

**Treasure Tip**

If you're starting from scratch, you should interview at least three advisors before making a decision.

## *Credentials*

What exactly qualifies your advisor as a professional? Some advisors hang a shingle outside their doors and go to work. The following questions will help you to separate the wheat from the chaff.

1. **Who are you registered with?** The advisor should be registered with at least one of the following:

   ➤ The Securities and Exchange Commission (SEC), 202-942-7040.

   ➤ Your state securities department (usually found in your state capitol).

   ➤ The National Association of Securities Dealers (if the advisor is commission based), 800-289-9999. If she is a CFP, the Certified Financial Planning Board of Standards, 303-220-1200. If not, you should avoid doing business with the advisor. You might want to check their registration status and ask whether there have been any complaints filed against them. Start with your state securities department, and then call the other agencies.

2. **Where did you graduate from college?** This might not be important to you, but it will sure answer the real question, which is, "Did you go to college and did you graduate?" If you doubt the answer you get, call the college and check. You shouldn't base your entire decision on whether the advisor finished college (I know several brilliant people who never went to college), but finishing college is a test of tenacity. If the advisor you're interviewing didn't finish college, make sure he can show you at least five good years of investment experience.

3. **How long have you been in the investment business?** Don't be a guinea pig. If this is the advisor's first few years in the business, you might want to wait. Most advisors make their biggest mistakes during the first year in the business. If you do hire a neophyte advisor, start with a small amount of money. The best advisor is someone who has experienced at least one big market correction (a period where many securities "crashed," or went down in value) such as in 1987.

4. **Who was your previous employer?** You might even ask for a resume. If your advisor has jumped around from firm to firm, you might want to reconsider. If you were hiring an employee, would you hire someone who has jumped between jobs each year over the last several years? There are certainly exceptions to this rule. Ask why the advisor jumped around. He or she might have done it by design to learn more about the business before starting an investment firm.

5. **What certifications do you have?** The most important certification a money manager can possess is a CFA (chartered financial analyst). This is a comprehensive three-year course developed and maintained by the Institute of Chartered Financial Analysts. It is not the most important thing to look for when hiring an advisor, but it is impressive. Comparing the CFA designation to the CFP is like comparing college to high school. The CFA is much more difficult and comprehensive than the CFP.

The only possible problem with the CFA is that it can make your advisor too academic. Academic investors can sometimes be rigid in their investment strategies, meaning they focus on certain kinds of conventional portfolio strategies but disregard others that also may be beneficial. Therefore, the most intelligent are not always the best money managers. As I explain in Chapter 11, "Building the Perfect Portfolio," it takes more than intelligence to be a successful portfolio manager.

**Wealth Warning**

Don't accept the opinion of a referral from a client who is related to your advisor. Ask for one of the advisor's first clients. They can tell you the most about the advisor.

6. **How many clients do you have?** The advisor can have too few or too many clients. Too few may imply that he has little experience. Too many may mean that he can't service all of them effectively. There is no magic number, and you'll have to judge for yourself. The more clients the advisor has, the more experience he has. If you are hiring a money manager, you also may want to ask how much money she has under management. If the manager has more than $30 million under management, she's built a significant business.

7. **Questions to ask yourself.** Are you impressed with this person? Are you comfortable with his credentials? Does he have enough experience to make you comfortable?

# Compensation

The way your advisor is compensated should be one of the key factors in your decision process. The two factors are commission and fee. The most respected professionals in the investment industry who do not work for full-service brokerage firms or loaded mutual fund companies will tell you to focus on the fee-only advisor. Do-it-yourself investors are the only exception to this rule. If investing is your hobby and you like to rely on a full-service brokerage firm's research, then by all means use these firms. They can be a great asset toward building wealth. However, if investing is not a hobby of yours, you should focus on fee-only advisors, who can't rack up commissions by steering novices into commission-heavy investments.

You've got to fully understand the costs involved before you hire anyone to help you manage your money. As noted earlier, an advisor's method of compensation will dictate the conflicts of interest you may encounter. Regardless of whether they are commission-based or fee-based, ask these questions:

1. **Exactly how are you compensated?** If the answer is "fee-only," then ask the percentage rate. Remember, it's not uncommon to pay 1.6 percent for an account less than $250,000, but that should include some financial planning. Accounts that exceed $1 million should be charged no more than 1 percent. These fees are usually negotiable, so don't be afraid to ask for discounts. Then, compare these rates with the other fee-based advisors you interview.

   If the advisor is paid commission, it may be difficult to compare apples to apples because of all the different investment products they can sell. One way to do this is to compare the commission of 100 shares of stock at a hypothetical price of $25. Most brokerage firms also have minimum commission amounts. Be sure to compare these, too. The most important thing to

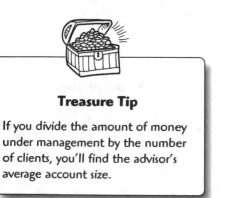

**Treasure Tip**

If you divide the amount of money under management by the number of clients, you'll find the advisor's average account size.

remember, if you hire a commission-paid broker or salesperson, is that there is always a commission paid somewhere, somehow. Unfortunately, it's your job to ask about it. It's also your job to double-check the accuracy of the answer you get. Numerous hidden costs can slowly eat away at your portfolio.

One common hidden cost is the underwriting fee that is added to a new issue or investment product. If a newly issued stock, fund, or other investment product is offered to you by a broker with no commission charge, ask for the total underwriting fee. Often, you'll find these underwriting fees to be in excess of 6 percent. What amount is too much? You'll have to be the judge. I avoid these fees altogether.

If a commission-based broker recommends to you a mutual fund, be sure to ask how you'll pay his commission. If he says the fund pays his commission, you should reply, "No, I'm paying your commission, just tell me how much it is and how I'm paying it." Listen to how he explains it. Ask him to explain the management fees and 12(b)1 fees. You might want to ask him to show you the explanation in the prospectus. If the fund has a 12(b)1 fee in excess of .5 percent (half of a percentage point), then this fund is a loaded fund and he should disclose that to you. The broker is paid to sell the fund and keep you in it. Many of these funds, especially the proprietary funds, pay the broker "trailers" that are extra commission payments paid to the broker as incentive to keep clients in the funds. Always remember to ask what the total 12(b)1 fees will be each year before you buy any mutual fund from a broker or advisor. Your knowledge will certainly get their attention.

2. **Explain to me all the costs involved in each investment.** You need to be aware of additional fees that do not go to the broker or advisor. The most common are the management fees that are charged by mutual fund managers. The average domestic stock mutual fund management fee is approximately 1 percent. Foreign funds charge a slightly higher fee, whereas bond funds charge lower fees. Another fee to look for is a custodian fee, which is normally charged by the brokerage firm for holding your account. If your advisor is paid a fee and uses a brokerage firm for trades, you also need to be aware of the commission and transaction fees charged by the brokerage firm.

### Wealth Warning

The primary influence over the broker is the investment firm's branch manager, who is also compensated based upon the amount of commissions and proprietary investment products sold. Proprietary investments are those that the broker's company underwrites and exclusively distributes or sells.

3. **What charges will I incur if I fire you?** Few people think to ask this question. It may seem a bit harsh, but you need to ask. If you are a positive person, firing the advisor may be the last thing on your mind, but you need to know the logistics and costs involved. You also need to know the cost of liquidating your account. Anything you buy should cost little or nothing to sell and should have a secondary market where it can be easily sold.

   For example, most full-service brokerage firms charge a 2 percent penalty (or $100 whichever is less) for transferring an IRA to another firm. You might not even realize this unless you read the fine print in the IRA agreement you signed when you opened the account. Many mutual funds have back-end loads that can add up to 6 percent if you decide to sell them within one year of purchase. As I pointed out in Chapter 7, "Stay Away from This Stuff," most proprietary or packaged products will also have heavy commissions and fees hidden in them.

   Most of the hidden costs are listed somewhere in the agreement you signed to open an account or go with an advisor or in the prospectus of the specific investment you bought. A few hidden costs aren't listed, but it would take another chapter to explain all of them. Just remember that nothing is free and that if it sounds too good to be true, it probably is.

4. **Questions to ask yourself.** After you have analyzed all the costs, do they seem reasonable? If you have hired a discretionary money manager, the total cost should not exceed 3 percent of your principal per year. Compare other money managers to see if they are more competitive. If your advisor's rates seem too high, ask for a discount. If you have hired a broker, compare the commission rates with other firms. If the rates seem too high, ask for a discount.

## Characteristics of Advisors

Each advisor has a unique personality that ultimately affects the contents and, therefore, the results of the portfolio. You need to understand this personality before you hire the advisor:

1. **Explain your investment philosophy.** The advisor's investment philosophy is important to your future. It dictates how your portfolio will be managed and how your wealth will be built and maintained. Most investment professionals either don't have a philosophy or they have difficulty explaining their investment philosophy within a few sentences. That frightens me. You want someone who can give you their philosophy easily, briefly, and with conviction. When you ask this question, look not only for these qualities, but also for understanding. Do you understand the philosophy? Are you comfortable with it? If you can't understand it, how will you know if you agree with what she thinks? How can you be comfortable with a philosophy you don't understand?

2. **Do you focus on the domestic market, foreign markets, or both?** The answer should be both. Many advisors focus only on the domestic market, which is a shame. To establish the proper level of diversification, you must have both domestic and foreign securities in your portfolio. If the answer is both, ask whether they use mutual funds or individual stocks for the foreign portion of the portfolio. If the answer is individual stocks, find someone else. There are only a few advisors in the world who can pick individual stocks and bonds all around the world successfully. If the advisor can show you a track record of success using both domestic and foreign stocks, then maybe you can consider working with him. For example, I think every investment portfolio should have both domestic and foreign stocks, as well as bonds. Instead of using individual stocks, I use mutual funds to accomplish this for my clients.

3. **Tell me a little about yourself.** Get to know your advisor as a person. You have to understand the person before you'll know whether she will be compatible with you and your needs. Ask her about her hobbies and interests. Ask what motivates her. Ask where the advisor grew up. Ask him about his values and goals. You should do business with an advisor who shares your values. Otherwise, you may run into a problem later.

4. **What is your specialty? What are you the best at?** You need to know what your advisor is good at. You need to know what she enjoys most about the investment business. What she enjoys most is more than likely where she will excel and provide the best results. My specialty, for example, is global portfolio management using no-load mutual funds and retirement planning.

5. **How do you view risk, and how does your philosophy keep me within my risk tolerance?** Let the advisor explain how your risk tolerance is calculated and how your portfolio will be designed accordingly. Don't be afraid to ask questions here. The stock market can be volatile, so make sure you understand the risks involved.

6. **Questions to ask yourself.** You have to consider compatibility. Will you be comfortable with this person? What kind of attitude does he have? Is he patient with you or just trying to sell you something? Do you trust this person? Is he trying to confuse you with investment jargon? Will you worry about your money after you hire this advisor? Is this person a good listener? Did the advisor ask about your goals and objectives? You need to make certain that your advisor will help you

**Treasure Tip**

You may find that most money managers will help you with the basics of financial planning. However, if you need more detail, find a fee-only financial planner who can help you. Make sure she spends time educating you so you can eventually do most of the planning yourself.

133

achieve your goals. If you don't have any, he should at least help you establish your expectations for risk and return.

# Customer Service

Many clients don't know what to expect from their advisors in terms of service. For many years, the markets made it easy for advisors to get away with little service. Things are different now. If you pay close attention to the level of service offered by the advisors you interview, you'll more than likely find a discrepancy. Most advisors offer a status-quo level of service. However, as advisory firms and full-service brokerage firms become more competitive, you will begin to see additional services. Be sure to ask about some of them:

1. **What services does your firm offer?** If you need a fee-only financial planner, ask what services are offered. The answer is different with each planner. The same is true with brokers and advisors in the money-management business. The level of client services offered varies with each firm. Some firms are competitive with the services they offer. Others don't seem to care. The following list of services will give you an idea of what advisors can offer you (if they want to) and the services you should ask about:

   ➤ Quarterly, if not monthly, brokerage statements (ask to see an example).

   ➤ Quarterly performance statements (ask to see an example).

   ➤ Advisor availability.

   ➤ A sufficient amount of client service people who can answer administrative questions.

   ➤ Yearly client reviews.

   ➤ Yearly tax information statements to help you prepare your taxes.

**Words of the Wealthy**

An advisor with **discretionary authority** is an advisor who has been authorized to buy and sell securities on behalf of the client, without the client's express permission. This authorization is given in the form of a limited power of attorney signed by the client.

2. **Where will my assets be held?** If you are considering an independent money manager, an independent third-party custodian should hold your assets for you. Normally the fee-only money manager will set up *discretionary authority* for your account at this custodian so he or she can place trades on your behalf. This custodian should be a brokerage firm that sends you statements every month. The money manager should have a limited power of attorney agreement with the brokerage firm that allows him to buy and sell securities for you, deduct his fee quarterly, and get a copy of your monthly statement and daily account information.

Having this independent firm separates your money manager from your account and reduces the possibility of fraud.

When you open an account with an independent advisor, make your check out to the brokerage firm where your account is being held, not to your advisor. Once your account is opened, call the brokerage firm and check your account number and balance. You should also receive a confirmation of the account being opened in the mail. Be sure to compare the statements you receive from the advisor with those of the brokerage firm.

### That Reminds Me...

Years ago, in a retirement community, one of my clients hired a man who called himself an advisor. She opened an account and began receiving statements showing above-average results. Other clients complained about not getting their monthly checks. Because she didn't need income from her account, she didn't have any problems—or so she thought. Soon, the advisor skipped town with her money. Every client this guy had was scared, furious, and embarrassed. How could he get away with this? Easy! He deposited the money in his own account and fraudulently produced his own statements. There was no independent third party producing a second statement. Approximately $10 million in client assets were lost.

3. **How accessible will he or she be?** It can be frustrating to not have access to information or answers when you need them. Who do you call when your advisor is on vacation? Make sure the advisor has hired other advisors who can help you. This is called "depth." A firm has depth if it has employed more than one advisor.

4. **What has been your year-to-year performance?** All advisors should be able to furnish you with a track record. This track record should be provided along with other relative indexes against which you can compare. It should reflect the combined performance of all the advisor's accounts and should mention that it was prepared using AIMR standards. The best broad market indexes are

   ➤ The Lipper Global Flexible
   ➤ The Morgan Stanley World Market Index

Lipper is a good comparison if you have a portfolio with both stocks and bonds. Morgan Stanley's World Market Index is good if you have a portfolio of stocks from all over the world. If the advisor lagged all of these indexes over a 3- to 5-year period of time, indicating lower than expected performance, you might want to ask why.

Remember, don't base your entire decision on the advisor's past performance. Just because the advisor did well last year (or the past 10 years), doesn't mean you can expect the same performance this year. Likewise, don't rule out an advisor just because the advisor had a bad year. Be sure to consider the philosophy of the manager before you eliminate him just because his track record is bad. His philosophy might be right on target next year.

If you are hiring a commission-based broker, you will not get a track record. Brokerage firms do not offer track records on their individual broker's performances, nor on the client's individual account. You'll get individual performance data on your account if you are in a wrap account, but otherwise, you're on your own.

5. **What was your worst year? Best year?** Wouldn't you like to know the advisor's worst year? Ask him what happened and listen to his answer. You want an advisor who takes responsibility for his results. If he defends his performance too much, he might not be willing to admit a mistake later. All advisors make mistakes. You want an advisor who's honest about it and willing to admit his mistakes. If he's willing to admit it, he's also more likely to correct it quickly.

### That Reminds Me...

The organization that administers the chartered financial analyst (CFA) course and exam is the Institute of Chartered Financial Analysts (ICFP), a subsidiary of the Association for Investment Management and Research (AIMR). If your advisor is a CFA, his performance numbers must comply with AIMR standards. Otherwise, he will lose his designation. The first objective of the AIMR standards is to establish a common, accepted set of ethical principles that ensure fair representation and full disclosure in investment managers' presentations of their results to clients and prospective clients. Their second objective is to achieve greater uniformity and comparability among such presentations. Without these standards, an advisor can manipulate performance data to seem more attractive than it actually is.

6. **Do you use AIMR standards in reporting performance?** The best industry standards for reporting investment performance comes from the Association for Investment Management and Research (AIMR). These standards are intended to foster a fair representation and full disclosure of performance results. The second goal of these standards is to promote greater uniformity and comparability among performance presentations. The guidelines are strict and comprehensive. If your advisor does not claim to use these standards, you should ask him why he's not willing to comply with industry standards. You can order AIMR's handbook of standards, *Performance Presentation Standards,* by calling 804-980-3647 or faxing 804-977-0350. The cost is $20.

7. **Do you offer financial planning, money management, or both?** If you hire a financial planner, he or she needs to know every aspect of planning, which includes spending control, retirement and estate planning, saving, asset protection, life insurance, and taxes. If you hire a money manager, he or she needs to know every aspect of investment management, which includes investment strategy, global investment trends, domestic industry trends, interest rates, and a full knowledge of all the best investment products available.

   I recommend that you find an advisor who can do both. Advisors around the country are realizing that they can't offer money management alone and survive. Clients are realizing that they need more than simple money management. They need someone to help with the whole picture. Therefore, it should be easy to find an advisor who offers both.

8. **How many clients did you lose last year? Why?** Every advisor loses clients each year for many different reasons. Before you hire an advisor, ask how many clients he lost and why. If he says none, you should be suspicious. There are many different reasons why advisors lose clients. It's a natural occurrence that cannot be prevented. If the advisor says he hasn't lost a client, he might have lost several for reasons he doesn't want you to know.

9. **Questions to ask yourself.** Do you feel that this firm will take care of your needs? Do they have a bias toward customer service? Are they open to your questions? Do they educate their clients? Find out specifically what makes this firm different. Do they have any unique services? Do they have sufficient staff to serve their clientele? How many advisors do they have who are registered? Do they have enough knowledgeable staff to cover their client's needs or are they understaffed?

# Client References

You must check references. It is standard procedure in almost any service business to ask for client references. The only thing different about the investment business is that advisors have to ask a client's permission prior to using that client as a reference. Once the client agrees, the advisor can offer their names and phone numbers to other prospective clients who inquire. Some advisors don't offer references and when asked, they reply, "My clients are confidential." Don't accept this answer. It ought to be a warning signal. If the advisor has a legitimate business and does a good job, then his clients should be willing to be references.

Get at least three references who have been with the advisor longer than one year. You might ask for the client who has been with the advisor the longest. You need to talk to clients who have been with the advisor during bad market years such as 1994 or even 1987. The advisor will naturally give you a list of his happiest clients, but you should still make the call. When you do talk to the references, assure them that their answers are confidential and that you have no intention of sharing them with anyone, including the advisor. Here are some questions you might ask:

1.  **How long have you known (the advisor)?** I have clients who have known me since I was five years old. They know much more about me than a client who hired me just last year.

2.  **What do you like best about (the advisor)? What do you like the least about (the advisor)?** These are my favorite questions. They are seldom asked, but they are probably the most powerful. The answers may tell you something about the advisor that you'd never otherwise know. You might find a personality trait that might make you feel more comfortable about working with the advisor. You might also find a monster in the closet! Whatever the case, the answers to these questions are usually by far the most interesting.

3.  **Knowing what you know now, would you hire (the advisor) again today?** This is called zero based thinking. The question is whether the client would hire the advisor if he had to do it all over again. The answer often gives you more insight into how the client really feels about the advisor. If the answer is yes, you might even add, "Do you mind telling me why?"

4.  **Has (the advisor) made you money?** You might want to be more specific and ask whether the advisor has beaten the S&P 500 or other indexes important to you. You might also ask whether the advisor achieved the return goal he set for his clients.

5.  **Did (the advisor) do what he said he was going to do?** Did he make any promises he didn't keep? This is the ultimate question that sums up the client's experience.

# Background Check

Finally, before hiring any type of advisor, broker, or planner, you might even want to call your state's securities department to see whether there have been any complaints filed on the advisor. If you want to get an idea of the kind of professional to avoid, ask about the most common complaints. Most consumer complaints involve financial planners, brokers, and advisors who earn their income solely by commissions, especially those advisors who represent only one company such as one mutual fund family.

The biggest scam in the investment business is the salesperson who calls himself a financial planner to disguise his true colors. If you hire a financial planner who charges you a fee for a financial plan and then gives you a plan with loaded (commissioned) mutual funds, you should run away as fast as you can. If the plan suggests proprietary funds (funds run by the firm the advisor works for), you should run even faster. This is one of the biggest conflicts of interest in the business.

---

### The Least You Need to Know

➤ Even if investing is your hobby, consider hiring someone to help you, but do your homework during your search.

➤ The best advisor to hire is a fee-only advisor who offers both money management and financial planning.

➤ Make sure your advisor is compatible with your personality, risk tolerance, and financial goals.

➤ Make certain the advisor is registered with either the Securities and Exchange Commission, your state's securities department, or the National Association of Securities Dealers.

➤ Ask your potential advisors for references, call at least three, and ask them about the advisor.

---

# Chapter 10

# Jumping into the Market

## In This Chapter

➤ What should your first investment look like?

➤ How much money will you need to start?

➤ Actual fund ideas that will get you started

➤ How to invest automatically

➤ Where should you hold your first investment?

Where exactly do you start? Just how do you get started with the first investment? In Wealth Stage 1, when you make your first investment decision, you might feel somewhat overwhelmed. This chapter will help you narrow your focus considerably and get you started on the right track. The first mistake most investors make when they begin investing is procrastination. Most investors fear their first investment decision so much that they procrastinate, sometimes for years. They think they have to buy a stock or something complicated that requires days of study and research. If you follow the five questions in the first pages of Chapter 8, "Investments That Do Work," you'll instantly narrow your choices. Therefore, the first investment decision should actually be the easiest, and this chapter will give you a nudge in the right direction.

Most first-time investors are also so afraid of making a mistake that they actually become frozen in fear. Don't let this happen to you. Remember from Chapter 3, "The Five Stages of Wealth," that the most important element initially is the amount of money you save, not total return. Your first investment decision is important, but the amount of money you save is much more important. Mistakes early in your journey can often be completely covered by one or two savings deposits down the line.

# Don't Swallow That Hook!

There are so many ways you can make mistakes. The one I hate the most is when someone takes advantage of me. Don't let this happen to you. Your best defense is knowledge. Now is the most important time to learn—when you make your first investment. However, it is also the best time to make mistakes. Why? Because it's best to learn from them early on instead of later when the mistakes are usually more expensive.

The first investment for most people can still be expensive. Why? The first-time investor usually knows the least, which means he or she falls pray to commission traps sold by brokers, insurance agents, and other salespeople. The typical first-time investor buys a fully loaded mutual fund or an insurance policy as an investment.

Some loaded mutual fund investments are sold as contracts that require monthly deposits, usually in the form of automatic checking account debits. The debit concept is great. Automatically, without any effort on the part of the investor, money is withdrawn from his checking account and invested for him. However, if you are buying a loaded fund, the commission usually bites heavily into the deposit before any money actually gets invested.

If you are a novice investor, it's difficult to prevent a smooth salesman from selling you an investment product with heavy commissions. They are trained to sell, and they are wonderful at it. Your best defense is knowledge. Chapter 7, "Stay Away from This Stuff," and Chapter 8 should help you with the basics of the good and bad alternatives.

For your first investment, pass on anything that seems to have a high commission attached. Also, trust your gut and pass if the salesperson is using heavy-handed tactics or is trying to rush your decision.

### That Reminds Me...

I have a client who was sold a mutual fund with a 50 percent commission charge on the first year's monthly deposits. This is still legal and promoted heavily in the armed forces by commission-paid salespeople. He was sold one of the most expensive investment products known to man. Fortunately for him, his tenacity and market performance prevailed, and his account grew substantially as he continued his deposits. However, he said, "If I had known there were such things as no-load mutual funds, my account might have performed a little better."

# A Portrait of Your First Investment

If you understand the necessary characteristics of a properly diversified portfolio, you'll find that the list of investments is quite short. Because the list is small, you might not need an advisor to help you. If you are uncomfortable with making a decision after reading this chapter, then you might want to get some help from a fee-only investment advisor, using the questions in Chapter 9, "How to Find Help," to help select one with whom you're comfortable.

Near the end of Chapter 8, I gave you a list of optimal wealth-building portfolio characteristics. Here's a reminder of the most important elements:

➤ The portfolio is built primarily of stocks.

➤ The stocks are diversified among many different countries and industries to help maximize return while reducing risk.

➤ The portfolio can be cost-efficiently adjusted.

One stock can't meet all these characteristics. However, if you think the preceding characteristics are boring, and if you have your heart set on buying a stock or another investment idea, go ahead and try it. Make your mistakes now while they don't hurt so much. Go with your gut, and with a little luck, you might do well.

The only way you can possibly design a portfolio of less than $100,000 using the portfolio characteristics listed here is with no-load mutual funds. Therefore, before you make your next investment decision, let's explore mutual funds again.

> **Treasure Tip**
>
> If you had to pick one investment idea that covered all the necessary characteristics of an optimal wealth-building portfolio, the single best investment idea is a no-load mutual fund.

## How Much Will You Need to Start?

All mutual funds have a minimum investment amount you must meet to initially buy shares in the fund. Therefore, you have to pay attention to minimums when you design your portfolio. If you have only $1,000 and you want to get started with a mutual fund, you might have difficulty finding a fund. Some funds have a minimum of $2,500, $5,000, and even $25,000. However, the average minimum initial investment is $1,000. If you have less than $1,000 to invest, you can either wait until you've saved that much or find a fund with low minimums. For example, American Century Funds (800-345-2021) offers a number of funds with low initial investment minimums. Some funds will accept less than $1,000 if you agree to purchase at least that amount over the course of a year using monthly deposits. You can start with as little as $50 if you agree to their automatic monthly investment requirement, which involves a debit from your checking or savings account.

You might want to go directly to the fund company to make your first investment, especially if you're starting with less than $5,000. If you go to a discount brokerage firm, they may charge you transaction fees, as well as a custodian fee. Your account isn't profitable for them at this size, so they don't encourage you to start there.

## Narrowing the List

Your first step should be to buy a single fund that is globally diversified. You need a fund that invests not only in the U.S., but also in other developed and emerging market countries. Few funds do this well, so your list of alternatives is small.

If you're looking for a globally diversified fund (that invests in the U.S. and foreign countries), you may encounter some confusion. These funds use different names depending upon which mutual fund rating service or publication you choose. The most common title is international funds, which include mutual funds that invest in the U.S. and foreign countries. You might also find the title global funds, which should be the same. Regardless of what they say, make certain you know how these funds are allocated. Be sure not to mistake a foreign fund for an international fund. Foreign funds invest exclusively in foreign countries.

The following is a list of funds I personally like that are globally diversified:

| | |
|---|---|
| Janus Worldwide | 800-525-8983 |
| Tweedy Browne Global Value | 800-432-4789 |
| Founders Worldwide Growth | 800-525-2440 |
| Scudder Global | 800-225-2470 |

Remember that these are just ideas to get you started. Please be sure to read the prospectuses before you buy these funds.

Because of the ever-changing market, I hesitate to mention any specific mutual fund ideas, but I want to help you get started. You have to keep in mind that markets change, funds change, and managers may leave the fund. You can't assume that any fund will remain profitable, will duplicate past performance, or will keep the same manager. However, the funds I'm suggesting next have seasoned managers who should be with the fund for a long time. They are only as good as their managers, and if the manager leaves the fund, you might want to find another fund.

Let me assure you that I receive nothing for mentioning these funds. I like the philosophies of the managers. They are all unique and brilliant at what they do, and I know they will take good care of your money.

# Risk and Return

Risk and return work hand-in-hand. Return is the reward you get for the risk you take. Risk is something that should be managed, not avoided. You may have heard of the term *risk/reward ratio*. This measures the relationship between risk and reward, which is not an easy calculation.

Stock market risk is normally associated with portfolio or market fluctuation. The stock market lost almost 80 percent of its value in the crash of 1929. The market did come back, but it took a few years to do it. The possibility of a crash like this is highly unlikely today; however, the risk is there. The more likely scenario is a 10 or 20 percent drop in stock prices. Many investors refer to this as a stock market correction. The question you need to ask yourself is whether you could handle the potential damage to your portfolio. If you can accept this risk, then you are an aggressive investor. An aggressive investor is one whose portfolio is fully invested in stocks or stock funds that are diversified throughout companies all over the world.

**Words of the Wealthy**

The **risk/reward ratio** is a term used to describe a security's return relative to its risk. If a security has the potential for a 10 percent return on the upside, you should only be willing to accept an equal or lesser degree of risk on the downside. For example, why risk a 20 percent loss for a possible 10 percent return?

## To Thine Own Self Be True

Most investors overestimate the level of risk they can actually handle. Unfortunately, it usually takes a big drop in the market to find a person's actual risk tolerance. What you want to avoid is this scenario taking place once you've reached Wealth Stages 3, 4, and 5. That's when it may be too late to make any adjustments. I consider Wealth Stages 1 and 2 training stages. Get to know your risk tolerance early in the game so you can reduce surprises later in life. As you learn more and your portfolio grows, you might want to change your risk tolerance either way. Keep in mind during the rough times that you are investing for the long run.

## What Kind of Return Do You Expect

During the years of 1995, 1996, and 1997, the market made some unprecedented gains. If you use these as benchmarks, you'll make a huge mistake. Be reasonable with your expectations.

No matter what you've accomplished in the last several years, an aggressive investor should target annual returns of approximately 14 percent, moderate investors should shoot for 12–13 percent, and conservative investors, 7–11 percent. You might get better performance, and you might get worse. The point I'm trying to make is that you shouldn't set yourself up for failure. Set reasonable expectations, and do the best you can.

Don't try to hit home runs, no matter how much risk you think you can tolerate. Investing is like baseball. It's won with base hits, not home runs. The more home runs you attempt, the more you'll strike out. However, if you're bored with base hits, go for the fence now, early in your career when the mistakes don't hurt as much.

**Treasure Tip**

Waschka's law of market corrections says the worst thing you can possibly do during a correction is sell. A correction is simply an absence of buyers amidst a flood of investors wanting to sell. If you join them, you'll completely miss the market rebound when there's an absence of sellers and a flood of buyers. Stay off the bandwagon.

## Learn from Your Mistakes

When you do make a mistake, learn from it. Spend some time learning why you failed. Ask yourself

➤ What could I have done to prevent this loss?

➤ If I had to do it all again, what would I do differently?

➤ What will I do next time to improve my results?

Take some time to learn from the loss, but don't let it discourage you. So many people take their mistakes personally. They say to themselves, "I guess that's just the kind of investor I am." I hear them say to me all the time, "If you want something to go down, just let me buy it." This is a horrible attitude to have, and ironically, it is self-fulfilling. If you think this way, you'd better believe you'll lose money. But if you take the time to learn from your losses, you'll be all the wiser.

# Don't Let the Market Control Your Life

If you are focusing on achieving Wealth Stage 2, now is not the time to look at your investments every day. In fact, I don't ever recommend this practice unless you are a professional. I know so many people who let the stock market dictate their total attitude toward life each and every day. They are happy when it's up and depressed when it's down. They usually lose sight of the long-term vision when the market is down.

There are two more important things to focus on. When you are in Stages 1 and 2, your savings amount and investment knowledge should be of key importance. At these stages, you actually want the market to fall and keep falling. Why? Because you are investing money each month. Don't you want to buy low and sell high? If so, you want the market to be down when you buy and up when you need your money at a later date.

**Treasure Tip**

On your way toward Wealth Stage 2, if your yearly savings deposit exceeds 10 or 20 percent of your total portfolio, then don't concern yourself with any possible stock market correction until after the first stage of Wealth Stage 2.

## The Tortoise and the Hare

Most beginning investors worry too much about picking the fastest growing investment. They focus too much on the market and not enough time on minimizing expenses or meeting their target savings goal. The result is portfolio mediocrity as their unbalanced portfolio never grows significantly in size. Such investors end up with a volatile portfolio that might be growing at a 15 percent rate, but it doesn't really matter. Because they didn't meet their target savings goal, their account never grew very large. It's the classic tortoise and the hare story. While the hare runs around frantically trying to buy the best performing stocks each month, the tortoise wins the race because he saved as much as he could each year. His returns might not be all that incredible, but his account value sure is. Try to be the tortoise, not the hare.

## Invest Automatically

Most mutual funds offer an automatic debit service from your checking account. This is a no-brainer, yet so few people take advantage of it. Over half of the people I suggest this to are afraid of it. I've narrowed down the list of fears most people have of the automatic debit service:

**Treasure Tip**

Waschka's law of savings says you should save automatically by letting a mutual fund debit your checking account each month.

➤ Fear of the mutual fund company taking advantage of them

➤ Fear of an invasion of privacy

➤ Fear of losing control

➤ Fear of forgetting to record the deposit in the check register

First, the mutual fund can't take advantage of you. Why would they jeopardize their registration with the SEC just to get a few more dollars out of your account? Second, the mutual fund can only debit a certain amount, not check your balance. Third, this service is a way to gain control over spending, not lose control. Fourth, post a big note to yourself where you pay your bills to record the debit each month. The debit service is too easy and powerful not to take advantage of it.

# Where to Put the First Investment

The smartest thing you can do when you begin investing is build your portfolio in a tax-deferred environment. Your first investment could be purchased within your IRA account, which would allow it to grow tax deferred. It doesn't matter whether you can deduct the deposit; what's important is the tax-deferred growth and the almost unlimited investment alternatives to choose from. Therefore, consider your first $2,000 investment going into an IRA. Any of the types of investments listed in this chapter can be purchased within an IRA.

An IRA is simply an investment account. An IRA at a bank may be invested in a CD, but it is actually an account. They may restrict you to CDs only, but it is still an account. Brokerage firms (full service and discount) offer the same account. However, they allow you to put several different securities or funds within that same IRA account. This is a confusing topic. Just remember, you can have as many different IRA accounts as you want. You might decide to do business directly with several different no-load mutual fund companies. That's fine. Each one will open an IRA account for you.

**Treasure Tip**

The best place to start saving is in a 401(k) plan or IRA because both allow your investment to grow tax deferred over time. The second best place to invest is in a regular investment account. The growth is taxable but only when you sell or receive distributions from your mutual funds.

You could also start out by investing in your 401(k) from your employer. In a 401(k), you're probably not going to find an international fund as an alternative. More than likely, you'll find a foreign fund that could be combined with a domestic stock fund to achieve a global balance.

You could also start your own investment account for yourself (and your spouse). The first decision you'll have to make is whether to buy directly from a mutual fund or through a discount brokerage firm. For now, as long as you are buying only one or two funds, going with the discount brokerage firm doesn't give you much of an advantage. Later, when you own three or more funds, the discount brokerage firm will let you consolidate your portfolio into one account. This is a real time-saver. Investing directly with several different funds can be time-consuming. To buy a fund, you have to call for an application, wait for the application to arrive, fill it out, send it in, and wait for them to receive it—and then they purchase the fund for you. This could take 10 days. This entire procedure can take place the same day if you have an account with a brokerage firm that offers no-load funds. Instead of getting many different statements in the mail, the brokerage firm will consolidate all your mutual funds on one statement. Instead of getting several different 1099s at the end of the year, you get one.

Remember, discount brokerage firms are somewhat limited in their list of available funds. Therefore, your favorite fund might not be on their list. You can call the firm and ask if they plan to add that fund, or you can just go directly to the fund itself.

# Graduating to More Than One Fund

The best advice I can give any novice investor who's looking to do more is to learn all you can. Graduating from one fund to two or three requires a little more knowledge and confidence, which are easily attainable from books and investment classes. If you want to learn more about mutual funds, read *The Complete Idiot's Guide to Making Money with Mutual Funds*. If you just can't stand this stuff, get a fee-only advisor to help you get started.

## *Graduating to Two Funds*

Assuming you chose one mutual fund in your investment portfolio, sooner or later you're going to have enough money to diversify into two, three, or more funds. There's no magic amount to begin this split; it's all a matter of preference and whether you can meet the minimums on the funds you select. If the minimum is $1,000, all you need is $2,000. You want to be sure to build a mix of domestic and foreign invested funds. If you tend to be a little conservative, focus on stock funds that buy relatively large companies using a *value-oriented* philosophy. You might also keep your foreign fund allocation at or below the 30 percent level, which leaves 70 percent of your money domestically invested. This may be difficult to do with $2,000. If you have $4,000 and want 30 percent invested in a foreign fund, you can put $1,200 in the foreign fund and $2,800 in the domestic fund.

If you are an aggressive investor, you might want to focus on stock funds that buy stocks of relatively small companies using a *growth-oriented* philosophy. Your foreign allocation could be as high as 50 percent.

**Words of the Wealthy**

A **value-oriented** manager searches for undervalued stocks that are priced below what the manager actually thinks they're worth. The goal of the value manager is to sell at a profit once the market realizes the stock's true value.

**Words of the Wealthy**

A **growth-oriented** manager searches for stocks with high earnings growth. Investors are willing to pay relatively higher prices for these stocks for the chance that they may be even higher later.

When you select each fund, look for a fund manager who thinks like you do. The only way to find this out is by reading the manager's objective and philosophy in the prospectus. You might get lucky and find an article or television interview, but chances are you're going to have to do some searching. Don't worry; the next five chapters should make the search a little easier.

## Graduating to Three Funds

You might consider three funds once your portfolio grows beyond $15,000. If you are a moderate-risk investor, your three-fund portfolio should look something like this:

| | |
|---|---|
| 35% | Small-cap domestic stock fund |
| 30% | Mid-cap domestic stock fund |
| 35% | Foreign stock fund |

Basically, you would add a small-cap fund to your portfolio at this point. If you are conservative, you can still use a value manager with a 30 percent or less foreign allocation. Aggressive investors can use a growth-oriented manager and up to 50 percent foreign.

You don't really need any more than 12 mutual funds in a portfolio. Graduating beyond the three-fund portfolio takes more time and effort. The next five chapters will help you be more effective and efficient in that effort.

### The Least You Need to Know

➤ The first thing you invest in should be a no-load mutual fund that invests primarily in stocks that are diversified globally and managed cost-efficiently.

➤ Try not to be sold by a smooth-talking salesperson who wants to take advantage of you by selling you an expensive investment product.

➤ Make your mistakes early when you're working with smaller amounts of money; you can learn a lot from them and they won't be as expensive as they will be later.

➤ If you are a conservative investor, focus on value-oriented mutual funds (funds that invest in undervalued stocks), and if you are aggressive, focus on growth-oriented mutual funds.

➤ Don't monitor your investment every day; you'll drive yourself and everyone else crazy.

➤ Focus on learning more about the market and maximizing your savings amount.

# Chapter 11

# Building the Perfect Portfolio

This chapter takes you to the next step in portfolio management—building the perfect portfolio. Okay, so there is no such thing as a "perfect portfolio." However, there is a perfect portfolio for you. This portfolio should be custom designed for you with your risk tolerance and goals in mind. Just like the concept of wealth, the perfect portfolio is a journey, not a destination. In this constantly changing investment market, you must be flexible enough to make changes when necessary. You must also be cognizant of how your own life changes. These changes will force you to keep an eye on your portfolio—or at least hire someone else to do it for you.

This chapter is designed to teach you the cycle of building wealth through the use of your investment portfolio. If you understand the principles in this cycle, you will be able to achieve any wealth level you desire. Once your portfolio exceeds approximately $10,000, which is large enough to easily diversify among more than three mutual funds, you're ready to take advantage of another level of opportunity called multi-fund portfolio management. You now have the ability to add additional layers of diversification to your portfolio, hire a team of investment specialists, and build a synergistically profitable portfolio.

How do you select the investments to build this portfolio? Most investors use past performance. All the fine print tells you not to do this, but investors do it anyway. Markets do change, meaning that your investment strategies should reflect these changes. That's what this chapter is all about: incorporating a portfolio management cycle that keeps up with the changing markets.

This chapter primarily refers to mutual funds because that's where I spend most of my time helping my clients. However, you can use the same principles in this chapter for stock investing. It's a lot more difficult to do, but it can be done if you have the time and passion.

*The Portfolio Management Cycle Asset Allocation*

Asset Allocation
- Hockey Puck Theory
- Ten Tactics (ch. 13)

Investment Selection
- Buy & hold
- Sector rotation

Maintenance & review
- Measure results
- Micro-delegation
- Zen-based thinking

# Asset Allocation

The first step in the portfolio management cycle is asset allocation, which is a fancy term for the strategy of dividing your assets among several different types of investments or asset classes for the purpose of diversification and profit. An asset class can be stocks, bonds, money markets, gold, or even real estate. The theory of asset allocation is based upon the idea that a portfolio diversified among many different asset classes will incur less risk than a portfolio invested in only one class.

**Treasure Tip**

Studies have shown that the asset allocation decision is the single most important factor in determining your portfolio returns, as well as risk.

For example, let's say that you decide to invest your $10,000 in domestic stock funds only, leaving nothing in foreign stock funds. If foreign stock funds outperform domestic stock funds, your portfolio will have underperformed—and you would have taken more risk because you didn't diversify your portfolio globally.

Asset allocation gives you the ability to diversify across many different asset classes, as well as securities. This step is powerful because it builds into your portfolio the opportunity for greater returns, and at the same time, it reduces risk. The idea is that each of the parts has its own risk and return characteristics (some high risk and some low), which together in one portfolio can balance each other out. In essence, you smooth out the ride.

## Asset Allocation Software

You don't need this yet, but I thought you might like to know that software can help you with the asset allocation decision. Several expensive software programs will calculate your "optimal" asset allocation based upon your risk tolerances. Unfortunately, the outcome is based upon years of past performances of each asset class. This means that the allocation you get assumes that the future will be similar to the past, which more than likely is not true. You can use these programs if you want to; they can be confusing. Just remember that they aren't perfect. If you're just starting out, you don't need this stuff.

## Asset Allocation Based on Age

How do you know how much to place in each asset class? Many brokers and investment advisors use a weird rule to decide how an investor's assets should be allocated. I don't know where it started, but I've seen it many times in investment classes, financial magazines, and even in financial books. It's based on the principle that an investor's bond allocation should be based upon age. If you are 25, then 25 percent of your portfolio should be in bonds and 75 percent should be in stocks. If you are 80, then 80 percent of your portfolio should be in bonds and 20 percent in stocks.

Instead, your allocation in any type of investment should be based upon your risk tolerance and how you feel about that investment, as well as the risk you are willing to assume to meet the goals you want to achieve. You can also take into account the Hockey Puck Theory, described next.

**Wealth Warning**

The market doesn't care how old you are; it will take your head off whether you are 25 years old or 80. If you had 80 percent of your money in bonds in 1994, your portfolio got hammered. Many bond funds were down 15 percent or more.

## The Hockey Puck Theory

It's said that Wayne Gretzky, the most popular hockey player in the world and definitely one of the best, was asked by a reporter one day, "Wayne, I don't get it. Why are you so much better than your teammates and opponents? You are not a faster skater. You are not a quicker puck handler. You're not even any meaner. What makes you so much better?"

Wayne stopped a minute and said, "Well, most of my teammates and players skate to where the hockey puck is. I skate to where I think the hockey puck is going to be."

This has nothing to do with investing, but it has everything to do with excellence in portfolio management. If you think about it for a minute, most investors don't even invest where the market is. They invest where the market has been, right? Your goal should be to invest where the market is going and not where it has been. You must be willing to invest your money based upon what you think is going to happen. To do that, you have to understand trends. A trend is a 3-, 5-, or 10-year series of events that affect a niche of the world economically, politically, and socially. The most dramatic trends affect the entire world.

The whole idea behind investing for profits is to position your money to take advantage of the best investment opportunities available. These opportunities are best found by focusing your attention on trends, especially the ones indicated by small revolutionary changes in the world that have the potential to

➤ Spawn new products and maybe new industries

➤ Improve the health and lifestyles of people all over the world

➤ Help emerging countries catch up with the modern world

➤ Help corporations be more productive and profitable

Therefore, instead of allocating assets the conventional way—using different asset classes—position your assets to take advantage of trends. By diversifying your money among several different unrelated trends, you dramatically increase your potential for returns and reduce your risk of loss.

### That Reminds Me...

If you really want to find examples of the most dramatic trends in the world, pick up a copy of *The Economist.* Its "Survey of the Software Industry" (5/25/96, p. 4) said that John Doerr, one of Silicon Valley's leading venture capitalists, has calculated that the introduction of the PC caused the largest creation of wealth in the history of the planet. The article also said that Morgan Stanley's Mary Meeker, one of the computer industry's most respected analysts, reckons that the Internet has the potential to become even bigger. This is a trend with a capital "T." They were both correct, and most of the stocks in both of these industries have done quite well.

If you are looking at trends, you must be able to develop scenarios based upon events that are currently unfolding. This requires some knowledge, imagination, and a heavy reliance on the latest flow of economic data. You need all this to provide some hint of a realistic prediction of the future. Your prediction doesn't have to be exactly on target; you just have to be close. It's a little like landing an airplane using only your instruments in the midst of a hurricane. It may be difficult, but it certainly beats flying completely blind.

1. **Finding Trends.** The first thing you do is find the most dramatic trends in the world. You can start simply by asking your spouse or parents what new things they are spending money on. You can also find trends in the news media. Instead of just listening to the news, spend time thinking about how you could profit from the events being covered. Look for statistics whenever you can (such as the number of people using cellular phones or beepers, for example). Select the three to six best trends you can find and design your portfolio to take advantage of these trends. If you select unrelated trends, your portfolio will have a certain amount of diversification. You have to expect to be wrong to some degree. At least one of these trends might not develop the way you anticipated. If you diversify among several trends, your mistake won't hurt so bad. You can divide evenly among the trends or over-weight some trends more than others. What does a trend look like and how do you find one? Chapter 13, "Waschka's 10 Easy Portfolio Strategies That Work," will help you easily identify these trends.

2. **Exploiting trends.** You can do this with individual stocks and bonds or mutual funds. The most convenient method involves mutual funds. While the mutual fund manager focuses on the micro-view of the corporate world, you have more time to focus on the macro-view of the world. If you allocate your assets among these funds according to the amount of confidence you have in the trends you've selected, your portfolio will be more customized to your personality and beliefs. That's the way it should be. You should invest in what you believe in.

Why not take a minute to write down the five most influential trends in your life? Observe what you have purchased in the last several months. Look at the magazines you read, especially any trade magazines you might use in your business. What's new? What changes do you see in the future? Here's a list to get you started:

➤ Advances in healthcare for the aging babyboomers who'll need it

➤ Advances in communications via cellular phones, pagers, and the Internet

➤ The growth of emerging market countries and their communications industries

➤ The aging babyboomers and their desire to travel more for pleasure as they approach the age of 50

➤ The European corporate restructuring and the introduction of the European Monetary Unit

➤ The currency devaluation in emerging markets and the return of economic growth there

This method of asset allocation is what I call real-life asset allocation. Most investment professionals and professors will argue that it doesn't work because it's not based on specific procedures, has no equations or formulas, and doesn't have any set guidelines for use. However, neither does the market!

Because of the market's tendency to continuously change, you can't expect quantifiable logic to work. If the market were quantifiable and easy to profit from, everyone would be rich. You could buy a software program, plug in your amount and poof! you'd get a quantifiably measured portfolio. But that doesn't work well. Therefore, if you want to flow with the market and make any money, you have to escape from conventional wisdom and remain flexible in your strategies. Your success will be directly related to your ability to stay flexible and adapt to the changes.

*Let me make this warning.* You are going to encounter *bear markets*, which are time periods when nothing seems to work—because everything is falling in price. Even if you had $1 million in the market, I would more than likely tell you to sit tight and ride it out.

**Words of the Wealthy**

A **bear market** is simply a time when few (if any) people are buying. Therefore, it's the worst time to sell. History shows that periodically, the market will pull back and correct itself. This is normal but often difficult to accept.

Your attitude toward a market decline should actually be one of excitement. If you are putting money into the market systematically each month, don't you want to buy stocks at the lowest prices you can get? Here's your chance.

Most people don't understand the concept of delayed gratification. It's a simple concept that's as old as the Model T Ford. To understand the stock market, you must understand delayed gratification. Stocks weren't designed to make people money instantly. They were designed to be a method of allowing business owners to raise capital for long-term projects. To own stock, you must have a long-term investment horizon. When the market is down, you face a faith and confidence issue. Don't lose the faith during the storms; they will occur.

# Investment Selection

Most investors start here by mistake. It's like picking a job without any consideration of needs, goals, and passion. The first step should be asset allocation. If your account is small, the biggest decision is how much you should have invested in the domestic market and how much in the foreign markets. Once you've made this decision, the investment selection process becomes easier. You may only need one domestic fund and one foreign fund, and that might be the extent of your asset allocation decision. The second decision is investment selection, which has already been simplified somewhat by your first decision. You know what you need now.

Most people just pick stocks or mutual funds without any thought to allocation. They grab a magazine from the shelf at the grocery store checkout stand, pick a great performing fund off the "top picks" list, call the company, and just like that, they're invested. As soon as their fund is off the "Top 10 list," they swap into another fund. This is the scary truth about investors today. They spend more time cleaning their car than they do planning their investment portfolio.

Understand that with these selection strategies, you have to be flexible and adaptable to change. The market is not dogmatic, and neither should you be when investing in it. You are also going to be wrong a certain percentage of the time. When you make a mistake, first you have to be willing to admit it without taking it personally. Then, you must be proactive enough to correct your mistake. Often, the best proactive thing to do is sit tight for a while and do nothing—which is hard when the market is down. If you're like most people, you'll want to fix it.

I've narrowed down the selection process to three strategies: buy and hold, market timing, and sector rotation. These strategies work, but you cannot be dogmatic with them. Each selection strategy is used in conjunction with your asset allocation decision. If you have decided to devote 20 percent of your portfolio to technology stocks, then you need to select one or two technology funds to fill that 20 percent allocation. These selection techniques will help you do that.

**Treasure Tip**

Morningstar (800–876–5005) is a company in Chicago that produces printed and computer-based research to make your mutual fund selection process easier. They offer a $55 trial subscription of their printed product, normally $395 per year, and trials of their computer-based products. I don't consult their opinions or fund ratings because they are based on several years of past performance, but I do use the factual information they offer.

## Buy and Hold Strategy

Buy and hold is the single most common strategy used by mutual fund investors. It simply is what it says: Buy a security and hold it through good times and bad. This strategy should only be part of your investment selection strategy. You should use the buy-and-hold strategy to build the core of your portfolio, which should deliver stability to your overall portfolio. Core funds are rarely traded and are usually held two to four years.

When using this strategy to purchase mutual funds, the most important thing is the manager. You want the fund to go with the flow of the market. If the market is over-priced, then you want the manager to take action toward protecting the fund from a possible correction. Whatever the market conditions are, you want the fund manager to be able to react properly and invest in almost anything he sees fit to buy. Therefore, you want the manager to have few restrictions. You can find a list of these restrictions in the prospectus. If you give someone few restrictions, you need to demand a lot of experience.

Make sure to look for funds that have a relatively steady track record in good times and bad. Don't overlook new funds. Most investors shy away from new funds because there is no 3-, 5-, or 10-year track record. The manager might have a great record at another fund that you can easily research.

The best fund managers in the world are interviewed regularly in publications such as *Barron's* and *Forbes*. They are truly giants in the industry. Here are a few of my favorites and the funds they manage:

➤ Robert Sanborn, Oakmark Fund, 800-Grow Oak

➤ Mason Hawkins, Longleaf Partners Funds, 800-445-9469

➤ Tom Marsico, Marsico Funds, 888-860-8686

➤ Jean-Marie Eveillard, Sogen Funds (low load), 800-334-2143

➤ Chris Browne, Tweedy Browne Global Value, 800-432-4789

**Words of the Wealthy**

Fundamental analysis is the study of the basic facts that determine a security's value. A fundamental analysis of a mutual fund includes the study of the securities within the fund, the manager, the philosophy, the expenses, and the average P/E ratio.

Don't buy one of these funds because it is listed here. Get their prospectus and annual report, and do some research (your own *fundamental analysis*). Chart the funds using the software listed in Chapter 12, "The Six Habits of Very Wealthy Investors," and select the fund with the best performance and least volatility.

During bear markets and times when the market makes a correction, the buy-and-hold strategy should be the key strategy. It's not smart to trade a lot when the market falls dramatically. Again, be flexible here, but remember that a correction or bear market is simply a time when few people buy stocks. It's not smart to sell out because you have no idea when the market will turn back up.

**Words of the Wealthy**

Using charts to read the price history and other statistical patterns of stocks or mutual funds is known as technical analysis. Many investors and most professionals use these charts to make investment decisions. A technical analyst is also known as a chartist.

## Market Timing

Market timing is simply the strategy of being in the market when it is going up and out of the market when it's going down. This is quite a seductive strategy, but it's almost impossible to accomplish consistently over time. Market timing is also known as *technical analysis*, which primarily includes the study of information in the form of charts. Technical analysts attempt to predict the movement of a particular market or security based upon past behavior in similar market circumstances.

Be careful with this strategy; your portfolio could get hurt. Don't take this strategy to the extreme. Over the past 13 years, I've seen a lot of people get scared in the markets, sell everything, and go to money market funds, only to see the market continue to rise for many years. This is the extreme. I use money market funds to a certain degree for market timing purposes, but the biggest position I've ever held for any length of time is 45 percent for a few months.

One of the biggest trends in investment strategy lately has been the growing popularity of momentum-based investing. This concept is highly publicized by several people in the investment industry. This is a form of market timing where you pick individual stocks based upon their recent price appreciation and their earnings growth. A momentum stock strategist would say, "If the stock is going up and the earnings look good, then buy it." They would also say, "If the stock is falling, sell it." The end result is a million investors playing a market-timing game who all end up overreacting on both sides of the market. This makes for some crazy volatile days in the market. I hope this trend will fizzle out, but I don't count on it.

## Sector Rotation

Many investors use the sector-rotation strategy for selecting investments without even realizing what it's called or how it actually works. It's a strategy based upon several theories. First is the theory that there are many markets or sectors of the market that can act independently of each other. These sectors can be industries, countries, or any specific type of security.

The second theory of sector rotation is the assumption that there will always be opportunity in the market. As my friend Dave Muller says, "There's always a bull market somewhere." For many years, he wrote a monthly investment newsletter titled *Foreign Markets Advisor*. It may be hard to find the bull market, but it's out there somewhere. That doesn't mean that you want to throw all your money in it! It just means that you should always take advantage of the opportunities available.

The third theory behind sector rotation assumes that an investor is able to be invested in the sectors that are performing well and can get out quickly before the trend changes direction for the worse. The fourth theory of sector rotation says that by maintaining a portfolio focused on the best performing sectors, you'll be able to beat the market over time.

The illustration in this section shows how the theory of sector rotation works in a perfect world. Remember that this is just an illustration, and your results are going to vary. After identifying a major

**Treasure Tip**

Some funds are managed by a committee instead of one manager. I prefer to have a single manager because they are usually more decisive and efficient than a committee. However, there are certainly exceptions to this rule.

trend and investing in the corresponding sector, the investor rides the growth of one sector (or trend) and rotates to another sector (or trend) before growth begins to slow. You can ride the growth of a sector by using mutual funds that focus on that particular sector, or you can use individual stocks. You strive to repeat this process over time to produce above-average returns. This strategy does require a lot of work, but it can be profitable.

*Sector Rotation*

You can compare this strategy of sector rotation to surfing in the ocean. First, you find just the right wave, and then you position yourself to take advantage of it. Before the wave crashes you against the beach or rocks, turn back and find another wave. This strategy may seem seductive, but it is difficult. It is a game of numbers, which means that you will fail part of the time. With patience, research, and diversification, your winnings will cover your losses. It is not a question of *if* you will lose; it is a question of *when* you will lose and to what extent. If you can win more than you lose, your portfolio will prosper. The only way to win is to buy an investment (from someone else) that you think is worth more than the money you paid. Then, you must hold that investment until someone is willing to pay you more than you feel the investment is worth. Both transactions involve other people being wrong. What you are in fact saying each time you buy and sell is that the other person is wrong. That's pretty bold, wouldn't you agree? But this is only half of the boldness required. To increase your chances of profit, you have to increase your chances that the other person is wrong. The more wrong they are, the cheaper you can buy, and that means more profit for you.

There is a group of investors who call themselves *contrarians*. They believe in the sector-rotation theory, and they increase their chances of making a profit in the stock market with strategies such as the following:

1. Buy the sector that has fallen or corrected the most—what everyone hates.

**Words of the Wealthy**

**Contrarians** are investors who like to buy stocks that are considered undervalued or out of favor.

2. Buy the sector that everyone fears—usually a sector that is somewhat new to the market.

3. Buy the sector that has the most negative media coverage; what does the media hate?

The objective of the contrarian is to find the most hated or feared sectors, wait until they have hit a bottom, and then buy. It's hard to know exactly when the bottom is hit without a chart. You don't need a three-year chart to do this. A 6- to 12-month chart usually works better. Make sure the fund's price chart verifies this bottom. What does a bottom look like? It doesn't really matter. What's important is whether the fund is trending upward after a long period of falling. Don't try to invest at the exact bottom. Buy the fund when you see the price trending upward. One of the most powerful things you can find is a sector that is out of favor and at the same time is involved in a potentially profitable new trend. This discovery of course is like the Holy Grail of investing and is rarely found, but it is possible to find such things occasionally. Junk bonds in 1990 and emerging markets in 1992 are two great examples.

The idea is to hold the fund until it hits a top. That's usually when everyone is talking about it or when it hits the front pages of *Time* or *Newsweek*. Then, sell it and find another sector. If you have access to charts, make sure the fund's price chart verifies this top. What does a top look like? Again, it doesn't really matter. What's important is whether the fund is trending downward after a long period of rising. Don't try to sell at the exact top. Sell when you see the price begin to trend downward. As funds top out and are sold, it's important to have other funds available to buy. The perfect scenario is to have another sector available to rotate into immediately. Therefore, you should always be on the look-out for other sectors that are beginning to trend upward.

The momentum investor does the opposite by buying sectors or stocks that are going up in price already in hopes that they will continue to go up.

## The Flower Portfolio

All three fund selection strategies are best illustrated by the flower portfolio diagram. The buy-and-hold strategy is used to build the core of your portfolio. The core funds are rarely traded and therefore make the base of the flower. The market-timing and sector-rotation strategies are used to build the next layer of sector type funds, represented by the petals. As market trends change, so does the portfolio. If the market is underpriced or in a bull phase, the flower may have many petals. If the market is overpriced or in a bear phase, you might only see one or two petals. The core funds tend to be somewhat of a safe haven when the markets are overpriced because they are usually less volatile. While the core remains in tact, the petals fall off occasionally and are sometimes replaced with different petals. Therefore, the flower does change its design as the seasons of the market change. The only problem is that the seasons don't always repeat themselves each year. Core funds are normally held two to four years.

*The Flower Portfolio*

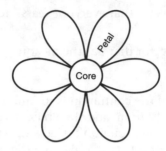

The second layer of funds (sector related) in the portfolio should be purchased based upon the hockey puck theory. They are selected based upon their potential ability to take advantage of a particular trend. These funds are normally held 6 to 18 months.

### That Reminds Me...

When using the hockey puck theory and sector rotation, I tend to use funds that usually focus on one particular industry, country, or specific security type. I call them "Orville Redenbacher funds." Have you ever seen an Orville Redenbacher commercial? The company motto is "Do one thing and do it better than anybody else." They do one thing—popcorn—and they do it better than anybody. That's what a specific objective fund manager can do for you. The manager concentrates on only one industry, country, or specific security type—and nothing else. This focus enables her to be a true specialist in that particular area. She does one thing and does it better than anybody else.

# Maintenance and Review

The third phase of the portfolio management cycle, maintenance and review, is most often neglected by investors. For example, most investors have no idea how well their portfolio is performing. They try to do everything and rarely ever make transactions when they should. Take some time each month to look over your portfolio. If this is absolutely no fun to you, you might need to hire some help.

## Measurement of Results

If you are in Wealth Stage 1, you should be measuring your deposits into your investment accounts to make certain that you are at least making your target savings goal. Do this once a year. If you're married, make certain that you include your spouse.

You could also measure your portfolio performance, but remember it is second in importance until you reach Wealth Stage 2. Once you've reached Stage 2, then you should pay equal attention to your performance. This should be done once a year. Let me warn you that unless you made good grades in mathematics, you should not attempt this calculation. It's very complicated, especially if you have been making regular deposits (or withdrawals). If you work with an advisor or brokerage firm, ask whether this can be calculated for you. Financial software packages can also help. All you have to do is enter each deposit and transaction for your account for the period you want to measure. This may seem tedious, but once you've got the data in, all you have to do is update it each month. The software is pretty simple to use, and it certainly does a lot more than calculate investment returns. Here are my favorite packages:

Quicken, produced by Intuit, 800-446-8848

Microsoft Money, 800-785-3448

Once you've done this, you might want to compare your performance to other indexes. If you have a global portfolio of stocks, use the Morgan Stanley World Market Index, which can be found every business day in *The Wall Street Journal*. Record this index as often as you measure your portfolio results so you can keep track of the index.

Your individual funds should also be compared to relatively similar funds. You don't have to constantly switch back and forth between the best performing funds, but if your funds consistently underperform other similar funds, then you might want to make a change. Also if other similar funds in a sector where you're heavily invested begin to slow down and head south, it might mean that the trend is changing. Your fund may still be going strong while all the other similar funds are going down. If you knew this, you could get out before your fund follows.

## Micro-Delegation Strategy

The macro-view is the study of major trends around the world, whereas the micro-view is the study of the specific stocks that take advantage of these trends. Most of the major trends can be exploited using mutual funds. If you want to focus on technology, for example, there are many funds that do so. If you do additional research, you'll find that some funds focus on hardware and some on software. Depending upon your particular interests, you can usually find a fund that matches your specific goals. If you can't find a mutual fund that takes advantage of the trend you choose, then select several stocks that will.

### Words of the Wealthy

**Micro-delegation** is simply the delegation of the micro-view responsibilities to other professionals. This strategy enables you to focus on the big picture. It also allows you to delegate the details to other people who are often better at them than you.

Even if your passion is investing, the amount of time you have to research the world markets and the fine details that go along with them is limited. Recognizing this limitation changed my entire outlook on investing. It brought me to the most powerful investment strategy I've ever used. I call it *micro-delegation.* If I'm going to really focus on worldwide trends, how could I expect to have the time to thoroughly study individual stocks and bonds? I couldn't answer this question, so I began to delegate the micro-view responsibility to mutual fund managers. The simple purchase of a mutual fund automatically means that you have delegated the micro-view responsibility to the fund manager. Compared to a portfolio with a handful of stocks, the net benefit you get with mutual funds is micro-delegation, similar potential for returns, and lower risk exposure.

As outlined in the next chapter, your efforts in keeping up with the world markets and different economies will be rewarded. The ten portfolio management tactics in Chapter 13 will help you interpret and exploit the information and market changes you'll encounter, which in turn will help you maintain the proper asset allocations necessary to beat the market averages.

## Zero Based Thinking

As I've mentioned earlier in the book, all sell decisions should start with this question: If your portfolio were all in cash today, would you buy what you own? If the answer is no, make the changes necessary to get to where you want to be. If the answer is yes, do nothing. Your decision should be based upon your continued research of world markets and trends. You can use this strategy with your entire portfolio or each individual investment. It makes every investment decision so much easier.

---

### The Least You Need to Know

➤ Use the Wayne Gretzky asset allocation theory to allocate your assets among several different trends in the world.

➤ Build your portfolio by using several different mutual funds that position themselves to profit from the trends you feel the strongest about.

➤ Maintain your portfolio by focusing on the macro-view of the world while rotating portions of your portfolio to take advantage of the changing market conditions.

➤ Always ask yourself, "If your portfolio were all in cash today, would you buy what you own?" If the answer is no, make the necessary changes.

# Chapter 12

---

# The Six Habits of Very Wealthy Investors

## In This Chapter

➤ A quick look at economic theory

➤ The best sources of investment information

➤ Charting mutual funds

➤ Unreasonable thinking

You've achieved the first part of Wealth Stage 2, and your portfolio's return now exceeds your target savings goal. It's here that portfolio management becomes vital to the wealth-building process. If portfolio management is your passion and you decide to manage your own money, there are a few things you must know. You need six habits to successfully manage your investments. They are easy to obtain, and they are the keys to unlocking the world of high-performance investing as you build your portfolio beyond two or three mutual funds or other types of investments, as described in Chapter 10, "Jumping into the Market."

I do not claim to be any smarter than you, nor do I have access to information that you don't have. The traits listed in this chapter have more to do with common sense than they do with genius. After you read this, you should have a different perspective on doing research and making investment decisions. This chapter may be just what you need.

# 1: Develop an Understanding of Basic Economics

To really do well in the stock market, you must understand the basics of economic theory. There are many books available on this subject. For example, Steven Landsburg, an associate professor of economics at the University of Rochester, wrote an interesting book titled *The Armchair Economist* (The Free Press, 1993). Economic theory is easy to understand if you take a little time to study it.

## Inflation and Interest Rates

You need a basic understanding of inflation and its effect on interest rates. A basic economics book will teach you the details if you want to get into them.

The key thing you need to understand is that the expectation of higher inflation will spur higher interest rates and vice versa. If investors anticipate inflation, they know that higher interest rates will follow, which will cause bond prices to fall. Therefore, they sell their bonds. Bond prices work on the age-old principal of supply and demand. No matter what inflation does, if a large number of investors sell their bonds at the same time, interest rates go up and bond prices fall. This is especially true for long-term Treasury bonds. However, once interest rates on Treasury bonds or corporate bonds approach an 8 to 10 percent yield, investors tend to sell stocks and buy bonds. Why? Think about it logically. Why would you want to own risky stocks that might (historically) have paid only 10 percent when you can get a guaranteed 8 to 10 percent with a bond? How do you anticipate inflation and interest rate movements? Watch the producer price index each month along with the consumer price index. (These are usually announced in major newspapers and on the national news.) The former will tell you how the latter will move in the future. I discuss more about this in Chapter 13, "Waschka's 10 Easy Portfolio Strategies That Work".

**Treasure Tip**

A basic understanding of economics will help you make so many decisions in life, including when to buy a house, when to borrow money to start a business, and when to buy a stock or bond. It will also help to clarify the three most important aspects of economics: inflation, interest rates, and corporate earnings growth.

## Corporate Earnings Growth

You also need to understand how corporate earnings can affect the stock market. Stock markets move primarily in response to anticipated earnings growth of different companies. If the economy does well and corporations in the U.S. are able to produce a higher amount of profit (earnings) than last year, then the stock market should do well.

The same idea applies to other countries around the world and their stock markets. If investors anticipate a country will grow economically, or if they see companies beginning to improve their earnings, they will buy stocks in that country. You can make a lot of money investing in these countries if you get there before everybody else does. How do you anticipate the earnings growth of a country? Watch the economic growth, which is measured by the gross domestic product (GDP) growth rate. My most favorite magazine is *The Economist*, which shows current and anticipated GDP growth rates each week. The best scenario is to look for a country that is turning around from slow or negative growth to faster, positive growth. Don't buy foreign stocks individually. They should only be purchased through mutual funds. If you want to focus on a particular country, look at the closed-end funds that invest there exclusively.

# 2: Find the Best Research Resources

You must have access to economic and market data worldwide. You can do this with a few publications or tap into the Internet. If you'll access the data at least once a week, you should be fine. When the market is volatile, you'll naturally want to check more often.

The best investment Web sites are

Pawws Financial Network, http://www.pawws.com

Lombard Institutional Brokerage, http://www.lombard.com

Investools, http://www.investools.com

Zacks Investment Research, http://aw.zacks.com

The Motley Fool, http://fool.web.aol.com/fool_mn.htm

Fund Link, http://www.webcom.com/fundlink

Fund Atlas, http://networth.galt.com/www/home/mutual/fund_atlas/fund_atlas.html

GNN Personal Finance Center, http://gnn.com/meta/finance

National Council of Individual Investors, http://com.promenet.com/nci

SEC's Office of Investor Education and Assistance, http://www.sec.gov/consumer/abotoiea.htm

The best investment publications are

| | |
|---|---|
| *The Wall Street Journal* | *The Economist* |
| 800-568-7625 | 800-456-6086 |
| $164 per year | $125 per year |
| Daily (except Sat., Sun., and legal holidays) | Weekly |
| Market data and news | World news |

| | |
|---|---|
| *Investors Business Daily* | *Forbes* |
| 800-831-2525 | 800-888-9896 |
| $189 per year | $57 per year |
| Daily (except Sat., Sun., and legal holidays) | Bimonthly |
| Market data and news | Domestic news |
| | |
| *Barron's* | *Business Week* |
| 800-544-0422 | 800-635-1200 |
| $140 per year | $49.95 per year |
| Weekly | Weekly |
| Market data and news | Domestic news |

# Charting Isn't Just for the Pros

A picture tells a thousand words—and so does a chart. You can't pick a fund by looking only at its performance numbers. So what if it's up 20 percent for the year? Its price might be trending downward, and it could still be up 20 percent for the year. The only way to know the whole story is to see a chart of its price over the past year or so. The pros use charts before buying; why can't you? It's easy. All you need is a computer and some specialized software. Here are three charting services that can help you. Call and get a trial disk from each one. Try them each for 30 days, and see what you think. Be careful: Once you see how much fun this is, you may never leave home.

➤ **Telescan** (800-324-8246, Web site www.wallstreetcity.com) costs $349 and is easy to operate. It even comes with a video to help you get started. The company allows you to download prices daily into your software, which produces price graphs. Telescan lets you chart almost all domestic stocks and mutual funds.

➤ **Livewire**, produced by Cablesoft (805-646-0094), costs $295 for the software. The data feed is $100 every six months. They offer a 45-day trial for only $45. What makes Livewire unique is that it allows you to overlay up to three different graphs to show relative performance. Livewire lets you chart almost all domestic stocks and mutual funds.

➤ **Monocle**, produced by Manhattan Analytics, (800-251-3863) costs $149 for the software, and monthly downloads are $20. It may take some time to learn, but it is the best software I can find to chart mutual funds. The primary advantage of this software is its ability to calculate and chart the *relative strength* of one fund versus any other fund or index. The only disadvantage is that they have data on only 1,500 funds. However, the program is so good it makes up for this disadvantage in many different ways.

There are charts available in publications such as *Morningstar*. However, they are usually at least one month old, and that's just too old. The charting services listed above offer current, up-to-date data, which is what you need.

Basically, you want to look at three things in a chart: the general direction of price movement, how it relates to a market index, and volatility. First, you want to look at the general direction of the price movement. Is the stock or fund going up or down? Obviously, you want a security that is going up. Maybe it has trended downward for quite some time but is now turning back up. This might indicate a turn-around opportunity. Second, you want to compare the stock or fund's price movement to a market index such as the S&P 500. Is the fund more volatile? Does it move with the market? Or does it move somewhat independently? If you think the market is too high, you might want to find investments that move independently of the market. Third, how volatile is the security? Does the price move inconsistently up and down or steadily across the page? If you are a conservative investor, you want to avoid the volatility and focus on stocks or funds that move steadily upwards. If you want to learn more about charting, read William O'Neil's book, *How to Make Money in Stocks* (McGraw-Hill).

**Words of the Wealthy**

**Relative strength** is a graphic illustration of the percentage (or fractional) difference between the price of a security and an index (or any other security). If the security and index rise and fall equally at the same time, the graph is a straight line.

# 3: Invest Time in Your Investments

It takes time to make money in the market. The time you choose to spend will depend upon your passion for and interest in investing. Therefore, if you find yourself not taking the time, get some help. You don't have to watch the market every day, but you do have to watch it at least every week. As your portfolio grows, you'll need more time for research and decision making. The majority of your time should be spent reading publications and thinking. You need to follow inflation, interest rates, the stock markets, and other trends, which I explain in more detail in the next chapter. The publications I mentioned earlier will help you do this. The charting software I mentioned will help you keep an eye on your funds as well as others you may be interested in.

# 4: The Disciplined Investor

You must have a certain amount of discipline to be a successful portfolio manager. You need the discipline to research, know when to sell, know when to buy, and know when to hold.

## *Research Is a Requirement*

The changes in the market aren't always big enough to catch your attention. You have to see them take place gradually. If you don't watch the world markets and trends consistently (at least on a weekly basis), you might not see the gradual changes. If you are working on achieving Wealth Stage 1 or 2, then don't worry too much about the economy; focus on your savings target. However, once you reach Wealth Stage 2 and you decide to manage your own money, you must pay attention to the world economy and stock markets. If you enjoy doing this and make this a hobby, it's easier than you think. All you have to do is read a few publications each month. *The Economist* will help you keep up with worldwide stock markets and trends. You don't have to read the entire magazine; read only what interests you. *The Wall Street Journal* and *Forbes* will help you keep up with the U.S. markets.

## When Should You Sell?

Knowing when to sell is the most difficult thing to do. It's easy to know when to buy, but it's really difficult to know when to sell. Here's an easy discipline to try. As I mentioned in Chapter 11, take a look at your portfolio at least once a week and ask yourself: If your entire portfolio was in cash today, would you buy what you own today? If your answer is no, make the changes necessary. Maybe you need money for another project or maybe you have a better investment idea; whatever the case, make the necessary changes. If your answer to the big question is yes, don't make any moves. This is what I call zero based thinking. I came up with this idea at lunch one day with Brian Tracy, who produced the tape series *The Psychology of Achievement*. It has helped me develop my own sell discipline.

Another helpful sell discipline I use is the last half of Sir John Templeton's second law of investing. He said, "Sell at the point of most optimism." Most people call this contrary thinking. Whatever you want to call it, just do it. The investment game is won by those willing to sell when everyone else is buying like crazy.

## How Do You Know When to Buy?

The best time to buy is when everyone else is selling. The first half of Sir John Templeton's second law of investing reads, "Buy at the point of most pessimism." If you have the discipline to follow this advice, you can make a lot of money in the stock market. Unfortunately, only a few investors have the guts or discipline to do it. Those who think and invest this way are called *contrarians*. What excites them the most is bad news because they know investors will overreact, and as a result, certain stock prices will fall lower than they should. That's when they buy.

**Words of the Wealthy**

**Contrarian** investors are those who invest contrary to everyone else. They buy when the market is correcting and sell when the market reaches new highs.

## Stay Committed to Your Investment Decisions

Make your decision and stick with it until the reasons you bought the investment change. You don't have to trade a lot to achieve an above-average return. This is especially true with mutual funds.

# 5: Keep an Open Mind

Albert Einstein said, "Imagination is more important than knowledge." Why do so many academically advanced investors do so poorly in the market? Do they know too much? Maybe they develop their brains but not their guts. Why do so many high school students beat investment pros in stock market contests? Your ability to process knowledge and data with an open mind is the first key to successful investment decisions. An investor can know too much. If your knowledge limits your ability to objectively see all the possibilities, you know too much.

## *Think Outside of the Box*

George Bernard Shaw once said, "All progress depends on the unreasonable man." He deduced that the reasonable person adapts himself to the world. The unreasonable person tries to adapt the world to himself and therefore improves the world for everyone. It is my belief that to be a successful investor, you must also be a little unreasonable.

First, the changes that are taking place in the world today are quite unlike the changes we've experienced in the past. They are unreasonable. They include social, economic, and political trends that most people don't even understand until they hit the local community. These changes often involve highly advanced technology that didn't even exist last year.

Second, these unreasonable changes will transform the way we work, live, and think. Never before has it been so important to pay attention to what the future can bring. Third, if these changes are unreasonable, then our thinking must be unreasonable to deal with them. We're going to have to turn our normal patterns of thinking upside down, even if such thinking seems outrageous.

### That Reminds Me...

There are two kinds of companies: the living and the dead. Companies that don't have a constant eye on the future will surely die. The living companies, those who will survive over the long run, focus on constant innovation and improvement. This is the kind of company in which you want to invest.

Companies today can design a product and put it on the shelf faster than ever, and they're getting even faster every day. This means that the software or appliance you are using today will most likely be obsolete in 12 months. Someone somewhere will come up with a better idea. That means that the company or even industry that produced the "old" product is at risk. If they don't stay in touch with their customers and the changes in the product, they are dead. I'm saying that, more than ever, complete industries are now subject to forced "re-engineering" at a moment's notice. To some, re-engineering might be creating a new, advanced product line to compete with the new model that was just introduced. Re-engineering might also mean layoffs and plant closings because no one saw the trend or paid any attention to the customer. This scenario applies to all products, and no one is safe from it. The possibilities are endless. The best defense for most companies is to distinguish themselves with outrageous customer service and extensive in-house research work by open-minded people.

### That Reminds Me...

After years of research and analysis, scientists discovered that if you put a live frog in a pan of cold water and slowly apply heat, the frog will not budge. Even after the water gets to a boiling point, the frog will not budge! It sits there and dies. Why doesn't the frog react? "Because each change in temperature is so slight that the frog continues to adjust to the water. It fails to realize that the net result of these changes should be an abrupt, energetic change in its behavior—a new approach to new conditions." How many reasonable investors have been boiled alive as small changes in the market occurred over time while no action was taken?

To achieve investment excellence, unreasonable thinking must be used. Successful investors today can no longer ignore the small market changes. They must be able to interpret the seemingly insignificant facts in order to beat the street.

George Bernard Shaw also said, "The only person who behaves sensibly is my tailor. He takes new measurements every time he sees me. All the rest go on with their old measurements." Take new measurements often, and don't be afraid to be a little unreasonable.

## Think Creatively

Sometimes thinking differently means applying completely different logic. I like to use the phrase creative thinking. For example, imagine you want to travel exactly two miles while averaging 60 miles per hour. (You might want to write this down.) If you average 30 mph during the first mile, how fast do you have to travel during the second mile in order to average 60 mph? (Let's disregard acceleration and deceleration to make it easier.)

I've asked this question in my workshops for over four years. Almost everyone answers "90 mph." They add 30 and 90 to get 120, which when divided by two, equals 60 mph. However, this answer is incorrect. In this case, it is impossible to average 60 mph no matter how fast you travel. During the first mile, if averaged at 30 miles per hour, two minutes are used, which is the exact required time needed to average 60 mph over the entire two miles. The problem here is that most people apply addition/division to a time/distance problem. Therefore, the answer can never be solved. Investors do the same thing everyday. They try to apply 3-, 5-, and 10-year past performance histories to a continuously changing investment world. To beat the stock market averages in this world, you often have to ignore past performance and use creative thinking instead.

To be a successful investor, you have to look at current data (such as 3-, 6-, and 9-month economic data) and then project into the future any possible trends this data might show. Investment selection techniques must be based upon these trend projections.

**Treasure Tip**

To be good at analyzing data and predicting trends, you must have a great imagination and be willing to make decisions that often fly directly in the face of conventional wisdom.

# 6: Is Investing Your Passion and Desire?

Show me an investor with passion, and I'll show you someone who's probably beating the market.

Those who do well in the market have a passion for it. They love the research and study that investing requires. They are natural sponges of information. They soak it all in and make decisions from the gut. They're confident and they take responsibility for their mistakes. They know that mistakes are necessary for learning and improving their work. Here is a list of the most common desires I've found among wealthy people:

➤ A desire to learn

➤ A desire to be a proactive investor

➤ A desire to learn from mistakes

➤ A desire to beat the market

➤ A desire to manage risk

You can't force yourself to have these desires. Your interests may lie in a completely different field. If this is the case, don't worry about it. Just find someone who does have these desires and hire her to help you manage your portfolio.

### The Least You Need to Know

➤ To be a successful portfolio manager, you must understand the basics of economic theory.

➤ Focus on the best business publications, and take advantage of the information available to you on the Internet.

➤ Use charting services to observe and compare fund performances with one another.

➤ Develop the discipline it takes to sell at the point of most optimism and buy at the point of most pessimism.

➤ Knowledge is important, but your creativity, passion, and desire make you more money.

# Chapter 13

# Waschka's 10 Easy Portfolio Strategies That Work

## In This Chapter

➤ How bond prices and interest rates work together

➤ How panic in the market can make you money

➤ How the economic cycle can make you money

➤ The baby boom generation and stock market boom

➤ How to take advantage of inefficiency

A strategy is a plan of action toward achieving a specific goal. The goal in this chapter is to build wealth in the securities markets. The strategy involves many different tactics that are simply procedures or maneuvers that will give you an advantage over most other investors. If you ever want to get to Wealth Stage 3 using your investment portfolio, you need to be better than the average investor. The 10 tactics in this chapter are primarily aspects of a mindset you assume. They are like binoculars through which you can view the investment world.

In our society, knowledge is power. For all practical purposes, it has become the most powerful tool in the world. Few people realize this, however, and much fewer understand it. It has been proven throughout history that whoever knows how to harness and use the most powerful tools has the potential to be wealthy beyond their dreams. Therefore, you must first focus on harnessing knowledge and information (which I covered in Chapter 11, "Building the Perfect Portfolio"). Then, you have to know how to use it. Specifically, you have to know how to think, and that's what this chapter is all about.

I have designed 10 portfolio management tactics that are essentially 10 different ways of looking at information. These are simply ways of thinking or methods of looking at the world. They are also funnels of thought through which information is poured and processed into a more useful form. Their purpose is to help you discover and better understand the magnitude of specific trends in the world. These tactics will also help you see each individual trend from different perspectives. The more you understand these trends, the better chance you have of profiting from them to contribute to your ongoing efforts to build wealth.

With the growth of the Internet and other forms of media such as cable television, never before in the history of time has information been more easily accessible. That's exciting. However, accessing the information isn't enough. You have to know how to process it. Your mind can be your greatest asset. It can also be your greatest liability. Here are 10 tactics to improve your investment mind.

# Watch the Interest Rate Seesaw

You can become a basic bond expert if you understand the following easy concept. You might even want to read this section twice. It is easier to understand than you think.

Bonds produce a fixed rate of cash flow (income) that investors are willing to buy for a certain amount of money. For example, if you buy a newly issued 30-year Treasury bond at $1,000 and it yields 7 percent, you get a $70 yearly fixed cash flow until the bond matures. If inflation drops dramatically, interest rates also fall. Therefore, let's say the government a year later is issuing the same 30-year Treasury bond, but now it's paying a yield of only 5 percent, which is a $50 yearly fixed cash flow. If the same bond is only paying $50 now, what would *your* 7 percent bond be worth? It's paying two percentage points higher (or $20 more per year), so it's got to be worth more, right? Yes, sir; your bond's worth more money. If you sell it, you will receive more than the principal you invested. How much more? By using certain yield-to-maturity formulas or a simple bond yield book, you can calculate how much more. You can find bond yield books at your local bookstore or library. Bonds do fluctuate in price over time; however, at maturity, that price fluctuation stops and the bond matures at its face value.

The most important thing to understand is how bond prices are affected by changes in interest rates. Let me explain using a seesaw. If you put interest rates on one side of the seesaw and bond prices on the other, you can get a better understanding of how bonds can fluctuate in price. When interest rates go up, prices of bonds currently trading in the market go down, and vice versa.

Notice how the seesaw is lopsided. This shows the effect interest rates have on bonds with different maturities. A 5-year bond (a bond that will mature in 5 years) will fluctuate much less in price than a 30-year bond. The longer the maturity, the bigger the potential swing in price.

*Interest Rate Seesaw*

Interest rates %

Years to Maturity

5  10  15  20  25  30

Bond Price

When interest rates go down,
bond prices go up, and vice versa.

Now that you understand this tactic, what do you think interest rates will do in the next 12 to 18 months? If you think they will fall, you might want to invest in the longest-term Treasury bond or bond fund you can find. However, if you think rates will rise, you might want to avoid longer-term bonds altogether and invest in short-term bonds (or even a money market fund, which is considered to be the shortest short-term bond fund).

If you are investing for the long-term, don't worry about the maturity of the bond. Regardless of whether you select a 30-year bond or a 1-year bond, these are liquid securities or tools that can be used to profit from short-term moves in interest rates. For the purposes of this tactic, they are never bought with the intention of holding until maturity. Interest rates normally trend up (or down) over a period of at least a year. Therefore, I'm not suggesting that you make trades more often than once a year.

### That Reminds Me...

One of the most important and influential forces in the stock and bond markets is the rate of interest paid on the 30-year Treasury bonds, which are bonds issued by the U.S. Government that mature in 30 years. When you hear someone mention the bond market, she is specifically referring to the price movements of this particular bond. All other bonds seem to fluctuate in price according to the movements of the 30-year Treasury bond. Interest rates such as mortgage, CD, and money market rates also are influenced by the 30-year Treasury bond.

### Words of the Wealthy

**Zero-coupon Treasury bonds** are bonds that are sold at a discount to their maturity; that is, you buy the bond at a particular price and then receive its full value when the bond matures.

One of the best places to be when interest rates fall is in *zero-coupon Treasury bonds*, which are also known as strips or zeros. The zeros with longer-term maturities are the most volatile because they offer no interest and only a principal payment at maturity. It is cheaper to buy these bonds individually, but you can also purchase them through a mutual fund. The Benham Group offers a Target 2020 Fund, which is a portfolio of zero-coupon bonds that mature in the year 2020. Remember that these bonds are also the worst place to be if interest rates go up.

# Investing in the Midst of Panic and Euphoria

What do you think moves the market: logic or emotion? Well, the answer is without a doubt emotion. You've heard the term "market psychology"? The reason is that the market moves when investors tend to panic one moment and then experience euphoria the next. If the market were a person, he would definitely need a psychologist.

The stock market has taught us over the years that its movements in the short term can rarely be explained or justified. The knee-jerk movements in the market (especially in 1987) have little to do with logical fundamental calculations. The most important discovery I have made during my 14 years of investing has been that emotion has more to do with market movements than rational thinking.

I often refer to the market as Mr. Market. When you go to Mr. Market's house, you never know what to expect. He's emotional, temperamental, and subject to wild mood swings. The headlines one week may be negative on interest rates. The next week, the negative report might cover the trade deficit. Most major news coverage with a negative outlook causes Mr. Market to think a crash is coming. If you rely on Mr. Market for advice, as most people do, you'll follow in his footsteps and you'll be persuaded to sell.

### Treasure Tip

Remember, Mr. Market has loads of money. If you can buy what he might want later, you will be rewarded. The reverse is also true. Once everyone in his gang is buying, you need to be selling. This will help ensure that you are selling at the higher price.

Then, out of the blue, good news will appear. It may be an earnings announcement or lower interest rates. It doesn't really matter; it's good news and that's what counts. Mr. Market jumps for joy and buys stocks like crazy. Most investors, just like clockwork, jump right in with him. Hey, the market's going up; can you blame them?

There's just one small problem with this story. Mr. Market and his followers never make much money. At best, if they are lucky, they might equal the averages. The biggest reason is that most stocks are bought at their high. Plus, the excessive transactions necessary for this strategy cost a lot of money.

The irony is that the true way to make money and build wealth is to do the opposite of what Mr. Market does. Whatever he hates or whatever he is selling is more than likely what you need to be buying. This will help ensure that you are buying at the lower price.

Also known as the contrarian theory, I call this tactic of doing the opposite of Mr. Market the panic-cycle tactic. It's the most powerful tactic in this chapter because it offers the most potential for profit. It also requires the largest amount of guts and faith because it flies directly in the face of conventional wisdom.

First, being able to identify the point of most pessimism (panic) or optimism (euphoria) is almost impossible. However, you don't have to be exact; you only have to be close.

Second, when you really get close to the point of most pessimism, buying what everyone tells you not to isn't exactly easy. The last thing your friends or advisors are going to do at that time is suggest that you buy. The opposite is also true. When you get close to the point of most optimism, when everyone is buying like crazy and telling you to do the same, the last thing you're going to want to do is sell. (However, you might want to sell and take a profit, especially if you bought at a much lower price.)

The pendulum illustration in this section clarifies how the panic cycle works. You can apply this to individual stocks, bonds, industry sectors, countries, geographic regions, and styles of investing. You can even apply it to real estate. The market pendulum swings between panic and euphoria. The middle equilibrium position of the pendulum represents fair value. Because investors tend to overreact, securities tend to be over-priced or underpriced. Securities in the market swing back and forth from an underval-ued position to an overvalued position as investors overreact both ways.

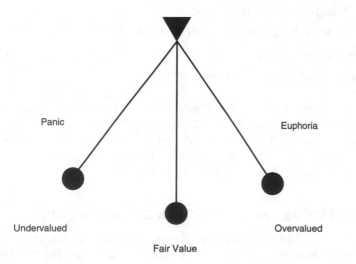

*Panic Cycle Pendulum*

Panic

Euphoria

Undervalued

Overvalued

Fair Value

When investors panicked in 1990 over banks possibly having the same trouble as the savings and loan industry, bank stocks fell dramatically in price. I purchased a closed-end bank fund in 1991. In less than two years, I made a 100-percent profit for many of my clients.

**179**

Ask yourself this: What is everyone panicking over today? What does everyone hate to invest in now? In a bull market, it might be hard to find stocks or funds that everyone hates. Likewise, in a bear market, it's easy to find things people hate. Therefore, this strategy is easy in bear markets and difficult in bull markets.

# Look for Industry and Geographical Growth

This investment tactic involves the search for industries or countries that indicate new growth prospects and the search for stocks or mutual funds that can profit accordingly. What you want to find is an industry or country that is in the early stages of a new wave of growth. Here is a list of the best industry growth opportunities:

➤ New industries in their early growth stages

➤ Mature industries that develop new products

➤ Mature industries going through a financial reorganization—we've seen this a lot!

➤ Mature industries going through a mission reorganization

➤ Mature industries going through a management reorganization

An example of the first is certainly the Internet, which has the possibility to make more people wealthy than any other industry in the history of the world.

Here is a list of the best country or regional growth opportunities:

➤ Emerging market countries in their early growth stages

➤ Emerging market countries adopting capitalism

➤ Developed countries experiencing economic cycle changes

➤ Countries establishing new governments

➤ Countries with falling inflation and economic growth

A great example of the first opportunity is Russia and China. They will be volatile in the short term, but they have enormous potential. Each one of these growth opportunities is also an example of a trend, and you can take advantage of almost every single one of them by using mutual funds. Most of these growth trends are long term, which means you often have plenty of time to take advantage of them.

# Invest in Anticipation of Economic Changes

This investment tactic is based on the cycle of economic expansion and contraction. It requires you to estimate the economy's current condition and the most likely future condition. You can do this by estimating the growth of gross domestic product, which is announced monthly in most financial newspapers. The actual growth rate tells you what happened. You have to guess what you think will happen. This is not an exact science, but you can make estimates using certain economic data. An economic expansion consists of increased employment, consumer spending, increased corporate borrowing, and corporate earnings growth. An economic contraction (recession) is the opposite of this scenario. The easiest way to predict economic expansions and contractions is to watch the monthly index of leading indicators. This index encompasses 12 leading economic indicators that move in advance of the business or economic cycle. If the index is rising, you can more than likely expect a growing economy. The opposite is also true.

Once you've made estimates, you make asset allocation decisions (deciding what percentages of your portfolio to put in which types of investments) based upon where you think we are in the economic cycle. The economic cycle is best illustrated by plotting the growth rate of the *gross domestic product (GDP)*. In the illustration in this section, you can see what this cycle looks like in a somewhat-perfect world.

As you can see, at certain points in the cycle, bonds perform well, and at others, stocks do well. If you know the current position of the economy on this curve and understand how different securities react to certain points in the cycle, you know how to allocate your portfolio.

**Words of the Wealthy**

The **gross domestic product (GDP)** is the total value of goods and services produced by a country during a year. The GDP's rate of growth is more popular in the news than the actual GDP number. When plotted on a graph, this growth rate illustrates the country's economic cycle.

**The Economic or GDP Cycle**

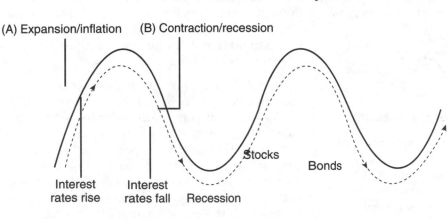

For example, when the economy expands (area A), interest rates usually go up and bond prices fall. Therefore, you might not want to own long-term bonds. At a certain point in the expansion as interest rates on bonds become more attractive, stock investors tend to sell stocks and buy bonds. This might cause the stock market to do poorly. Therefore, at some point, you might want to build a position in money market funds.

181

When the economy contracts (area B), interest rates fall and bond prices rise, which is a great time to own long-term bonds. At some point during the contraction, stock investors will anticipate a turn-around in the economy and begin to buy stocks—even as the economy continues to do poorly.

When is a good time to own stocks? When a contracting economy is predicted to turn expansionary, stocks tend to do well. They continue to do well until interest rates are predicted to go up. Notice that in both cases, I said "predicted." Investors usually don't wait to see the actual economic change. They make moves in anticipation of these economic changes. Therefore, stocks prices often move well in advance of economic data.

# Monitor Market Cycles

At any given point in time, the overall stock market can be considered too high, too low, or just right. There are a lot of ways to measure this specifically. It's not enough to just say the market is up 25 percent in 10 months. Relative to 10 months ago, yes, the market could be too high. However, relative to corporate earnings, the market prices could be low.

How do you measure the market's price relative to corporate earnings? You have to look at the average *P/E ratio* of the S&P 500 index each week in publications such as *Barron's*. This is the average P/E of the market, and it's listed under "P/Es & Yields" in the "Market Week" section. When the average P/E of the market exceeds 20, the market is believed to be overpriced. Investors tend to get a little nervous. At this level, they want to sit on the sidelines and let earnings catch up with stock prices. If earnings are predicted not to grow fast enough to catch up, investors will sell and cause a correction. Therefore, the average P/E ratio of the market is important to watch when you're investing in stocks and stock mutual funds.

If you consider the market to be overpriced, you might want to be conservative and focus on value-oriented stocks—stocks that have already corrected or fallen in value. This strategy is very conservative; when stock prices fall, value-oriented stocks seem to fall less than the average. You might even begin building a position in a money market account. If you are right and the market makes a correction, you will have some of your assets protected in the money market account, and you'll have money to invest at lower prices. If you are wrong and the market doesn't correct, you'll still be participating. If you consider the market to be underpriced or fairly valued, you want to be fully invested.

There are other ways to measure the market, such as the average market to book and the average dividend yield

**Words of the Wealthy**

The **P/E ratio** is the price of a stock divided by the yearly earnings per share. It is the price of a stock relative to its earnings, which is important to know when you compare one stock to another. It is also important in determining whether a stock is underpriced or overpriced relative to other stocks.

of the market indexes. I don't use them much, but they are also listed in *Barron's* under "P/Es & Yields" within the "Market Week" section.

# Study Demographics

Demographics affect the market more than most people realize. One of the most significant demographic concepts this century is the effect of the baby boom generation on our economy. It is important to understand the ripple effect this wave of births caused. The baby boom generation is 80 million strong.

The baby boom wasn't just one wave; it was three—two small waves and one big one. The first peak is 1942, the second is 1946, and the big third wave, 1955. If you knew when these people statistically spent the most money, you would be able to predict a super-strong economy once the average baby boomer reached that age.

According to the U.S. Bureau of Labor Statistics *Consumer Expenditures Survey*, conducted in 1987, the average American family spends the most money per year between the ages of 44 and 46. Harry Dent, author of *The Roaring 2000s* (Simon & Schuster, 1998) took the graph of baby boomer birth year peaks and moved it out 46 years to see when each particular segment of the boomer population would reach 46. If you add 46 to each of the peaks, you know when these people would theoretically spend the most money—1989, 1993, and 2007. This would also have an effect on the stock market. Dent says, "The correlation between spending and the stock market is remarkable, and it's no accident." He says that consumer spending trends and the stock market have moved together historically time after time. He predicts that as the huge third wave of babyboomers approach the average age of 46 (2007), we will experience the greatest bull market in history.

What do these people buy? Vacation homes, durable goods, entertainment items, and cruises. These people also now have money to invest for retirement. Where do they invest? The stock market! Why not get there before they do?

What happens later when this segment slows its spending? The economy will slow also. This should take place approximately in the year 2010. Where do you want to be invested? Probably in long-term Treasury bonds. If interest rates fall as I predict they will, bond prices will rise.

# Take Advantage of Information Gaps

The information gap is the gap in time between when a newsworthy event occurs and when the general public recognizes the profit potential of the event. The wider the gap, the bigger the profit potential. The information gaps were quite a bit wider before the Internet came into play. However, you can still find them if you look. The key is researching well and making correct assumptions. Whether you invest in the market or own a business, you have to make educated assumptions based on a limited amount of information.

Successful investors know the cycle of research:

1. Study information that you gather.
2. Make assumptions about the future.
3. Test your assumptions.
4. Measure results.
5. Gather more information.
6. Make adjustments.
7. Test again.
8. Measure results.
9. Gather more information.
10. Test again.

The quality of information you gather can significantly affect your outcome. Therefore, your goal must be to continually put yourself in front of the best quality information available.

Knowledge of this gap alone gives you several advantages. First, we know that mainstream media enjoys covering blood, guts, and conflict. Stories such as the North American Free Trade Agreement (NAFTA), the Turkish Stock market up over 200 percent in 1993, and post-healthcare reform in 1995 all had a lower priority.

Second, we know that the general public tends to focus its attention on poor quality media—usually sensational journalism. People seem more interested in a two-headed Martian baby than in the economic events taking place in Singapore. Only a fraction of the general public read high-quality publications such as *The Economist, Barron's,* or *Forbes.* They are the only ones who get to take advantage of this knowledge. The reality in my opinion is that even fewer people take the time or have the imagination to project this knowledge into the future.

The goal therefore is to narrow your gap by being an avid reader of high-quality information. Narrowing your information gap is all about getting the information first before the general public sees it. To profit from narrowing the gap, you must act. Remember that not acting can often be a good idea too.

# Identify Technology Gaps

The technology gap is the gap between the best technology available today and the technology currently in use today. The bigger the gap, the bigger the profit potential. The technology gap can be applied to countries, industries, and individual companies. Technology in its simplest definition is the key to efficiency and ultimately profits. The profitability of most companies today has a lot to do with the level of technological sophistication in place. If a company, industry, or country installs or incorporates a higher level of technology, its efficiency should improve and increased profitability should follow. Therefore, if you identify companies, industries, or countries who are (for whatever reason) using out-of-date technology, you might find an opportunity.

The key is to invest in entities that can benefit the most from improved technology. Small improvements in technology can exponentially increase production and efficiency. This is the name of the game today. Where are the biggest gaps right now? Look in your own home or business; they surround you, but you may not have noticed them before. They could be in the following areas:

➤ **Technology industry.** Consumers who are not connected to the Internet. The technology is there, but the majority of consumers are still not connected.

➤ **Healthcare.** New drug therapies. We have the technology to cure so many diseases, yet certain areas of the world such as emerging market countries are just now getting the benefits of these drugs.

➤ **Entertainment.** Surround sound and virtual reality. We now have the technology to produce theater-quality sound in every living room, and the price of the equipment is dropping dramatically. Yet the percentage of homes with these systems is quite low.

➤ **Emerging market countries.** Building infrastructure and basic industries. We have the technology to build extensive infrastructures and basic industries for cities and countries, yet many of the emerging market countries have yet to build them.

# Profit from Market Inefficiencies

Whether you agree or not, all investment markets, to some degree, are inefficient. The inefficient market gap measures this level of inefficiency. This gap is not an exact measurement; it's more of a relative measurement. Specifically, the inefficient market gap is the difference between a market's current level of efficiency and its ideal level of efficiency. This is of course impossible to measure exactly. I'm referring to a more subjective measurement—certainly quantifiable, I'm sure. For our purposes here, I want to stay relatively simple.

The efficiency I'm referring to is the ease by which information that helps people make investment decisions flows to the public. If there was an even distribution of all relative information about a particular market to the entire investing public, you would have a perfectly efficient market.

An efficient market assumes first that there is an even distribution of all relative information to the public. Second, it assumes that the public can make investment decisions based on this information quickly and efficiently. Third, it assumes that these decisions can be made with no restrictions.

As you can probably imagine, a perfectly efficient market is not only hard to profit from, but also quite boring. If it's perfectly efficient, there's no way you can strategically take advantage of the market. Therefore, your chance of return is the same as anyone else's. You want to look for pockets of inefficiency—where you can strategically take advantage of a market.

The two basic types of inefficiencies are natural and forced. Natural inefficiency occurs in the market when information is distributed chaotically. Improper information distribution can include

➤ Distorted or exaggerated information

➤ Lack of information

➤ Incorrect information

➤ Misunderstood information

The most commonly occurring natural inefficiency I see in the market is the obscure and forgotten stocks. These stocks aren't often followed by the multi-national brokerage firms and are followed even less by the media (at least positively). There are many of these stocks out there, but only a few are worth investing in.

The best way to take advantage of these stocks is to hire the best value-oriented stock pickers in the world. With all the mutual funds available, this is relatively easy to do. (See the "Buy and Hold Strategy" section of Chapter 11, "Building the Perfect Portfolio," for these managers.)

### Words of the Wealthy

A **junk bond**, also known as a high-yield bond, represents an IOU issued by a company whose ability to repay its interest and principal in a timely manner depends upon the economy and its ability to sell its products or services. Standard & Poor's as well as Moody's investment services offer corporate bond ratings. A junk bond is any bond with a rating below BBB or Baa.

The second type of inefficiency is forced inefficiency. There are few examples of this, but I have a feeling that with more government regulations, many forced inefficiencies will occur this decade.

The best example I can give you is the *junk bond* market in the early 1990s. Back in the days of Michael Milken and Drexal Burnam Lambert (the late '80s), junk bonds were considered evil. Once loved by many insurance companies, these bonds became the enemy of all insurance companies and many institutional investors.

Have you seen the commercial showing a wrecking ball swinging toward a building while a voice says, "Back in the '80s, most insurance companies invested in junk bonds?" The ball hits a building and takes an enormous hunk of concrete and steel with it. In the next scene, the same ball is falling toward a similar building while the voice says, "However, we only invested in investment-grade bonds." Then, the ball hits the building and explodes while the building stays perfectly intact.

This is an illustration of forced inefficiency. Because of events in the past and the resulting new written policies, most (if not all) insurance companies cannot purchase non-investment-grade corporate bonds, otherwise known as junk bonds. But you can! The minute your junk bond becomes investment grade, insurance companies will trip over themselves to buy it. Therefore, once the junk bond gets a more attractive credit rating, the market for the bond is more efficient. Until that point, however, the inefficiency is there.

### That Reminds Me...

You don't have to buy individual junk bonds any more. All you have to do is find a good junk bond fund. My favorite is a little known no-load junk bond fund called Northeast Investors Trust. It is still managed by Ernie Monrad and his son Bruce. This fund was not only the top-performing junk bond fund, but it was also the top-performing overall bond fund in 1994. It was one of the few bond funds with a positive return that year. If you ever see an opportunity in the junk bond market, be sure to include Northeast Investors Trust in your research.

# Watch the Leaders and Laggards

I personally believe that a list of the top-performing mutual funds in the past 10 years is useless information. The world economy is completely different from what it was 10 years ago. However, I do keep an eye on the top 10 list for the week. By watching the top-performing funds and stocks list each week, I get an idea of both the leading and laggard industries or sectors in the market. Why is this important?

If a mutual fund or stock from a particular sector is new to the leader's list, it may indicate an opportunity. This is especially true if this same sector has been on the laggard list in the recent past. Likewise, if an industry that was previously growing is new to the laggard list consistently for a few weeks, it might indicate a correction in that industry.

I also use these lists to compare my sector fund's performance to other similar sector funds. If I see a fund in a similar sector hit the laggard list, I immediately begin to watch other similar funds. As other funds in the same sector begin to correct, I tend to sell in anticipation of a correction in that industry. Because the funds with less quality management tend to fall first, you might have a chance to sell before the correction.

Where can you find a list of the top-performing funds last week? You can't find it in your grocery store; I can promise you that. But you can find it on the Internet. In Chapter 12, in the section "Find th Best Research Resources," you'll find a site called Fund Atlas. This site allows you to keep up with the top 25 funds for the past week, month, three months, and so on. This site can be a powerful tool for your wealth-building arsenal.

---

### The Least You Need to Know

➤ Learn the interest rate seesaw and keep your eyes on the economic cycles, interest rates, and the general public's feeling toward inflation.

➤ Buy when everyone panics and sell when everyone and his dog is experiencing euphoria.

➤ When you think the market is overpriced, put a little money in a money market fund and watch for opportunities.

➤ Unless something totally unexpected takes place, the baby boom generation should support the stock market at least until the year 2004.

---

# What Your Broker May Not Tell You

You want to be a successful manager of your own portfolio, right? Well, this chapter will help you do just that. It takes years to learn how to be a successful investor unless you learn from other's mistakes. Some people rely strictly on their own experience, and that can be expensive. Others read books and learn from others, and that's the key to success. I've found that the most successful investors do a little of both, but by studying the experiences of others, you can save a lot of valuable time.

Learning from others who have gone before you can help speed up the learning process and prevent years of mistakes. I know this from experience. I've always said that if you want to be good at anything, find the people who are the best at it and imitate them. I might not be the best investor, but I sure have learned a lot from some of the best investors in the world. This chapter is a list of investment laws I've learned from others, as well as on my own. I've also summarized a few laws I've mentioned in earlier chapters.

# Investing According to Larry's Laws

These strategies and philosophies have taken me more than 10 years to find, refine, and develop. I hope they are as profitable for you as they have been for me and my clients.

## Don't Believe the Sales Hype

About 90 percent of the investment advice you will hear or read in your lifetime is marketing related. As in most businesses today, most people in the investment industry want to sell you something. It may be a subscription, a security, or an insurance policy. Whatever it is, just be careful to evaluate the facts and disregard the marketing fluff before buying.

## Stand on the Shoulders of Giants

**Treasure Tip**

One of the ironies of the investment world is that if you really are a long-term investor who regularly puts money in the market, you should hope the market stays down until the year you need all of your money. The whole idea is to buy low and sell high, right?

I've said this before; it's so important. Take advantage of other people's talents when you can. At the very least, learn from them. Sir Isaac Newton once said, "If I have seen further, it is because I stood on the shoulders of giants." He was giving credit to all the mentors and philosophers who came before him. I do the same thing as an advisor and investor. I first select specific themes that I think will be profitable during the next five years. Then, I hire Orville Redenbackers (fund managers) to help. Remember Orville Redenbacker's wisdom, "Do one thing and do it better than anyone else." The fund manager who is targeting Hong Kong, Malaysia, and Singapore will know more than you and I do about that region. He travels there, knows the language, and will find opportunities years before we will in the U.S.

## What You Don't Know Really Can Hurt You

If you don't know that the investment you're making will cost you 8.5 percent and there's no secondary market for it, it's going to hurt. If you don't do your homework, you might not realize it until it's too late.

## If It Sounds Too Good to Be True, It Probably Is

The too-good-to-be-true rule says it all. How many times have you been suckered into something that turned out really bad? I know I've fallen victim more than a few times. If you want to substantially reduce the chance of getting your financial hide skinned, learn to separate the wheat from the chaff before you invest. Look for all the possible signs of deception: hidden fees, misleading information, absence of disclosure documents, and conflicts of interest.

## Be a Smart Risk Taker

Risk managed properly can be your key to wealth. Return is what you get for your willingness to assume risk. Learn how to manage risk through diversification and market knowledge. Don't hide your head in the sand. Learn all you can about the risks of an investment and understand that risk management is easy. It just means that you need to know the worse thing that can happen with each investment, and don't put all your eggs in one basket.

## What Goes Up...

Most investors live in fear of a correction. Some worry about it more than others. The successful investors I know focus on the long term and seem to welcome an occasional correction. They see corrections as buying opportunities. Don't be suckered into thinking that the market will rise 20 percent every year. That is a fairy tale. The market is just like anything else in life. It works in cycles.

## Be Proactive

Don't just throw your money in a fund. Do some of your own research, and make investing your hobby. If not, consider getting some help from a fee-based advisor. Read all you can so you understand the basics.

## Beware of Rumors

Don't use rumors to invest. Most of them are wrong. If they are even remotely close to factual, it's probably too late to do anything. Do your own research first before you invest any money.

## Beware of Conflicts of Interest

Just as a note: ADV doesn't stand for anything! Believe it or not. It's just the first three letters in Advisor, I guess. Even the SEC couldn't tell me years ago. Find out how your source of advice or information gets paid. Unless you are an experienced do-it-yourself investor, don't pay for investment advice with commission. Pay for it with a fee so that you don't have any possible conflicts of interest.

## Give First Priority to Value

A great deal of this book is dedicated to reducing your investment costs. However, it would be a shame for you to know the cost of every investment yet completely overlook the value they offer. Some funds may have larger than average fees but

**Wealth Warning**

You might think you're paying a fee, but does your advisor benefit from security purchases directly or indirectly? Be sure to look at all the disclosure documents available such as the broker's fund prospectus or the advisor's "ADV," is the disclosure document the SEC requires them to have on hand for you.

may well be worth the extra expense due to the management's experience or specialty. This is the exception and not the rule, but the point is that some relatively expensive funds out there happen to be worth the cost.

## Don't Worry About Things You Can't Change

There are two sets of variables in the world of wealth and investing: those we can control and those we cannot. We cannot control the price of a stock in our portfolio, but we can control the amount of money we save, invest, or spend. Most investors focus on the stock market, which is completely out of our control, whereas only a few focus on what they can control. The few who focus primarily on controlling their savings and investment and spending dollars tend to get wealthier. The key to happiness is also the key to investing: Focus on what you can control and let go of what you can't control.

**Treasure Tip**

Yes, some loaded mutual funds are worth the load. Yes, some brokers are worth the commissions you pay. And someday, there will be a variable annuity with enough investment alternatives to make it worth investing in. Don't overlook the value of an investment just because of the cost.

## Don't Panic

The worst thing you can possibly do during a brief stock market correction is sell. A correction is simply an absence of buyers amidst a flood of investors wanting to sell. If you join them, you'll completely miss the market rebound when there's an absence of sellers and a flood of buyers. When you panic, you become irrational, and that can kill your portfolio.

# A Note to Brokers and Advisors

Here's some great advice for brokers and advisors, which I always keep in mind: Your clients and prospective clients aren't idiots. They are your parents, your relatives, and your friends, and they are the sharpest investors in the world. At first glance, they might not seem that experienced, but if you feed them a bunch of garbage, they'll know it. Treat them with the respect they deserve. Communicate with them, teach them all you can, and take good care of them. If you do, you'll be rewarded with success beyond your wildest dreams.

## Avoid Custodian Fees

A custodian fee is a yearly expense charged to your account by the brokerage firm (or custodian) simply for having the account open. Not all firms charge custodian fees, especially the discount brokerage firms, if you keep a certain minimum balance. The brokerage firms justify the fee by offering services such as cash management accounts. These accounts allow the investor to hold all securities in one account, which can include a money market account, whereby all credit balances (extra cash) are automatically swept into a money market fund (or interest-bearing account). This usually happens on a weekly, if not daily, basis. This is called the "automated feature" of the account. Cash management accounts also feature a checkbook and debit Visa card with which you can withdraw money. Remember, the Visa card in this case is not a credit card. It directly debits money from the account.

The last main feature of the account is margin capability. If your cash management account has securities but no available cash or money market balance, you can still write a check and borrow against (margin) your securities. You'll pay interest on that loan, but the rate is usually reasonable.

Before you open an IRA account with a brokerage firm, you might also want to inquire about custodian fees. Often, you'll find brokerage firms that offer to waive the fee if the account exceeds a certain balance. If you are a do-it-yourselfer, be sure to shop and compare the custodial fees for these kinds of accounts at varying discount brokerage firms. The discount companies offer all the bells and whistles of the full-service brokerage firm accounts without the heavy custodian fees.

**Wealth Warning**

If you do business at a full-service brokerage firm and decide to take your IRA to another firm, be aware of any exit or transfer fees. These fees can add up to as much as $200 or 2 percent of your account, whichever is less. This might seem expensive, but don't let this fee keep you from seeking a better opportunity at another firm.

## Buy Discounted Closed-End Funds

Closed-end funds are mutual funds that offer a set amount of shares when they are initially offered, after which they are openly traded like stocks on the stock exchanges. What makes them so unique is the difference between their market price and actual net asset value price (NAV—what they are actually worth per share). If the market price is higher than the actual NAV, the fund is selling at a premium. If the market price is lower than the actual NAV, the fund is selling at a discount. If you want more information about these funds, refer to Chapter 8, "Investments That Do Work," in the section "Closed-End Funds."

Any premium you pay on a closed-end mutual fund is like adding another potential expense item to your portfolio. Therefore, only buy these funds when they offer a discount to their net asset values. Because these mutual funds are traded like stocks on the exchanges, they don't necessarily trade at their actual net asset value. Due to the emotional nature of the stock market, these funds often trade at prices below the actual value of the fund portfolio. They also can trade at prices above their net asset value; that's when you want to avoid them. These funds give the internationally minded investor access to most of the world's individual stock markets, often at bargain basement prices (discounts). For example, the Latin American Discovery Fund (LDF) traded at an average 96 cents on the dollar in 1993 and had a total return of 112 percent for the year. That's very nice.

## Avoid Limited Partnerships

Stay away from investment products such as limited partnerships or anything not traded on the open market. They are typically illiquid, very expensive, and difficult to accurately price. The successful investors I know avoid these; you should, too.

## Don't Stay on Margin

Brokerage firms will allow you to borrow money against your securities. The rate of interest you will pay is usually competitive with bank rates. This service can be handy if you are fully invested and you need money on a short-term basis. However, on a long-term basis, it's not such a great idea. Borrowing money to invest in the stock and bond markets over a long period of time is not a good idea. It's too expensive and just not worth the risk.

## Look for Profit, Not Tax Shelters

If you have doubt in my wisdom, just ask any wealthy individual over the age of 45 about tax-sheltered investing and limited partnerships. Your first and second priorities of investing should be profit and proper management of risk (or capital preservation). My first long-run priority has to be not to lose my client's money. My second priority—a very close second—is profit. If you manage your own money, you might reverse the order of these two. However, never make tax savings one of the top two priorities. Until we have absolutely zero tax shelters or loopholes, there will always be a "tax-advantaged investment product" that will offer to save you tax dollars. They are usually expensive and have little or no profit potential. Avoid these like the plague.

## Don't Buy from Strangers

Never buy over the phone from someone you do not know. If the investment sounds good, ask for references and do your homework.

**Wealth Warning**

If anyone tries to sell you a variable annuity in an IRA, take your portfolio, turn around, and run.

## Variable Annuities Don't Go in IRAs

Run, do not walk, from anyone in the investment business who tries to sell you a variable annuity within an IRA or qualified retirement plan. I covered variable annuities in Chapter 7, "Stay Away from This Stuff." If the gains and income in the IRA are already tax deferred, why would anyone buy a variable annuity? I'll tell you why—because a money-grubbing commission-based salesperson sold it to them. I've seen it happen and it's ugly. The penalty to correct this scam is expensive.

## That Reminds Me...

A prospective client at one of my workshops decided to open a $450,000 IRA account with my firm. He said that his money was currently with a full-service brokerage firm, invested in a money market fund. He planned to buy a variable annuity. This made the hair on the back of my neck stand up. I asked why he wanted to include that in his IRA when it was already tax deferred. He said, "Because the broker suggested it." When I explained that the broker's commission would have been at least $27,000, it nearly blew his mind. Not only was the annuity expensive, but it also had only five investment alternatives. Buying it would have been an expensive nightmare.

## Take Advantage of Breakpoints

Focus on larger transactions when possible for *breakpoint* discounts. For example, if you have to buy a loaded mutual fund, ask at what amount of investment your commission rate falls; it may require a purchase of several thousand dollars or a few hundred shares. If you know you're going to eventually put enough money in the fund to meet one of the breakpoints, ask for a letter of intent. Such a document says that you intend to invest enough to exceed the discount and therefore will get you the breakpoint discount.

**Words of the Wealthy**

The more you invest in a loaded fund, the cheaper the commission will be. The dollar amounts at which this commission rate falls are called **breakpoints**.

# Other Investment Laws Revisited

The second section of this chapter is designed to summarize other key investment laws presented earlier in the book. They are vital to the wealth-building process, and I thought you might enjoy reading them again for review.

## The Bulls Are Always Running Somewhere

There may be certain short periods where all markets are falling. However, there are always markets that have a long-term trend upwards (if not most of them). There's always something doing relatively well, even if it is a money market account. Just make sure you have a little of what's doing well in your portfolio. Don't chase returns and buy only what's doing well at the moment. Remember to diversify and spread your risk among many different investments. If everything is falling in price in your diversified portfolio, it usually means that the market overreacted. If so, it's usually best to sit tight.

## The Market Is Full of Inefficiency

Where there's inefficiency, there is profit potential. Look for the inefficiencies in every market. The last chapter touched on many different types of inefficiencies that almost always exist somewhere in the market.

## Be an Unreasonable Investor

Think differently with more imagination and creativity than other investors. Don't be too traditional or dogmatic about any strategy or tactic. Always remain openminded to new ideas and concepts.

## Cut Your Teeth on an All-Purpose Investment

If you are investing less than $5,000, can accept some volatility, and can do without the money for at least four years, you should start with a mutual fund that invests all over the world. Choose the one investment that meets all your criteria.

**Treasure Tip**

After every market correction, there's an opportunity to buy an investment at an undervalued price. The reverse is also true: After every major market rally, there is an opportunity to sell and take a profit. Most investors overreact as much in a negative direction as they do in a positive direction. For example, what is hated the most often seems to be quite popular later. Inefficiency breeds opportunity.

## Loads Versus No-Loads

There are two kinds of open-end mutual funds—those that have commissions, or loads, and those that do not. All mutual funds have management fees (the average is about one percent), but only loaded funds have extra commission charges attached to pay the broker or pay for advertising. By doing a little more of the legwork yourself, you can save as much as 8.5 percent on your purchase. Avoiding a commission means more of your dollars are actually invested.

One type of hidden commission is 12(b)1 fee. I covered this in Chapter 7, and it's important to the wealth-building process that you understand how 12(b)1 fees work. It doesn't matter whether your fund says it's no-load; check the prospectus's expense chapter for 12(b)1 fees. Be sure to avoid 12(b)1 fees in excess of .25 percent. If the 12(b)1 fee is higher than .25 percent, the fund is somewhat of a loaded fund. 12(b)1 is a securities regulation that allows mutual funds to charge a fee in addition to the management fee for such things as "marketing expenses, distribution expenses, or sales expenses." In reality, these expenses disguise the commission, which is paid to the salesperson either in advance, each quarter, or a combination of both.

## Avoid Loaded Variable Annuities

Loaded variable annuities are one of the most exciting things for a broker to sell; they make in excess of 6 percent commission on these. Vanguard's (800-462-2391) true no-load variable annuity is the most inexpensive variable annuity I have found with only 1.08 percent in yearly expenses. Two other companies that offer no-load variable annuities are Charles Schwab & Co. and Fidelity.

If you want to research the mutual funds within these variable annuities, call Morningstar (800-876-5005), which offers research on the mutual funds of variable annuities.

**Wealth Warning**

Just because a variable is inexpensive, it doesn't mean that it's a good investment idea. If you're limited to only a handful of investment alternatives, the chances of your portfolio performing well is also limited.

## Account Consolidation

If you like buying no-load funds, but you don't like multiple statements, multiple phone numbers, and doing business by mail, you might want to contact a discount brokerage firm.

## Consider Starting a Simple Plan

If you are self-employed, a Simple plan is certainly the least expensive qualified retirement plan to start and maintain. It's easy to start, and you can contribute up to $6,000 per year. It's similar to an IRA, only better.

## Never Use Life Insurance for Investment Purposes

Life insurance policies were never intended for investment purposes. Use life insurance for what it was originally intended, which was to provide money for your surviving family to pay for things such as debt coverage, living expenses, and estate taxes.

## Be Careful Purchasing Mutual Funds in December

Most mutual funds issue capital gains distributions in the months of November and December. If you own the fund the day of record (the official day the shareholder is given the dividend), you are given the capital gain—which means you pay the tax on a gain from which you might not have benefited. Some funds make distributions earlier in the year, so you may want to call prior to a big purchase just to check and see when their next distribution might be planned.

## Check Twice for All the Fees and Commissions

When you purchase anything from a full-service broker, investment advisor, insurance agent, or anyone in the financial industry, ask at least twice about all the costs and fees you will be charged.

## Educate Yourself with Free or Low-Cost Resources

Attend local investment workshops and seminars. Call your local college and ask whether they offer any non-credit investment courses.

## If Interest Rates Are Rising, Don't Buy Long Bonds

Remember, when interest rates rise, bond prices fall. Therefore, avoid intermediate and long-term bond funds when interest rates are rising. The best time to be in these bonds is when rates are falling. You can do this directly by investing in individual Treasury securities or using a mutual fund. One of the best funds you can buy when interest rates are falling is Vanguard's Long Term U.S. Treasury fund (800-662-7447). With a management fee of only .2 percent, it is the most inexpensive long-term U.S. Treasury bond fund available. You can also buy individual Treasury bonds directly from the Federal Reserve with no commission.

## Don't Buy Proprietary Products

Avoid loaded proprietary mutual funds, loaded annuities, and packaged products such as UITs (Unit Investment Trust).

## Don't Be a Trader

You don't have to trade often to make money in the market, especially if you are using mutual funds. Many people ask me whether I day trade stocks, which is trading in and out of stocks within a day's time. My answer usually includes a lecture on the risks of market timing and the fact that you can day trade stocks during volatile times and eventually you'll lose. Stocks are not meant to be traded within a day's time. They were meant to be bought and sold over a long time period, which gives you much better odds. Day trading is like going to a casino. It might be fun, but the odds are against you.

## Utilize No Transaction Fee Programs (NTF)

When you can, take advantage of the NTF programs available at discount brokerage firms.

## Don't Buy Individual Foreign Stocks or Bonds

If you are a do-it-yourselfer, don't buy individual foreign stocks and bonds; use foreign mutual funds instead. How can you keep up with stocks in Switzerland and Singapore at the same time?

## Ask for a Discount

It's all negotiable, so ask your advisor how you can get breaks on commissions and fees.

## Eliminate as Many Barriers or Limitations as You Can

Make certain you can purchase any type of investment you want from your brokerage firm, including no-load mutual funds.

## Demand Liquidity

Stick with marketable securities that have available secondary markets.

## The Secret to Successful Portfolio Management Is to Make It a Passion

If portfolio management is your passion, you'll work at it harder, smarter, and longer than most people. The end result will be wisdom and profits. If your passion lies somewhere else, find someone to help you who has a passion for portfolio management.

### That Reminds Me...

The happiest wealthy people I know focused on having fun at work. Most people don't enjoy their work. That's why most people don't get rich. Their attitude prevents them from ever getting anywhere in life. So many of them hate their jobs, their bosses, and their coworkers. They bring this frustration home, and it can result in divorce and even abuse. This cycle of misery eventually affects every aspect of a person's life. The only way out is with a change of attitude—away from selfishness and toward helping others and getting along with others, including the boss.

My hope is that these ideas will help you achieve investment excellence—the cost-efficient balancing of risk and return.

## The Least You Need to Know

➤ Know when you're being sold, and don't be suckered by marketing material.

➤ If an investment sounds too good to be true, it probably is.

➤ Profits are your reward for accepting risk and learning how to manage it properly.

➤ Focus on the things you can control, such as the amount of money you spend and save.

➤ Always study the costs of doing business before you invest in anything.

# Chapter 15

# Avoiding the Investment Boo-Boos

If you plan to reach Wealth Stage 3 or above, you're more than likely going to make some serious mistakes along the way. This chapter is designed to prevent most of them from taking place. The best way to learn anything is trial and error. Unfortunately, we seem to learn the most valuable lessons from our mistakes. Even the most successful investors make mistakes. In fact, investment management could also be called "the management of mistakes." If you are an investor, you're going to be wrong some of the time. It's not a question of *if* you're going to be wrong; it's a question of *when*. The key to the investment game is to be right more than you are wrong.

The good news is that you can learn just as much from the mistakes of others as you can from your own. Learning from your own mistakes takes a lot of time and money. Learning from other people's mistakes saves you time and money and can catapult you far ahead of your natural learning process. That's what this chapter is all about: learning from the mistakes of others. You'll recognize some of these mistakes because they are the opposite of what I've suggested in other chapters.

# Beginner's Mistakes

If you are a beginner at investing, this section will help you prevent some of the most common mistakes. There are certainly many more possibilities; this is just a list of the most common ones I've seen (or experienced firsthand):

## Wealth Warning

How far could you get in your car (in a forward direction) if you had to look in your rearview mirror 95 percent of the time? The same theory applies to using long-term past performance of mutual funds to make investment decisions. If markets repeated themselves, past performance would give you an indication of future returns. Unfortunately, the market changes on a daily basis.

## Treasure Tip

Unless you know exactly when you're going to pass away, you don't know how much time you have or how much money you'll need. The perfect financial life would consist of exactly enough money to live on until the day you die. Because of all the variables, there is no perfect financial life; you have to plan for an uncertain future. How do you do it? Start saving now!

➤ **I just met a broker over the phone, and he's great.** Brokers still make cold calls every day. Some day, this practice will be against the law. Until then, be careful.

➤ **I bought the fund because it had a great year last year.** The most common mistake investors make is investing where the market hockey puck has been. No matter how well a fund did last year, it is a new year now, and everyone (including the fund manager) is faced with completely different circumstances—completely different markets. Investing is a forward-thinking game. You place a series of diversified bets on your best judgment of the future, watch your bets, make changes when necessary, and maintain watch on the world for more new bets.

➤ **I'm not willing to take any risk.** Many investors don't understand that risk is something you accept and manage. If you avoid it, your assets will be subject to inflation risk (meaning, you'll make interest, but that interest won't help your investment grow faster than inflation). Most people unwilling to take risk become lenders. They lend money to banks and the government in exchange for interest payments on their CDs and bonds. What they don't realize is that in order to build wealth, you have to be an owner. You have to buy stocks or start your own company.

➤ **I've got plenty of time to start saving money.** This is definitely one of the most common mistakes Americans make today. They put off saving money until some arbitrary date in the future when their ship supposedly comes in. They honestly believe that in order to make it worthwhile, they have to save big amounts. That's not true. It's the habit of saving that's important—that the little amounts over time add up.

➤ **It's too late to start saving money.** This is the opposite of the last mistake. People wait until they have enough money to save (which to them is never) and wind up believing that they don't have enough time to save the amount of money they need. This is double jeopardy. They feel like they're stuck between a rock and a hard place. However, it's never too late to start saving money.

## Intermediate Investors Make Mistakes, Too

An intermediate investor is someone who has been managing her own portfolio for more than a year. As your wealth grows and you become more aware of the basics of investing, you'll begin to make subtle errors that you might not realize for years. Here is a list of a few common errors I see intermediate investors make:

➤ **I picked a good mutual fund family.** Because discount brokerage firms offer hundreds of no-load mutual funds to their clients, it makes absolutely no sense to do business with one mutual fund family. Buying exclusively from one mutual fund family is like saying all the funds that start with "P" are the best. You're destined for mediocrity with one fund family. Why limit yourself? Give yourself the opportunity to invest in at least 1,000 different funds by using the discount brokerage firms I mentioned in Chapter 10, "Jumping into the Market."

➤ **It's OK to have this much money in one stock.** Too much money in one stock is a typical problem for those who work or who have worked for a publicly traded company, particularly one that offers a 401(k) or employee stock option program. Granted, an employee might know a great deal more about that company than most other investors. However, if one small thing goes wrong with the company and the stock price plummets as a result, his portfolio will also plummet. It's not worth the risk. Do what it takes to diversify your portfolio. If you have a huge capital gain and you hesitate because of taxes, sell off some of your stock each year and spread out the tax. Consider gifts to charities. Talk to a tax attorney about setting up a charitable remainder trust (CRT).

➤ **My account's so big, I need five brokerage firms to do business.** Many investors get spread out among several different brokerage firms. They get so many statements each month that they have to add up and recalculate their portfolio allocation. They get several 1099s at the end of the year. If they want to make a trade and they have only a little

**Treasure Tip**

A rational investor might say that the stock market moves with expected earnings, inflation, and interest rates. An irrational man might say that the stock market moves with the whims of human emotion. The irony is that they are both correct.

money in each account, they have to write several checks or transfer money from one account into another. To check their account between statements, they have to call each firm and get the numbers. Basically, they live in a busy nightmare. Why not keep it simple? I have yet to see why anyone needs more than two brokerage firms.

➤ **Look at this great yield in the paper!** Don't be fooled by what I call "yield bait." An ad in the paper last month read, "Free conversion of your low interest IRA to our eight percent IRA. No equity risk. Call our IRA help desk without obligation." CD and Treasury bond rates last month were well below eight percent on all maturities. With interest rates as low as they are, how can this company offer "eight percent" and "no equity risk" and give you "free conversion?" Answer: It is selling an annuity with a one-year guaranteed rate only. The penalty if you sell the annuity the first year is approximately six percent, and it declines to zero after six years. The annuity company will take the money invested and more than likely purchase corporate and long-term government bonds. If unsuspecting investors buy this IRA and keep it for a year, one of three things is likely to happen:

1. They will be happy with the new yield declared each year and keep the annuity.

2. They will be unhappy with the yield and will want out.

3. They will find a better opportunity and will want to get out.

Yield bait is a term I invented to describe the many different tools (such as annuities, bond funds, and proprietary investment products) that commission-based firms use to attract unsuspecting investors who need income. These investments are usually advertised as high-paying investments with little or no risk. Most of the time, investors purchase these investments without any idea of the expenses and possible penalties involved. The moment they try to sell or get out, boom! Reality sets in. They immediately see how expensive the investment actually is, but the withdrawal penalty will more than likely prevent any change. In the case of the annuity, the real question is, "Why do you want to limit your alternatives when you don't have to?" Why not purchase individual bonds or a no-load bond fund that costs little or nothing to sell next year if you want out? Remember, both fixed and variable annuities have sharp hooks with barbs. Once you get in, you're limited to whatever the annuity company offers you regardless of other possible opportunities. They may attract you with the yield as bait, but the consequences can be heavy commission charges or fees.

The most dangerous yield bait today is the long-term (10 to 30 years) government or municipal bond fund. If rates continue to go up, the fund's price will fall. Most of these government and municipal bonds funds are bought with safety of principal in mind. "Full faith and credit of the U.S. Government" means little to someone who loses 15 percent of principal on her government bond fund after only a one percent rise in rates. Remember, not all funds are bad. Just be smart and do your homework before buying any bond fund. This is especially important when buying any fixed-income security from a commissioned broker or insurance salesperson. If you buy, they can make commission income of 8.5 percent off your money. It's what you don't know that will hurt you.

➤ **When there is a bear market, it's best to sell everything and buy bonds.** This is a trap for many investors. The belief is that during a stock market correction, you can simply sell part or all of a portfolio, buy bonds, and sit there until the market settles out. This sounds oh-so-attractive and easy, but it's a trap. To win at this strategy, you must make two market timing moves and be right each time. First, when you sell, you must be right that the market will go down further. Second, when you buy back in, you must be right that the market is at a bottom. If you are wrong at either point, you most likely will lose money—to say nothing about transaction costs. My advice is to sit tight during corrections and buy more stocks. If you are dollar cost averaging by adding money systematically to the market, continue to do so. You're buying stocks at lower prices, and that will help your returns in the long run.

➤ **I heard a rumor.** Using rumors for investment research is like playing Russian roulette. One rumor might be accurate every now and then, but the odds are against making money. Typically, if the rumor has any truth to it at all, by the time you hear it, it's too late.

### That Reminds Me...

Where do rumors start? I have a theory. Many people in the world have entirely too much free time on their hands. Free time can often result in insecurity. Victims of insecurity spend a lot of time talking, trying to prove to others and themselves that their insecurities don't exist. One way these people disguise financial insecurity is to talk about everything they've heard, most of which is insignificant, yet easy to sensationalize. Abraham Lincoln once said, "It's better to keep one's mouth shut and be thought a fool than to open it and resolve all doubt."

➤ **The fund's up 10 percent this month; I think I'll take some profits.** Regardless of whether you use stocks or mutual funds, you don't have to trade often to make money. If fact, most of the wealthy investors I know maintain a long-term outlook. They hold most of their securities over the long term in good times and bad. For the most part, they don't try to time the market. They consistently add money to their portfolio or at least let some of the gains be reinvested, knowing that in the long run, they will be rewarded for their patience. However, when they feel an investment is no longer worth keeping, they sell it—so they do some trading, but not a lot.

➤ **I bought a no-load fund from a broker.** I was driving down the street last year and saw a full-service brokerage firm advertisement on a sign that read, "Ask us about our no-load funds." Some brokers advertise (unlawfully) 12(b)1 mutual funds with declining back loads as "no-load funds." They say that they are "no-load" after six (or so) years when the back-load disappears. Don't be fooled. If there is a 12(b)1 fee in excess of .25 percent, then the fund is loaded. Where do you find the 12(b)1 fee? Ask the broker (this will surprise him), and then look in the prospectus under "Expenses." The normal 12(b)1 fee will add an additional 1 percent to the management fee, making it too expensive.

➤ **I'm waiting for the market to go down.** Many investors try to time the market. Many wait to buy or sell in anticipation of a market drop. But no one knows when the market will correct. It's a guessing game that I guarantee you'll lose if you play it short term. You can only play long term. It's the only way to win. If you really are convinced that the market is too high, divide your portfolio into four pieces. Invest each piece at a different time. You could invest once each month for four months or once each quarter over a period of a year. Either way, you win. If the market does correct, you will be purchasing at lower prices. If the market continues higher, you are participating.

### That Reminds Me...

A client hired me to manage a piece of his portfolio. He had been waiting for a market correction since 1990 to invest. For years, his $5 million portfolio sat in CDs and money market funds. This is a long time, especially because the market is up dramatically since then. As you can imagine, he's spent a lot of time beating himself up over this. He keeps thinking about all the money he could have made if he had invested in the market in 1990. I asked him, "If you had $3.5 million more in your portfolio, would it change your life?" He said, "No. You're right. I don't need to look back any more."

➤ **I can't sell yet; I've got a loss and I'm waiting for the fund (or stock) to break even.** This one of the craziest statements I've ever heard. What difference does it make whether the stock goes back up to the price at which it was purchased? While you're waiting, your money could've been in another investment, making money. What's important is whether you would be willing to buy the stock today if you had your money in cash. If not, sell it, even if you do so at a loss.

➤ **I can't sell now; my capital gain is too big.** So many people forget that this is a profit game, not a tax game. If you base your decisions on how much tax you're going to pay, you will lose. You should use zero based thinking to make this kind of decision. No matter how much tax you have to pay, if the investment is bad, sell it or give it away to charity.

➤ **I don't need any help; I can do this myself.** Many investors make the mistake of not delegating any of their work. This is okay to an extent, but I've seen some pretty stubborn investors who sacrifice profits for pride.

# Advanced Investors Also Make Mistakes

Advanced investors are people who have been managing their own money for more than five years. They have a lot of experience, but even they make mistakes. This section is a list of the most common mistakes I've seen in the last several years:

➤ **My bond allocation should match my age.** I've covered this before, but it's worth repeating. I don't know who started this garbage, but it sure is a common theory. Just because you're 50 years old doesn't mean that your portfolio should be 50 percent in bonds. The percentage of money you put in bonds should be based upon two variables: your risk tolerance and what you think interest rates will do in the next 12 months. If you are a conservative investor, you might want to keep a large portion of your portfolio in short-term bonds. If you are a moderate risk investor who thinks interest rates will fall in the next 12 months, you might want to build a position in long-term Treasury bonds or zero-coupon bonds.

➤ **I know what I'm doing.** Many investors think they know too much and don't follow their own instincts. They get a "big head" because they follow all the market data and think that quantitative measurements win the investment game. This strategy is referred to as *quantitative analysis*, which says that markets are measureable and predictable. I can certainly tell you from experience, they don't win. If they did, anyone who could operate a computer would consistently beat the market. Quantitative measurement is important, but the market moves more on emotion than anything else. Learn all you can, and then listen to your gut and go with your instincts.

➤ **If you need income, you must have mutual funds and stocks that produce big dividends.** This is the most common misconception among retired investors today. They shun capital gains in search of interest income and dividends. Why? There are two reasons. First, using interest and dividends is the traditional way to produce income for the retired person. Second, most investment professionals think that interest- and dividend-producing securities are necessary for income-seeking investors. They all seem to live in a world where capital gains never take place; it's as if they don't exist. But there's a better way. It's almost so simple that it seems stupid to even mention. A better way to furnish income is to harvest not only the regular cash flow from income and dividends, but also some capital gains (by selling selected shares for a security that's up). I've done this for many years, and my clients are very happy about it.

➤ **I've made too much money, and I've got to stop paying so much in taxes.** I've had clients tell me I made them too much money. No kidding! Two years ago, I called one of my favorite clients. She is retired and single and lives in a small town in Arkansas. She lives a simple life, yet she loves to travel with friends both here in the U.S. and abroad. I explained to her that her account performed very well this year. For 1993, her account grew 25.5 percent (total weighted average). (Remember what should follow any statement like this: "Past performance is not indicative of future results.") She made $104,844 on a beginning balance of $433,707. During the year, she wrote checks totaling $42,149, which still left her $62,695. To anyone else on the planet, this would have been music to the ears. However, her reply was, "Larry, you made me too much money!"

### Words of the Wealthy

Financial **quantitative analysis** involves the study of numerical information for the basis of decision making. Under the idea of quantitative theory, everything is expressed in measurable form and is therefore also predictable. Investors who use this theory believe that by studying specific market data, they can accurately predict the market's movements.

I told her, "You know, I don't think any client has ever told me that." She said, "You might have put me in a higher tax bracket." This could be true considering the fact that she also received income that year from timber sold on her farm. I said, "You may be right, but I also made you enough money to pay the additional taxes. I also made you an additional $25,000 that was reinvested back into your account." She paused a minute and said, "Well, I guess I should be happy." To which I replied, "Yes, ma'am."

This client worries too much about taxes. When I met her, her account was 90 percent municipal bonds with maturities beyond 15 years. Her goal in working with me was to diversify and increase her return. She wanted a 10 percent return with minimal fluctuation on the downside. I exceeded her return goal without coming close to her downside limit. But all she could think about was the taxes she would have to pay. Don't be blind to profits when you're faced with taxes.

## The Least You Need to Know

➤ Don't buy any investment from a stranger on the phone whom you've never met.

➤ Past performance should not be the only reason you buy a mutual fund.

➤ Don't buy on rumors, beware of yield bait, and don't do business with only one mutual fund family.

➤ Don't try to time the market.

➤ Beware of the broker who sells you a "no-load" mutual fund.

# Part 3
# Building Wealth with Your Own Business

*Wealth Stages 3 and 4 are achievable using most of the strategies you've learned so far. However, if you want to increase your chances of achieving Wealth Stage 4 and maybe even Wealth Stage 5, you might want to start your own business. It may not be a requirement for achieving Wealth Stage 4, but it's almost impossible to reach Wealth Stage 5 without your own business.*

*Most business owners who achieve any significant wealth use the principles of saving monthly and investing, but their business gives them an extra boost both in terms of additional income and growing equity value—which are the two keys to building your wealth with your own business. If you build a business that you can sell, you have the potential to build your wealth as fast as the business grows. A fast-growing small business that is nimble, flexible, and easily modified to meet customers' needs could be just the ticket to get you to the upper wealth stages.*

*First, I help you select a business that you'll enjoy. Second, I explain what you can expect working for yourself. Third, you'll learn how important a CPA can be to the wealth-building process. Fourth, I explain how important a good banking relationship can be. Fifth, you'll learn the most common mistakes made by business owners. Sixth, I share with you one of the hardest things I've ever experienced—finding good employees and delegating. Lastly, you'll learn the keys to building a profitable business that can be sold in the future.*

# Chapter 16

# Start with Your Hobby

---

### In This Chapter

➤ What you should focus on before you start your own business

➤ Why you should use your hobby to start a business

➤ How to write a successful business plan

➤ The new business checklist that can save your life

---

Most people don't start their own businesses because of the fear of risk. Ironically, the reason people make so much money in their own businesses is because they chose to accept the risk.

Another reason why most people don't start their own businesses is also a big reason why most businesses fail. When most people begin considering their own businesses, they focus on what they think will be successful or make the most money. The focus is primarily on making money, which might sound smart at first, but it's actually a mistake. Many initially successful businesses fail because the owner gets burned out or loses the drive to push forward. They lose their interest.

If you shouldn't start a business to make money, why start a business? The answer lies in your passion and dreams. Can you imagine starting your own business with one of your favorite hobbies? It's a dream that only a few people realize. Why? First of all, most people don't even think it's possible. They think you have to be extremely talented, rich, or famous to start a business. Second, they think that making money should be hard. One of my former associates loves to do research, and after spending days at the library, she said that she feels guilty because she doesn't feel as if she's working. She thinks work must be hard. It's simply not true. Your work should be enjoyable. It's okay to have fun at work. The third reason most people don't start a business doing what they enjoy is because they haven't taken the time to figure out what they enjoy doing, much less make a plan to implement it. This chapter begins to explore how your own business can be part of a plan to achieve the wealth level you want to achieve using a hobby or career that you enjoy.

If your target is Wealth Stage 4, you'll have to accumulate enough assets to produce a total return sufficient enough to substantially increase your desired lifestyle and keep up with inflation. That charge may seem overwhelming at first; it was for me. However, once I started my own business and saw the dividends and equity growth, I realized just how fast a business can build wealth. If you want to achieve Wealth Stage 5, starting your own business is almost a requirement.

# Why Start Your Own Business?

Here is a list of the most common reasons why people want to start their own businesses:

- ➤ To achieve financial independence
- ➤ To pursue their dream jobs doing what they enjoy
- ➤ To escape corporate bureaucracy
- ➤ To achieve creative independence
- ➤ To achieve a more flexible schedule
- ➤ To build wealth
- ➤ To enjoy life more

Do any of these reasons apply to you? Have you ever asked yourself why you want to start your own business? Now is a good time to do it. Ask yourself these questions, and if the answers are positive, you should definitely explore business opportunities:

1. Why do you want to start your own business?
2. What would starting your own business accomplish for you?
3. Would you enjoy working for yourself? Why?

**Treasure Tip**

The primary key to success in your own business is to be passionate about what you are doing. Passion creates tenacity, and if you're tenacious enough to give it everything you've got, the money will follow.

# What Business Will You Start?

Deciding what business to start is the hardest question for some people to answer, once they've decided that they do want to start a business. Unless you have had a burning desire to start a particular type of business, you might get stuck here. I'm going to coach you through this process and make it easier for you.

The first step is to review your answers to the five questions in Chapter 5, "The Secrets of Millionaires," in the section "Follow Your Passion":

1. Your doctor calls you and tells you that in exactly six months, you will die a peaceful death due to a weird unknown virus. What would you do during this six-month period? Who would you spend time with? What activities would you spend time doing? What would be important to you? (List at least 20 answers.)

2. An unknown relative died and left you a portfolio of cash totaling $2,000,000. What would you do? Who would you spend time with? What activities would you spend time doing? What would be important to you? Would you quit work? How would you spend your money? (List at least 20 answers.)

3. What three great endeavors would you dare to attempt if you were guaranteed you could not fail?

4. What do you want more of in your life? (List at least 20 answers.)

5. What do you want less of in your life? (List at least 20 answers.)

If you have not answered those questions, do it now. This simple exercise may just change your life for the better. Remember the rules:

➤ Sit in solitude.

➤ Find a quiet place outside in a natural setting.

➤ There's no such thing as a stupid answer.

➤ Anything is possible; don't judge your answers yet.

➤ Complete at least 20 answers to the first two questions.

➤ Complete at least three answers to the last question.

Do not read any further until you have completed this exercise. The answers to these questions should give you a clear picture of your goals and values in life. Basically, you list your passions and dreams. Use them to find and design the business of your dreams.

If you don't see a business idea coming right off the page, you might want to take some time and use the answers to at least design the parameters of the business you're going to start. For example, if you enjoy spending time at home, you might declare this as one of your business parameters. If you know and enjoy working with computers, this might be a key parameter also. If you continue listing your desired parameters, it will be much easier to select the perfect business for you.

**Wealth Warning**

Most people think that to start a business, they need some incredible new invention or product that will change the world. It would certainly help if you do have such a product, but it is in no way a requirement to start a business. All you need is a passion for producing a product or service and a customer who will buy it from you.

After you have a list of parameters, your next step is to screen every business idea you have. The perfect business might not meet every parameter for you, but it should satisfy at least your top three. Therefore, it is necessary to prioritize your parameters. Which one is the most important to you? Which is second? Third?

### That Reminds Me...

Everyone's parameters are different. I wanted to be able to manage money for people, live anywhere, hire others to run the company for me and manage them, focus on what I enjoy (money management), take vacations, build a source of residual income, keep clients for life, work even if I was physically disabled, and continue working until I was 80 years old if I wanted to. Once I decided upon these parameters, it was easy to make a decision.

If you are still having trouble finding the perfect business, here are some extra questions that might help you:

➤ What do you enjoy doing in your free time?

➤ What do you like to read in your free time?

➤ What do you excel in? What are you good at?

➤ What do others say you are good at?

➤ What do you want more of in your life?

➤ What do you want less of in your life?

Whatever you decide to do, make sure your business enables you to achieve at least your top three priorities. Your goal should be to get more life out of your business. If not, you might not be able to maintain the necessary passion you'll need to be successful. If this is the case, redesign the business concept to meet your goals.

I tell people that no matter what kind of hobby or passion you have, you can build a business around it. My favorite example is Gordon Rathbun whose passion is competitive water skiing. Most people agree that there's no way you can make money water skiing. Well, don't let Gordon hear you say that. As a teenager, he skied every morning and waited tables in the afternoons. Later on, he sold cable television services, but still skied every morning. In 1984 at the age of 34, he was ranked 10th in the world as a slalom skier! Gordon lived and worked to ski. Skiing is Gordon's passion.

After taking some friends to Acapulco to ski one winter, Gordon had an idea. At the age of 38, he started Ski Paradise, year-round ski schools in Acapulco, Mexico, and Lake Tahoe, Nevada. Gordon is now 48 and living his dream. A six-time national champion,

Gordon spends his winters in warm Acapulco and his summers in beautiful Lake Tahoe teaching people from all over the world how to ski like champions. Gordon says, "If you become an expert at your field of passion, you will become a natural sponge for knowledge, you will work harder than most other people, and you will be in demand for your service."

Once you have decided upon the business ideas that fit your parameters, you need to focus your market (potential customers). Who will buy your product or service? Do some research to find a market willing to buy from you. Here are some questions to ask yourself about your market:

➤ Will your business fill a need (of your customer)?

➤ Who is your competition?

➤ What is your strategic advantage over your competition?

➤ What makes your product or service better?

➤ How can you create a demand for your product or service?

# Writing a Winning Business Plan

Before you get started building your wealth further with your business, make sure to take time out to design and plan exactly what you're going to do. Some people hate business plans. I'm crazy about them. I wrote more than 15 different business plans before I found my dream business—a money-management firm. Planning is the most important part of starting a successful business. Your success will not necessarily depend on whether you complete a business plan, but it sure does help.

To write a good business plan, you'll have to do some research. The following is my business plan outline. This business plan was not only used to help plan and develop my business; it was also used to secure a $100,000 loan from a local bank. I was 31 years old at the time and had very little collateral. I'm convinced the bank gave me the money primarily because of the organization of the plan. Use this outline to help you organize your plan. Record the outline on paper or in your computer, and fill in the blanks, adding in the supporting documents where needed. You'll notice the term "pro-forma" with several of the financial statements that are needed in the plan. *Pro-forma* refers to the projected financial statements of a company.

**Words of the Wealthy**

**Pro-forma financial statements** are used to project the estimated financial results of a new company. They consist of an income statement, balance sheet, and cash-flow statement.

**Part I: The Proposal.**

What Is Waschka Capital Investments or WCI?

Loan Request and Purpose (Estimated Start-Up Costs).

Method and Terms of Repayment.

**Part II: History of WCI and the Investment Advisory Business.**

History of WCI and Larry Waschka.

Mission Statement and Investment Philosophy.

Ownership and Corporate Structure.

Description of Services.

The Investment Industry.

What Makes WCI Different from the Competition?

**Part III: Marketing Plan—How We Build Our Business.**

Who Is Our Market?

Marketing and Advertising Strategy.

Pricing Strategy.

The Competition.

Economic Overview.

**Part IV: Management.**

Principals and Key Associates.

Organizational Chart.

Research and Development.

**Part V: Financials. (This is a view of the beginning.)**

(pro-forma) Balance Sheets.

(pro-forma) Income Statements (Profit and Loss Statement).

(pro-forma) Statements of Cash Flow.

Ratio Analysis (if you are an existing business).

**Part VI: Financial Projections—Short Range (First Year).**

Assumptions.

Projected Income Statements (Profit and Loss Statement).

Projected Cash-Flow Statements.

Projected Balance Sheets.

Projected Ratio Analysis.

**Part VII: Financial Projections—Long Range (Three Years).**

Assumptions.

Projected Income Statements (Profit and Loss Statement).

Projected Cash-Flow Statements.

Projected Balance Sheets.

Projected Ratio Analysis.

**Part VIII: Supporting Documents.**

Gross Income Projections on a Worse Case Scenario.

Related Estimates for Expenses, Payroll, and Net Income.

Graphs and Data.

Gross Income Projections on a Best Case Scenario.

Related Estimates for Expenses, Payroll, and Net Income.

Graphs and Data.

Gross Income Projections on an Outrageous Case Scenario.

Related Estimates for Expenses, Payroll, and Net Income.

Graphs and Data.

**Part IX: Appendix.**

Principals' Resumes.

Job Descriptions for All Associates.

Business Advisors and References.

Client References.

New Office Lease.

New Office Improvement List.

Automobile, Equipment, and Furniture List.

Results of Recent Client Survey.

Larry Waschka's Personal Financial Statement.

Personal Budget.

Copy of Life Insurance Policy on Larry Waschka.

Every business plan is different, so some of the titles in this plan may not apply to you. This is just an example of a plan that worked. Where necessary, I have inserted optional items that you might consider. The bottom-line question is "Will your company make money?"

My business plan filled a three-ring binder. I explained every assumption and added all the necessary supporting documents. It was (and still is) a blueprint of my business. Some of my friends told me that my plan was too long; it was overkill. After I got my $100,000 loan and my net income grew by 1,000 percent the next year, I knew that the plan was just right!

If the task of writing your business plan and doing your financial statements seems overwhelming, buy one of the many business plan software packages available.

# Business Plan Software

Several different business plan software packages can make this process a whole lot easier for you. Make sure your package will do what you want it to. If you need good pro-forma financial statements, make sure the software will provide them for you. If not, a good CPA will help you. Remember that no single software package will ever completely personalize your plan. Automation is great, but if you take it too far, especially in building your business plan, the results may disappoint you. Make sure you do all you can to personalize your end product. Get your CPA or a friend to read it before you go to your bank with it.

Here are a few of the best software packages:

> **BizPlan Builder**, $129.00
> 800-827-0597
> Produced by JIAN.
> Also available:
> Employee Manual Builder, $129
> Safety Plan Builder, $129
> Marketing Plan Builder, $129

> **PlanMaker**, $129.00
> 800-955-3337
> Produced by Power Solutions, St. Louis, MO.

> **Business Plan Pro**, $149.00
> 800-229-7526
> Produced by Palo Alto Software, Eugene, OR.
> Also available:
> Marketing Plan Pro
> Decision Maker

> **Business Planning Advisor**, $129.95
> 800-441-4132
> Produced by Enterprise Support Systems, Norcross, GA.

Also available:

Situation Assessment Advisor

Product Planning Advisor

And several books by William B. Rouse

Before you select one of these packages, do some homework. Use the following table to compare features in each of the programs.

## Competitive Analysis for Business Plan Software

| | Business Planning Advisor | Business Plan Pro | BizPlan Builder |
|---|---|---|---|
| Formats—DOS, Mac, Windows? | Windows Only | Windows Only | DOS, Mac, Windows |
| Complete financial statement analysis? | Yes | Yes | Yes |
| Requires other software? | No | No | No |
| Onscreen sample business plans? | Yes | Yes | Yes |
| Quickstart manual? | Yes | No | Yes |
| Can create multiple business plans simultaneously? | Yes | Yes | Yes |
| 100 percent mouse support? | Yes | Yes | Yes |
| Text formatting? | Yes | Yes | Yes |
| Spell checker? | Yes | Yes | No |
| Computes amortization and paydown schedules? | No | Yes | Yes |
| Factors loan paydowns into projections? | No | Yes | Yes |
| Calculates depreciation and factors into projections? | No | Yes | Yes |
| Computes payroll costs and includes them in projections? | Yes | Yes | Yes |
| Onscreen help feature? | Yes | Yes | Yes |
| Tech support? | Yes | Yes | Yes |
| Can accommodate separate sales categories into projections? | No | Yes | Yes |
| Offers complete financial statements? | Yes | Yes | Yes |
| 30-day money back guarantee? | Yes | Yes | Yes |
| Can tech support handle business-oriented questions? | Yes | No | Yes |

# The Pro-Forma Financial Statements

If you plan to achieve Wealth Stage 4 or 5 using your own business, you have to understand financial statements. They are the key measuring tools of your business efficiency and profitability. The first critical element in your financial statements is your return on investment. Before you start a business, you need to make sure your business passes the return on investment (ROI) test. Many business owners don't understand this test. They jump into a business without even considering (or knowing) what their ROI will be. To pass the ROI test, you must prove to yourself that your return on investment can exceed the historical returns of the stock market (which have been more than 10 percent for the last several years). Your ROI can be calculated by dividing your net income by the amount of capital you've invested in your company. The obvious goal of your business should be to maximize the ROI, and this can be done two ways: reducing expenses or increasing gross income.

Why is the ROI so important? If you can't beat the stock market's return, why start a business when you can invest your money in the stock market? Why work so hard in your own business when you can invest money in the stock market from the comforts of your own home without any employees?

How do you know what your ROI will be? You need to prepare pro-forma financial statements using accurate or best judgment data. Pro-forma statements are simply estimated financial statements based on several assumptions. They enable you to answer questions such as, "Given a certain amount of estimated sales and expenses, how much profit can be produced by your business?" The easiest way to complete these statements is with software or a good CPA. Understanding how these statements work can make or break you in the first few years. Take some time to learn the basics of how these statements work and how to read them. You might hate accounting, but I promise, you'll hate failure and bankruptcy more.

### That Reminds Me...

A 61-year-old business owner told me one day that he wasn't in business to make money. He was trying to say that his focus was more on the welfare of his employees and customers. I couldn't believe his statement. This guy was either full of garbage or had his priorities completely backwards. I quickly responded, "The best thing you can do for your employees and customers is make money. If you don't, there will be no business, no salary for your employees, and no service for your customers."

A critical element of your pro-forma statements is cash-flow management, which is measured using a statement of cash flow, or cash-flow statement. This statement measures the actual beginning and ending balance of cash within a company. If you've never owned your own company, you might not realize how important cash flow can be. I know businesses that grew more than 100 percent per year in sales, but they went bankrupt because of poor cash-flow management. Because their clients didn't have to pay for the goods for 30 days, the business found itself with great sales growth but no cash to continue operating.

The key is to plan in advance with estimated monthly cash-flow statements and know exactly how big your line of credit at the bank should be. I discuss bankers and how to get an adequate line of credit in Chapter 20, "Find Great Talent." You and your banker will want to know where your break-even point will be. If you want to ensure success in business the first few years, take the time to learn all you can about cash-flow management. Buy a book or take a class if you have to. Many tricks of the trade can help you when you get into a crunch.

# Taking on a Partner

If you want to achieve Wealth Stage 4 or 5, don't take on a partner unless you have to. The potential problems are extensive, but not insurmountable. The fight for control is the biggest problem. The second most common problem is trust and support. If one partner does most of the work, the other becomes resentful and loses trust in the other. The third biggest problem seems to be the inability to keep a single vision. If the two partners are both strong willed, they often want to go in different directions.

Try your best to hire or *outsource* everything you need to start your business. Only if you can't hire or outsource what you need should you consider a partner. If it's money you lack and someone's offering you money for a partnership or equity, try every other angle first before you accept it. If at all

**Treasure Tip**

In a cash crunch, ask your suppliers and vendors to let you push payments back. Big companies do this all the time. Your supplier would rather be paid late than never.

**Treasure Tip**

A great way to test compatibility with a future partner is to take a short vacation together. Don't bring the entire family. Only the two (or three) of you should go. You'll know in three days whether you can work together.

**Words of the Wealthy**

**Outsource** simply means to pay someone outside your firm to do a job for you. It's an alternative to putting someone directly on your payroll.

possible, don't trade control for money. You should always maintain control over your business. A partnership may take away from that control. However, there are exceptions. Not all partnerships are bad. Before considering one, get to know the person well. Ask yourself whether you can work together in good times and bad.

## A Last-Minute Checklist

The following is a list of other items you might want to think about:

➤ Where will your business be located?

➤ What will be your legal structure? (See a CPA or attorney.)

➤ What insurance coverage will you need?

➤ How will you compensate yourself? What is the minimum amount of salary you need each month?

➤ Will this business help you do more than make a decent living?

➤ Can you do this without a partner?

➤ Can you sell this business later?

# Don't Get Too Anxious

**Treasure Tip**

I spent more than three months setting up my company before I left my employer. After giving my final notice, I walked into my own office ready to do business on the first day.

If you want to achieve Wealth Stage 4 using your own business, don't quit your existing job until you know that your venture can eventually produce an equal or higher income for you. Make sure you have adequate capital or income for the first year of living expenses. Be sure to finish your business plan, and then test your theory on a small scale before you jump out on your own. Don't get caught up in too much planning. Do a small-scale test of your business. Test-market your product, and test your production idea. Then, learn from those tests. Don't go into a full-scale business until you know your idea will work. I know from experience that this can save you hours of time and thousands of dollars later.

# How to Tell Whether You've Arrived

You know you've arrived when you reach the point where you can afford to spend a week every quarter on vacation somewhere in Europe or the Caribbean, but you don't because you're having too much fun at work. In 1995, my goal was to take a week of vacation every month. I did it for about four months and actually found myself missing my work. Once you reach this mindset, achieving Wealth Stage 4 is easy.

You also know you've made it when someone calls you on the phone and asks whether you might be interested in selling your business. This just happened to me recently; it wasn't an accident. I built the business so that I could sell it later if I ever want to retire. I have no plans to do this, but the concept of building my wealth through the equity value of my company was done by design. It needs to be part of your plan, too. Make sure you can sell your business one day. Find a way to build equity. Even if you offer a service, teach someone else how to do it. Hire an intern or apprentice who can take over later. I've hired five capable people in my firm who someday will be able to run my company without me. That's the ultimate dream. What will I do? I see myself becoming like Sam Walton, who continued to support his employees by helping them achieve their personal and business goals. He was like a cheerleader for his team. What a great job!

---

### The Least You Need to Know

➤ Don't start a business just to achieve a certain wealth stage; start a business that will give you an opportunity to focus on your passion and make money at the same time.

➤ All you need to start a business and achieve Wealth Stage 4 (and maybe 5) is a passion for your work, a market for your product or service, and a potentially sellable business.

➤ Planning is the most important part of starting a successful business, and a good business plan is the key to that planning process.

➤ Be patient and start your business slowly while maintaining your current job; get it off the ground before you jump out of your job.

---

# Chapter 17

The Boss

# Be Your Own Boss

---

**In This Chapter**

➤ How to design a business planning notebook

➤ Why systems and procedures are important for your business

➤ Marketing is the key to income

➤ When things go wrong, what do you do?

➤ Why businesses fail

---

After spending countless hours studying wealthy people, I've come to one definite conclusion: The key to great wealth is ownership of something unique and attractive that either produces income and capital gains or has the potential to do so in the future. A successful business can do this for you faster than any other strategy because of the extraordinary growth rates that are possible.

There is a price to pay if you want to be your own boss. However, if you took my advice in Chapter 16, "Start with Your Hobby," and you love what you do, the price will be easy to pay. When I started my money management firm in 1990, I didn't expect to take many vacations. I knew it would take a lot of work to be successful, but I didn't realize how much more time and money it would take. This chapter reviews the sweat equity you'll have to invest to build wealth through your own business.

# Playing Quarterback

With your own business, you are your own boss, and you're faced with more responsibility than ever. But you love it because you are building your wealth doing what you love to do. To be profitable, you have to be able to single-mindedly focus on each area of your business. If you're not organized, you'll be stretched to the maximum every day of your business life. You're going to be overwhelmed with responsibility—some of which you hadn't planned on. Many business owners get in this circle of overwhelming frustration and are never able to grow their business. They're too busy sawing the log to stop and sharpen the saw.

### That Reminds Me...

A few years ago, I spent some time with Roger Lane, a business consultant in San Diego who taught me a lot about planning and setting goals for my business. He said that in order to have a successful business, I had to achieve two goals: a 50 percent or better profit margin with a payroll that didn't exceed 20 percent of my operating income and a set of procedures and a staff that could run the business without me. These are good goals to start with. Once you achieve them, they are easy to maintain.

You need a tool to help keep you on track. The best way to manage your business effectively is to build what I call a "business planning notebook." It is an extension or working model of your business plan. You can build this notebook in your computer as a file or simply take a large three-ring notebook and divide your business plan into separate segments using titled dividers. Your business plan should already have identified these segments, but you might want to modify them a bit. Here is a list of the most common areas:

### Treasure Tip

Sweat equity is the hard work you pour into your business, which results in equity value. It's like buying a home and doing some of the remodeling yourself. The work you do actually increases the value of the house and, in this case, your business.

➤ Product/service development

➤ Marketing

➤ Management/personnel

➤ Administration

➤ Financial

➤ Competition

Every business is different, and your segments will be different from mine. Just make sure you cover what's important to you. Within each segment, include the business plan copy that corresponds to that segment. You can even use different color tabs to break down each area's heading into other additional segments. Marketing could be further divided into pricing, target market, publicity, and advertising. Each segment should include at least these four basic items:

1. Corresponding business plan copy

2. Goals in process, including the plan to achieve them

3. Future goals (ideas to consider in the future)

4. The systems or procedures that run each part of the operation

If you will take the time to maintain this working business plan, you will keep your business and your life on track. You'll also escape the inevitable overwhelming feeling that keeps most business owners running in circles.

The ultimate goal is to work on your business, not in it. First, you design the systems that run the business. Second, you hire the appropriate staff to run the systems. Only then will you be able to focus on strategic planning.

**Treasure Tip**

Maintaining your business planner on computer will enable you to update and modify your plan more conveniently.

# Systematize Your Business

After you have designed your business planning notebook, you need to take time each month to build the assembly lines or systems that make your business run successfully. If you take the time to do this, your business will not only run more efficiently, but also it will be better positioned to expand and grow. This in turn will help you build your wealth much more quickly.

Every business is different, but there is always some type of assembly line. My assembly line produces diversified portfolios and financial plans for my clients along with quarterly statements, monthly newsletters, and client memos. Each of these products is assembled using a separate assembly process. My responsibility is making sure my assembly lines run as efficiently and effectively as possible. One way to do this is to make sure my employees fully understand their roles in this assembly process. These assembly lines are also called systems, and they are the basic framework that all businesses are built upon.

### That Reminds Me...

Why do you think a little local hamburger franchise such as a McDonald's location can sell for as much as $1,000,000? Sure, the profit margins are great, but I think the main reason is that the systems and procedures are so efficient and well maintained that anyone can manage the franchise. Every task in that franchise, from pouring a drink to turning off the lights at closing, is written down and delegated to an employee. That's what your goal should be. You should develop a procedures manual within your business plan notebook that everyone in your company can see and improve upon every day. That's what it takes to build a successful, profitable, and sellable business today.

Your job as a business owner initially is to identify and build your own systems. These systems must be designed and written in the form of a systems or procedures manual. This working manual must coincide with your business planning notebook (or computer file). Every segment of your business has certain procedures that make up the assembly line of your business. These procedures are initially developed out of goals that you set. Here are the steps to developing a procedure:

1. Focus on your goals or your biggest frustrations that you'd like to see eliminated.
2. Brainstorm the tasks necessary to achieve the goal or eliminate the frustration.
3. List the necessary tasks and resources you'll need.
4. Prioritize the tasks; develop the procedure.
5. Implement and test the procedure.
6. Measure the results.
7. Improve the procedures.
8. Implement and test the tasks again.
9. Measure the results.
10. Continue to improve the procedure as technology allows.

This process goes on forever. Any business not dedicated to constant improvement is doomed. Eventually, someone smarter will come along with a concept that is just a little improvement on your basic product or service. He or she will kick your rear end right out of the game with some simple, stupid idea that you should have come up with in the first place. How do you prevent this from happening? Develop a procedure for constant product or service improvement, and dedicate yourself to enforcing it on a regular basis.

Written procedures do more than help you run your business. They will

➤ Enable you to develop new products and services.

➤ Enable you to train new and promoted employees.

➤ Help you find procedures you can outsource.

➤ Help you find ways to automate your business.

➤ Enable you to see inefficiencies in your business.

➤ Enable your employees to cross-train each other.

➤ Make your business more attractive to potential buyers one day.

Once the procedures are built, you must focus your efforts on making them as efficient and effective as possible. You can't do this alone. This is best done with your employees. If you have no employees, get a friend, spouse, or supplier to help you. You can also call on other business people in your industry.

The next step is delegating all the procedures you can so you can focus on the most important ones. The key is to find the right employees who are responsible enough to take the ball and run with it. You don't want employees who just do the task; you want associates who are eager to help you improve your mouse trap. One way to do this is to reward them with extra bonuses. This can be done individually, but it's best if you reward your whole team of employees. Any innovation or new idea that you implement can help your business for years to come. It's worth the expense.

## Focus on Marketing

You must focus on building your business, especially in the first several years. If you don't sell anything, you don't make any money. If you don't make any money, you can't save any money. The value of your business will decline as well as your wealth. Therefore, the most important segment or procedure of your business is marketing. Your business must have a marketing plan or procedure that you know will bring in business. How do you develop one? You follow the steps to building a procedure that were listed earlier.

The whole idea of marketing is to identify your target market and find the most cost-effective way to sell to it. This is done by testing your approach or advertising. Continue testing until you find an approach or ad that works. Once you find one that works, use it, but don't stop trying to improve it. You must continue the process. If you stop improving, your market will change and you'll miss out.

**231**

### That Reminds Me...

When I began teaching my "No-Load Funds—How to Build an All-Star Portfolio" work-shops, attendance was great, but after two years, it declined. I renamed it "No-Load Funds—Top-Picks for 1994." Attendance rose but fell off after a year. My associate Sharon, a registered investment advisor, came up with "How to Manage a Large Portfolio." Atten-dance rose, and attendees were better qualified with more money to manage than in any of my other workshops. That title helped my company's gross income grow more than 70 percent that year. Other money management firms heard about our growth and began using the title. Little did they know that an advisor in Little Rock, Arkansas, came up with the idea. Thanks, Sharon!

## Ten Marketing Questions You Need to Ask Yourself

Your marketing efforts are vital to the value of your business and therefore your wealth. The following is a list of marketing questions for you to think about. They will enable you to develop your marketing procedure:

1. Can you explain and identify the demand for your product or service?
2. Who is your competition?

### Treasure Tip

An advisor once told me that at least 50 percent of every business expense dollar should be spent on marketing and advertising during the first few years of business. His advice helped me increase my gross income more than 100 percent per year for the first four years.

3. What are the distinct characteristics of your product or service?
4. Who exactly is your target market?
5. Where does your target market live?
6. How will you determine the price?
7. How will you advertise and get the message out?
8. How will you test your advertising on a small scale?
9. Can you describe in detail your advertising budget for the first year?
10. How will you deliver your product to your customer?

# When Things Go Wrong

Things are going to go wrong occasionally no matter how smart or hard you work. It's how you handle the problems that makes you a good or bad business person. The wealthiest people I know seem to expect mistakes to happen occasionally. They learn from every mistake they make and do whatever they can to avoid letting it happen again. You have to accept the fact that you will have failures in your business. No matter how much you plan, things are going to go wrong. If you're not experiencing some failure on a regular basis, you're probably not trying very hard to succeed. As a business owner, you are under the constant threat of sudden changes in the economy, competition, customer needs, and employee needs. You can take some preventative measures, but you still have to be ready for surprises.

How do you plan for things to go wrong? How do you prepare for it? First, imagine the worst things that could happen in your business. Sit down and design measures that could prevent these things from happening. Second, develop a "damage control plan." The following is a damage control plan I designed to use when things go wrong. Every problem is unique and every question may not apply, but it's a start:

**Treasure Tip**

My employees are fantastic problem solvers. They come up with some of the best ideas. Each of them is unique, and they all see the business in a different light. I encourage them to think creatively, and I try not to be judgmental. The results have been outstanding.

➤ Separate the symptoms from the true problem.

➤ Describe the exact underlying problem in detail.

➤ What are the true obstacles?

➤ What elements can or cannot be controlled?

➤ How will you change the things you can control?

➤ What are the possible solutions? (List at least 10.)

➤ Prioritize the best solutions and implement the best.

➤ How can you prevent this from happening again?

If you want some creative ways to solve your problem, get your employees involved. They may come up with ideas that you haven't even considered. If you don't have any employees, get a group of your friends or even your best customers if you have to. Don't give up without getting some ideas from other people.

If you have a cash-flow problem, you'll want to immediately preserve all cash. This can be done by pushing back payables, postponing expenses, expanding your line of credit, and giving customers discounts for early payment. Visit your banker immediately if you have to. If your banker is smart, he'll help you get through your problem. If the problem continues, examine all your expenses and cut back where you can. If you have to sell off assets to survive, do so. You could also ask your employees for help by allowing you to postpone payroll. They might be willing if the alternative is a layoff. You could also offer equity in your business as a partial substitute for salary.

## Give Yourself a Break

If at all possible, make yourself take breaks. If you are excited and on fire about your business, you must take some time off for yourself and your family. The wealth-building process requires a lot of motivation and creativity. The richest man in the world on his death bed would trade all his wealth for another pain-free and peaceful week of life. The cemeteries are full of wealthy business men and women who worked themselves to death. To maintain your motivation and creativity, you have to take time out from your business.

When I started my business, I lived across the street from my office in a 500-square-foot apartment. For four years, I spent day, night, and weekends at my office working. My friends almost forgot about me. If it weren't for my desire to stay in shape and work out, I would have never left my office except to sleep or eat. Looking back, I could have been a bit more productive if I had taken a little time to relax. I simply felt guilty for not working. I had made a commitment to myself to be the best money manager in the state of Arkansas, and I knew that not one of my competitors was willing to work as hard as I did. I accomplished my mission, but I almost lost my soul, and that would have been tragic. Don't let this happen to you. Give yourself permission to take some time off occasionally. Spend that time in a relaxing atmosphere where you can rejuvenate yourself.

**Treasure Tip**

Most business owners think that if you work hard all the time, you'll eventually be successful. This is not true! You have to work smart. This implies a lot of thinking and planning. Thinking and planning require time and a peaceful, relaxed mind. Without either of these two, your business cannot prosper. Therefore, don't forget to take some time out.

## What's Really Important?

Don't do what I did during the first five years of my business. My business is my favorite hobby, and it was easy to lose myself in it. Unfortunately, I lost a lot of friends in the process because I was never around for them. When I was with them, all I could talk about was my business. You could not have met a duller person in your life!

No matter how excited you are about your business, it's not worth trading your family or soul for it. Don't lose sight of your priorities in life. First, you must live your life from your soul—not your business. Your business is not your life. If it is, you will die a dull, unsatisfied human being. Yes, it's great to work smart and hard on your business, but it would be a tragedy to lose your soul in the process.

Second, you must take time for your family. Don't use your business as an excuse to get away from what should be much more important to you. If your business is an escape, you may end up a successful business person, but you may lose something more valuable.

### That Reminds Me...

The author and lecturer Stephen Covey told a story in one of his speeches about a man who approached a lumberjack who was sawing a log with a big hand saw. The lumberjack was sweating, panting, and sawing like crazy, but his saw was dull. He had made some progress, but at the rate he was going, he was probably going to be there all night sawing this log. The man asked the lumberjack, "What are you doing?" The lumberjack replied as he caught his breath, "I'm sawing this log." The man then asked, "Why don't you stop and sharpen your saw?" To which the lumberjack replied, "I can't. I'm too busy sawing."

## The 22 Most Common Mistakes Business Owners Make—Why Businesses Fail

I've spent a lot of time talking to wealthy business owners about why statistically so many businesses fail. You've heard all the pessimism regarding new businesses. They say that more than 90 percent of all new businesses fail. I've also been told that more than 95 percent of new restaurants fail. However, the human spirit never ceases to amaze me. Regardless of all these horrible odds, new businesses start up every day.

What you need to understand is that most of the businesses that fail do so for similar reasons. Knowing why they failed is important to someone who might be considering starting a new business. Here are the 22 most common reasons business owners fail:

➤ No clear goals or objectives.

➤ They don't dream big enough.

➤ Failure to plan or don't know how to plan.

➤ Not enough discipline to follow the plan.

➤ Can't manage their own attention.

➤ Not enough cash—cash-flow problems.

➤ Hiring bad employees.

➤ Forgetting to test on a small scale.

➤ Spending too much money personally.

➤ Spending too much money on the start-up.

➤ Starting a business just for the money.

➤ Not knowing how to work with a banker.

➤ Refusing to borrow money.

➤ Not testing a big-ticket item before buying.

➤ Making hasty decisions that could—and should—have been researched.

➤ Not making customer service top priority.

➤ Not listening to the customer and empathizing.

➤ Not listening to employees.

➤ Ignoring industry trends and new product developments.

➤ Starting a business in the wrong location.

➤ Letting the competition steal your market.

➤ Failure or the inability to delegate.

Don't get caught up in these traps. They are easy to avoid if you pay attention and plan properly. You may want to take each one and change it to a positive context. For example, you could take "Not listening to employees" and change it to "Listen to employees." Take this new list and pin it up somewhere. Who knows, it may help you avoid a lot of mistakes.

---

### The Least You Need to Know

➤ You must build a business planning notebook or computer file that allows you to set goals and make plans for their accomplishment, as well as the systems that will maintain them.

➤ Use the goals you set and the frustrations you feel to build a set of systems and procedures that will allow you to run your business more efficiently.

➤ Use these written procedures to delegate tasks to your employees so you can focus on strategic planning.

➤ Identify your target market and find the most cost–effective way to sell to them by constantly testing new ads and different approaches.

➤ Plan on things going wrong with a damage control plan that will help you identify the problem, solve it quickly, and prevent it from happening again.

➤ Don't work yourself into the grave; take a break from your work and sharpen your saw.

# Chapter 18

# Wealthy People Have Great CPAs

---

**In This Chapter**

➤ Why a CPA is vital to your wealth

➤ The IRS is here to audit; who ya gonna call?

➤ The importance of financial statements

➤ How to get the most out of your CPA

---

Behind almost every wealthy person is a great CPA. Almost without exception, every wealthy individual I've ever met had a CPA. Many business people still don't understand the value of a good CPA. I think it's because most people don't understand the value of measurement and accountability, which are vital to the success of a business. Most people think a CPA is someone who will fill out your income tax forms. However, a good CPA can do so much more than your taxes. She can help you solve problems, plan for your future, maintain financial statements, set goals, set up a financial plan, offer second opinions, and refer you to other professionals who can help you. CPAs are in essence the coach and statistician in the wealth game. Best of all, they can be like silent partners in your business venture, assisting you with difficult financial decisions. I just don't know how to run a business without one.

## How to Find the Perfect CPA

The best way to find the perfect CPA is to get references from friends or business owners like you. If you don't own a business, I still recommend working with a CPA who can help you start one if you decide to later. If you are just starting your business, ask someone who has a small, growing, non-competing business that's only a few years old. A few more sources of CPA references are family, friends, successful individuals, and the Yellow Pages.

Don't hire the first CPA you meet. Interview at least three in person before you make your decision. Here are some questions you might want to ask them:

➤ **Are you a licensed CPA?** If you want an expert in accounting, make sure your accountant is a licensed Certified Public Accountant or CPA with a permit to practice. You might even ask to see his or her license. You might also ask whether he has an undergraduate or master's degree.

➤ **What type of tax work do you specialize in?** You need a CPA who specializes in small businesses and tax work. You also need a CPA who understands the basics of corporations, partnerships, and investments.

➤ **How do you charge your fees? What is your hourly rate?** Every CPA is different. Most charge by the hour, but there are flat fees as well as fees based on a percentage of your return. I prefer an hourly fee for corporate work such as monthly financial statements and advising, but a flat fee for preparing tax returns.

**Wealth Warning**

You may want to hire a CPA who has experience in your field. However, if at all possible, don't do business with your competitor's CPA.

**Treasure Tip**

You might want to call your state's Board of Public Accountancy, who can tell you whether your prospective CPA is certified and has a permit to practice. You might also want to ask whether there have been any complaints filed on her.

➤ **If I hire you, would you or someone else prepare my tax return?** If you are hiring a CPA, you want that CPA doing your work. It may not be a big deal to you, but at least have your CPA review the work if it's done by others.

➤ **How long have you been in business?** Make sure your CPA has been a practicing accountant for at least five years and has experience in start-up and fast-growing businesses.

➤ **How many employees do you have? CPAs?** It's nice to know how much depth your CPA's firm has. Does she have a qualified support team? Do any other CPAs work at the firm?

➤ **How accessible will you be for me?** This unfortunately might have to be a judgment call. You may never know how accessible your CPA will be until you need her. Ask her what she's doing to make herself available.

➤ **What percentage of your clients had to file extensions last year?** If the answer is more than 20 percent, the CPA probably has too much going on to take care of you. There may be a legitimate reason, so ask why. Her clients might have procrastinated and not sent their information in time.

➤ **How can you help me reduce my tax burden?** This may seem like a silly question, but it's a great way to see exactly how the CPA thinks. You might even ask about how she's helped her other clients reduce their taxes.

➤ **Will you furnish me with a letter of engagement?** The *letter of engagement* will list in detail all the services that will be performed for you, as well as the fees that will be charged.

➤ **Ask yourself whether this person is a good listener.** It really bugs me when people don't listen to me. What I really enjoy is someone who not only listens, but also empathizes with me. I want my CPA to do just that. I want her to put herself in my shoes for a minute so she can better understand my situation. Will your CPA do that? If not, find someone who will.

➤ **Will you furnish me with a list of client references?** If the CPA is unwilling to furnish you with a list of client references, scratch her off your list. Once you do get references, call them and ask them what they like and dislike about the CPA. Ask them how accessible she's been.

**Words of the Wealthy**

A **letter of engagement** is a prepared statement by the CPA that outlines in detail what he will do for you. The letter should also illustrate how the CPA will be compensated and at what rate.

**Treasure Tip**

Ask the prospective CPA for a list of client references. Call each one and ask how accessible the CPA has been for them.

## Measuring Your Way to Wealth

I've learned that whatever is systematically measured seems to improve. Whenever I pay close attention to my financial statements, I see my weaknesses and I begin to focus on ways to improve my company. It's a natural tendency. If you don't get a chance to see your company financial statements on a monthly basis, you might be putting your head in the sand. If you want a successful company, you must measure your success at least every month. You can do this yourself with financial software, have someone in your office do it for you, or hire a CPA.

I chose the last option. Why? First, CPAs are Orville Redenbachers. They do one thing, and (I hope) they do it better than anybody; at least they do it better than I do! I want someone who single-mindedly focuses on tax planning and financial statements. Second, there are too many tax code changes to keep up with yourself. Third, it's better to have someone outside your firm measuring your success. I think he will be objective and unbiased. Fourth, if you'll pay a CPA to do what he does best while you continue to do what you do best, you'll both make more money in the long run. Fifth, most creditors require audited financial statements prepared by a CPA. Your basic set of financial statements should include

➤ Income statement (profit and loss statement)
➤ Balance sheet (assets, liabilities, and equity)
➤ Cash-flow statement

## That Reminds Me...

If you expect to build your wealth through your business, you need to understand the basics of financial statements. Take advantage of classes available at your local university. Some local banks also offer similar classes on cash management. If you can't find a class, go to the bookstore for help. This can be a boring subject, but it is vital to your success in business. If you can't read a financial statement, you won't know how well your company is performing.

A full service CPA can also help you with additional services and measurements such as

➤ Pro-forma financial statements
➤ Financial ratio analysis
➤ Personal financial statements
➤ Financial statement forecasting
➤ Depreciation schedules
➤ Payroll management
➤ Business valuation

In fact, a good CPA will teach you how to read and understand all of these statements. If you have a good understanding of financial statements, you can do your own financial statement forecasting using several software packages that are available:

**Profit Mentor** 3.0 ($495.00)
800-682-1908
Produced by Management Advisory Services, Seattle, WA.
Self-contained needing no additional software.
Windows version only.
30-day money-back guarantee.

**The Financial ToolKit** ($129.00)

800-966-7797

Produced by Money Soft, Phoenix, AZ.

Stand-alone DOS system—no Windows version available.

Self-contained needing no additional software.

30-day money-back guarantee.

If you don't understand financial statements or just hate working with them, it might be better to ask your CPA to do your financial statement forecasting for you. It's worth the money each year to have this done. This kind of forecasting has three steps. First, you make a few key assumptions such as future sales growth and expense projections for the next several years. Second, using financial statement forecasting software, you enter your assumptions as well as your last several years of financial statements. Third, you let the computer calculate the expected effect of the assumptions on your financial statements. If you don't like the desired effect, you can make certain changes in your assumptions. This kind of business forecasting not only allows you to find the optimal amount of sales growth for your company, but it also gives you the opportunity to project your company's profitability. Therefore, if you can do this successfully, you also are able to measure, project, and keep track of your wealth.

**That Reminds Me...**

Profit Mentor is an outstanding, comprehensive program used by many small businesses. According to Management Advisory Services, more than 163 small business development centers around the country currently use Profit Mentor software to help their start-up clients get funding from local banks. These centers are normally affiliated with local universities and colleges. Banks and other financial institutions are using Profit Mentor to teach their clients how to improve cash management systems. This in turn improves the chances for their clients' success and brings the financial institution more business.

# When the IRS Calls

When the IRS calls you to set up an audit, the first thing you're going to want is some help. You're going to need someone who knows your business as well as or better than you. Who's going to know you better financially than your CPA?

**Wealth Warning**

How do you prepare for an IRS audit? The best tool you have before, during, and after your audit is a good CPA who has been with you for years.

**Treasure Tip**

A business can report net income, and at the same time have a negative cash flow. Without cash flow, your business will probably go bankrupt over time. That's why I always remember the phrase, "Cash is king."

**Treasure Tip**

Be sure to review your financial goals with your CPA. If he's aware of your goals, he'll be more likely to come up with ideas that can help you achieve them more quickly.

Call your CPA and have him go over with you verbally what you can expect from an IRS audit. Discuss what you two can do together to make it less likely to happen and easier to handle if it does.

CPAs cannot do everything. If you need additional help in an audit situation, you might want to seek the council of a tax attorney with a lot of IRS audit experience. Find a firm with a good track record. Make certain that it has successfully defended clients who faced the IRS.

# Problem Solving

The most common problem business owners face in their first five years of business is cash flow. One of the single best solutions can be a good CPA. First, he can measure your cash-flow situation each month for you. Second, he can identify your problem faster using your company financial statements. Third, he can recommend ways to solve the problem quickly, and he can show you ways to prevent further problems.

The second most common problem business owners face is maximizing the profit margin (the profits of the business divided by the revenues, which is the key measurement of profitability). Business owners and investors have a common problem. Most investors don't know their portfolio's yearly return, and believe it or not, many business owners don't even know their profit margin. If they don't know their margin, they don't know whether they've maximized it either.

# Goal Setting

Many business owners don't think about using their CPAs when it comes to setting goals. They don't understand the value the CPA can add to the goal-setting process. Not only do CPAs prepare your financial statements, they also see things you don't. They have the capability of forecasting your financial success for you. Your CPA can help brainstorm and plan financial goals for your business. She can also help you achieve those goals by helping you monitor your progress each month.

# Basic Personal Financial Planning

Your CPA can be a great source of basic personal financial planning. If you are ever going to achieve Wealth Stage 3, 4, or 5, you must spend time maintaining your personal financial plan. The two obvious aspects of financial planning that a CPA can help you with are retirement planning and personal budgeting. Not all CPAs are good at this, but if you take the time to find a good-quality CPA, she can be instrumental in your wealth-building process, which must include budgeting and retirement planning.

Retirement planning is key to the wealth-building process and is simply a matter of planning to save and setting up the vehicle to save in. As a business owner, you can take advantage of one of the last great tax shelters—the qualified retirement plan. I discuss these further in Chapter 24, "The Last Word on Wealth." For now, it's important to know that your CPA can help you a great deal in deciding what plan is best for you and your company. If you don't have a retirement plan established, stop and do it now. Achieving Wealth Stages 3, 4, and 5 is almost impossible without one. Retirement plans are without a doubt the most common denominator among all the wealthy people I've met.

Budgeting is something most people naturally dread, but it can make you rich. A good CPA will help you budget your business expenses, as well as your personal expenses. Once he sets you up initially, you can monitor yourself or use the CPA for accountability. If you know someone is monitoring your actions, you might be more inclined to make improvements.

**Treasure Tip**

Your CPA could be a key ingredient in your wealth-building recipe. Be sure to ask her for help when you set up a budget or retirement plan. She may have some valuable ideas that you overlooked.

# Second Opinions

A good CPA is someone who knows you and your business and is willing to give you advice whenever you ask. During your wealth-building journey, you are going to be faced with many decisions. Some will be easy, and some will be difficult. Using a good CPA who knows your situation is like having a partner. Use this partner when you can to help you with the big decisions. My clients use their CPAs to help them with many different decisions. Here is a list of the most common:

➤ Business expansion

➤ Mergers and acquisitions

➤ Business deals with others

**Treasure Tip**

Your CPA may even be a good source of information regarding prospective employees. Because she works with other businesses, she may know of an employee who is looking for a promotion or other employment.

➤ Lease versus buy decisions

➤ Investment ideas and tax consequences

➤ Investment professionals

➤ Investment performance evaluation

## CPAs Are Well Connected

If you are serious about reaching Wealth Stages 4 and 5, you definitely need help from other professionals. Your CPA works with many other clients who have similar needs and problems. This can make him a great source of referrals. If you need help from other professionals, why not ask for a referral from your CPA? Be sure to ask for at least three referrals. Here is a list of different types of professionals your CPA should know:

➤ Investment advisors

➤ Investment brokers

➤ Financial planners (fee-only)

➤ Tax attorneys

➤ Insurance agents

➤ Bankers

## Helping You with Your Banker

Wealthy people have strong relationships with their bankers. Bankers are an excellent source of inexpensive capital that can be used to start or expand a business. Most business owners don't think of their CPAs when it comes to banking. However, the banker does. Anyone who's ever borrowed money from a banker knows that good, accurate accounting is important to a banker. Before you visit your bank looking for a loan, visit your CPA. Make sure your personal financial statement is up to date. Get him to help you with your loan proposal. Get your financial statements in order, and consider bringing your CPA with you when your banker wants to discuss your loan proposal.

**Treasure Tip**

If you decide to sell your business to retire or when you've achieved the wealth level you'd like, your CPA may know a potential buyer.

After you have started your business, you might also want to send copies of your financial statements each quarter to your banker—even if they're not required. This makes a banker feel good about you as a client.

# Your Corporate Setup

A CPA can do most of the initial framework involved in helping you decide how you want to legally set up your company. However, you might want to get additional assistance from an attorney who is experienced with the different ways to incorporate.

# Maximizing Your CPA Benefit

One of the best ways to minimize the cost involved in hiring a good CPA is to provide him with accurate and organized records. I know people who show up on the CPA's doorstep with a box of unorganized invoices and canceled checks. This is no way to run a business and no way to build wealth. Wealthy people keep their records organized and automate their accounting. Automate your business accounting from the beginning by utilizing one of the many accounting software packages available. Here is one:

> QuickBooks Pro ($149.95)
> 800-446-8848
> Produced by Intuit, Palo Alto, CA.
> Self-contained needing no other software.
> Windows 95 and higher and Mac versions available.
> 90-day money-back guarantee.

---

### The Least You Need to Know

➤ If you plan to build serious wealth, you need a great CPA to watch after your company's finances, keep up with tax laws, give you an objective opinion, and give you the opportunity to focus on what you're the best at so you can build wealth more quickly.

➤ Take the time to get to know your CPA and help him learn more about your business, and you'll have an inexpensive partner who can help you solve problems, plan for your company's future, and build your wealth to your desired level.

➤ Use your CPA to help improve your relationship with your banker by systematically offering copies of your financial statements, even if they're not required.

➤ Wealthy business owners automate the basics of their business accounting using one of the many accounting software packages available.

# Chapter 19

---

# Wealthy People Have Great Bankers

## In This Chapter

➤ How to establish good credit

➤ How to build the perfect loan proposal

➤ What to ask your banker

➤ What if your loan is denied?

➤ What if you can't pay off your loan?

Behind every great wealthy person is a great bank. To reach Wealth Stages 4 and 5, you almost have to have a good relationship with your banker. You're going to eventually need money to invest in your business, and bankers are the key to inexpensive money. All you have to do is pay yearly interest, which is usually offered at the most competitive rate available. If you go anywhere else for a loan, you're almost guaranteed to pay a higher rate. Therefore, you must make a habit of getting to know your banker. The wealthy people I know take their bankers to lunch, play golf with them, and invite them and their spouses to dinner parties.

Two things never seem to change in the business world:

1. Businesses need to borrow money to survive and be profitable.
2. Banks need to lend money to survive and be profitable.

If it's that simple, why are so many people turned down for loans? They don't understand how to borrow money from a bank. Bankers look for specific documentation before they can lend money. If you have the qualifications and know the documentation needed and how to present it, you should be able to borrow all the money you need.

A professor at my college taught me one thing I will never forget. He said, "Larry, there will always be more money chasing good ideas than good ideas chasing money." I consequently found out that he was right. There are many different sources of capital or money for your business venture. There are banks, venture capital firms, investment bankers, pension funds, insurance companies, and private placement firms. What you must understand is that some sources are more expensive than others. The least expensive is a bank loan. Banks don't usually ask for equity positions (ownership) in your company. All they want is interest paid on the loan and the principal paid back on a timely basis. The rate of interest they ask for is usually the lowest of all the sources. Therefore, a bank loan is the most efficient and cost-effective source of capital.

A good relationship with a banker who understands your company and your needs is key to your wealth-building success. A good relationship must include both financial and personal character. Your financial character is measured by your net worth as well as your proven ability to produce cash flow from your business. A good personality isn't enough to satisfy a banker. You must develop a track record of cash flow (actual profitability from your work). A large net worth also helps, but cash flow can be just as important. Fortunately, you can do this in your existing job before you start your business. Start keeping records of your own success and ability to produce results. Illustrate this for your banker before you start your company, and your chances of landing a loan are much greater.

## Good Credit Is Essential

What's the key to dealing with a bank? Good credit. The first thing you must have before you approach a bank is good credit. Establishing good credit is vital to the wealth-building process. How do you do it? Borrow money and pay it back on time. It's as simple as that! Make this a habit and never be late on a payment. The first thing a banker will want to know is how well you've done in the past regarding your ability to pay back loans on time. He finds out using a report called the *credit history*. This report will tell you (and your banker) about most of the loans you've had, as well as any late payments on bills or loans. Considering how important this report is, I suggest you get a copy before your banker does.

When you call a credit agency, don't get frustrated with the automated answering service. Stay on the phone until you get what you need. You can also write the agency and request your report. Be sure to give your complete legal name and Social Security number.

When your credit report arrives, review it carefully and look for anything that might be detrimental to your credit. If you see any discrepancies that might disturb your banker, write an explanation of your side of the story. Include all the facts, names, and dates. By law,

**Treasure Tip**

Without a good credit record, you can't borrow money to buy a car, home, or anything without paying exorbitant interest rates. A bad credit rating gone unattended will kill your chances of building wealth.

you can insert up to 100 words into your file at the credit agency. When your banker sees the discrepancy, he'll also see the explanation, which might calm his fears.

Here are the largest of the credit agencies:

**Experion**
National Consumer Assistance Center
P.O. Box 949
Allen, TX 75002-0949
800-682-7654
(They offer a free report once a year if you were denied credit within the last 60 days.)

**Equifax**
Credit Information Services
P.O. Box 105873
Atlanta, GA 30348
800-685-1111

**Trans Union Corporation**
P.O. Box 390
Springfield, PA 19064-0390
440-779-7200

If you cannot find a bank to loan you money after all this effort, find a family member or friend (with good credit) to co-sign the loan for you. This will enable you to re-establish your credit. Once you've paid off that loan without missing a payment, the bank will be more inclined to loan you money again.

## The Perfect Loan Proposal

You need money to start and maintain your business so you can expand and achieve Wealth Stages 4 and 5. Your banker needs to lend money, and all he wants is a client who can borrow money and pay it back on a timely basis. The best way to prove you can do that is by preparing a proper loan proposal. Your business plan should double as a loan proposal. Some of the segments will be more important to your banker than others. What will he be looking for? Here is a list of the five most important items:

➤ Your loan request and purpose.

➤ The collateral you have to back the loan.

➤ The amount of liquid assets you have available.

➤ Your personal and business cash flow, as well as corporate financial statements.

➤ Your own personal character.

These items can be presented several ways. It's best to include them all in your loan proposal. Let's take a look at each item.

First, the proposal must include a summary of the loan request and purpose, which can be a simple sentence. My proposal read, "WCI is requesting a loan of $100,000 for new office equipment, furniture, and additional working capital."

Second, you need to list your own personal and corporate *collateral* that can be pledged against the loan. The easiest way to do this is to provide a financial statement that summarizes your own personal assets, liabilities, and sources of income. All banks have a standard sheet that you can fill out or redesign on your computer. The bank will want to know what it has to fall back on if you can't pay your loan. Providing this list may seem weird to you the first time you do it, but it's part of the process.

Third, the proposal should list all the possible sources of liquid collateral that can be used to back the loan. This includes stocks, bonds, CDs, and anything of value. The bank will want you to personally guarantee the loan, which means that you are willing to pledge everything you have to pay off the loan.

Fourth, the proposal must include a cash-flow statement. This should be included in the financial statements of the proposal. This statement shows exactly how much cash your business generates as well as a projection of future cash flow over the next three years. You'll need to also illustrate your own past history of personal cash flow. The easiest way to prove this is to provide copies of your tax returns for the last three years.

You also need detailed financial statements, which include at least a balance sheet and income statement. These statements should include the past three years as well as projected statements for the next three years. Your banker will pay particular attention to the effect of your business operations on your corporate equity. This figure is calculated by subtracting your company's liabilities from its assets. She will also examine how you have balanced your assets and liabilities.

### Words of the Wealthy

**Collateral** is something of value that is pledged against a loan in case of default. When you list collateral such as furniture, equipment, property, or accounts receivable, you should also include documents that will verify the value of these items.

Fifth, you might want to offer a resume or biography of yourself along with character and business references, such as successful business owners you know, your banker, your CPA, and your largest suppliers.

You might want to include additional items such as copies of your personal and business credit reports. Call the credit agencies listed earlier in this chapter and request both. Your banker will be impressed that you took the time to get these for her.

The proposal should include a list of more than one source of repayment. Your banker will want to know whether there is any source of income other than your business that can be applied to payments if you have trouble.

Your business plan or loan proposal should also be considered a wealth plan. It is your ticket to the capital you'll need to build your business and ultimately achieve your desired wealth level. Be sure to prepare the best proposal you can, and always maintain it as a working plan.

## That Reminds Me...

When a bank takes care of you, don't forget them. It makes money from deposits as well as loans. Be sure to maintain a significant amount of your company's deposits in an interest-bearing checking account with that bank. You could use a brokerage firm money market account for a higher rate, but the marginal interest rate you'll make isn't worth spoiling your relationship with your banker. You might need to borrow more money later.

Use the following checklist for items you'll need before you build your loan proposal:

➤ Personal (and business) tax returns for the past three years.

➤ Articles of incorporation, bylaws, corporate resolutions, and partnership agreements.

➤ A detailed expense budget. (A personal budget will also help.)

➤ A detailed marketing plan, including a list of your top three customers or prospective customers. If applicable, be sure to ask for your customer's permission.

➤ Your competition and what makes you better.

➤ A personal resume for you and any partners you may have.

➤ Letters of recommendation (clients, previous employers, and so on).

➤ Proof of life insurance.

➤ Copies of your property titles.

➤ Copies of all your current bank and brokerage accounts statements.

Gathering these documents is a lot of work, but it will increase your chances of getting the loan you want under the terms you ask for. The less information a lender must ask for, the more credibility you'll earn. If you skimp on information, the banker might think you are trying to hide a negative aspect of your business or personal history. Bankers are more likely to make loans on a marginal transaction if the lender believes in the customer. Make certain your proposal is completely free of spelling errors and grammatical mistakes. The newest word processors are great, but they are no substitute for getting another person to look over the document for errors, especially if he is a good editor. The errors just might kill your chances of getting a loan. Hire an English teacher if you have to. They're inexpensive and will probably appreciate the extra work.

### That Reminds Me...

If you want additional help with your loan proposal, look for a software package called LenderPro. It's produced by Money Soft ($295, 800-966-7797) in Phoenix, Arizona. It is a stand-alone DOS system, and no Windows version is available yet. This self-contained program needs no additional software and comes with a 30-day money-back guarantee. It offers several amortization options and lets you create different funding scenarios, and the written text of your plan can be exported to word processing software such as Microsoft Word.

## Finding the Right Banker

The right banker can help you reach Wealth Stages 4 and 5. Notice I said *banker* and not *bank*. I prefer someone who can make a decision. The two bankers I use currently are the president and CEO of the bank. They can make any loan decision I bring to them. That's important to me. Most large banks don't like smaller businesses. They focus on medium- and larger-size companies. Smaller loans are usually delegated to the junior lending officers, where both inexperience and turnover can be problems.

### Treasure Tip

You can also ask your CPA for a bank reference. Ask him for the names of three bankers he knows and recommends.

The best way to find a good banker is to get recommendations from other successful small businesses in your area. Find at least three bankers. Stop by and introduce yourself. Tell them you are looking for a banker and that you will have a proposal soon to present to them. Get to know a little about them personally. Do they seem easy to talk to? Are they interested in you and your company?

### That Reminds Me...

When my company was nominated for Arkansas' Small Business of the Year, many different banks called me. What infuriates me is that they didn't call until my business was five years old. When my company and average deposits were much smaller, banks didn't care about me. I had to find a bank that could understand my needs as a small business owner, something larger banks never seemed able to do. I chose a smaller, growing bank that could identify with my situation. That bank was and still is Bank of Little Rock, and if you're lucky enough to have a banking relationship like mine, you'll understand the peace of mind it can give you.

## What to Ask Bankers

The banker you select will be a vital part of your wealth-building journey. Don't settle for the first one who says yes. Spend some time getting to know them. You're about to start a long-term relationship that could be beneficial for both of you. Get to know the banker as a person before you do business. Make sure you can communicate with him.

### Treasure Tip

Be sure to dress professionally when you meet and interview your prospective banker. Be candid and honest, and be yourself. Bankers want to do business with people with good character and integrity.

Once you have your loan proposal ready, set appointments with at least three bankers. Before you give them the proposal, get to know them as people. What are their interests? What do they enjoy about being bankers? Then, ask the following questions:

➤ **How much capital does your bank have?** A national bank can lend a customer only up to 15 percent of its capital. Some states will allow their banks to loan as much as 20 percent of their capital. If the bank has only $500,000 in capital, it can only lend you $75,000. This might be enough now, but what about later? Will the bank be large enough next year for your needs?

➤ **What is your bank's capital ratio?** *Capital ratio* is the ratio of capital to assets, and it measures a bank's strength and availability of capital. Make sure your bank's ratio exceeds 6 percent. A ratio lower than 6 percent might mean the bank is having some difficulties.

**Words of the Wealthy**

A bank's **capital ratio** is calculated by dividing the bank's capital by its total assets. This ratio measures the bank's availability of capital, as well as its financial strength.

➤ **What is your non-committee loan limit?** This is the amount of money your banker can approve without presenting your loan to a committee. I don't like committees and prefer to deal with bankers who can approve my loan. If you need a great deal of money, you may have no choice. You want to deal with a banker who can approve a significant amount of money.

➤ **What is your loan-to-deposit ratio?** All banks are required to publish this ratio in the local paper every quarter. If your bank's loan-to-deposit ratio is less than 50 percent, you may be dealing with a bank that's too cautious about

lending money. They would rather invest in government and municipal bonds, federal funds, and items other than loans because those securities offer less risk. Make sure your bank has a loan ratio exceeding 50 percent. A ratio above 50 percent shows that your bank is eager to make loans. That's the kind of bank you want.

➤ **Has your bank recently merged with a larger bank?** Avoid banks that have merged with larger similar-size banks. The confusion, disturbance in job security, and chances of your getting a different loan officer are too great to worry about.

➤ **Does your bank have areas of emphasis or expertise?** Some banks specialize in consumer loans and some focus on business loans. Some banks do a lot of business with a particular industry such as real estate. Knowing this about your prospective bank might give you some insight into how well the bank might be able to serve your credit needs.

**Treasure Tip**

Be sure to ask your prospective banker whether he and his bank are accustomed to working with small companies. Prove it to yourself by asking for a small company client reference and calling it.

➤ **Can you give me a list of client references?** This might completely blow your banker's mind, but you need to know what other people think about him and the bank. Even if you were referred to this bank by a friend, you might want to do some of your own research. Ask for clients who also have small businesses who can relate to your needs and concerns. When you call the references, be sure to have some specific questions ready. Use as a guide the questions in Chapter 9, "How to Find Help." If the banker refuses to call any of his clients to ask whether they mind being a reference, go to another bank. Don't waste your time with that bank.

## Dealing with Rejection

The wealthy people I know didn't build their wealth by being timid or shy. They were tenacious in their efforts, and when they were faced with a no, they continued to look for a yes. If you get turned down by a banker, ask why and try to correct the problem. Then, resubmit the proposal. Make sure the problem isn't bank related. If they give you a vague answer, ask them to be more specific. If they continue to be vague, don't do business with them. They might be having some problems of their own.

Don't give up. Go to several banks, and present your proposal. After my own bank turned me down in 1994, I presented a proposal to four other banks and got four offers.

In my fourth year in business, my banker made the mistake of telling me over the phone that he wouldn't even consider helping me structure a $100,000 bank loan to expand my business. This was a complete surprise to me. It just didn't make any sense. I had been with this bank for several years and had, in a timely manner, paid off all my loans except for my company car loan, which I was still making payments for. Well, I took it personally, which was wrong, but it sure motivated me to shop around at other banks. I presented my loan proposal to four other banks, and all four wanted to loan me the money (structured the way I wanted). I picked Bank of Little Rock and paid off the five-year loan within two years.

This is not the end of the story. Three months after the first bank refused to consider my loan request, I called to draw on my $20,000 line of credit, which was still at the first bank and had been in force for two years. When I called, the teller said that my line of credit had been canceled. I called the same guy that turned me down for the loan and said, "Can you explain why my line credit has been canceled?" He replied, "Well, I assumed that you were going to another bank, so I canceled it." The bank canceled my line of credit without even sending me a notice. However, good things come from bad, and this story does have a happy ending. I called my new banker and told him I needed a $40,000 line of credit. He said, "Come by now, and we'll have the paperwork ready for you." I just love these guys, and they love my company. Don't be discouraged if the bank initially tells you no. Find one that wants your business.

## What If You Can't Make Your Payments?

Wealthy people will do whatever takes to make their loan payments. However, occasionally, you can experience unexpected problems. Fortunately, bankers understand this. They're human too. If you see a potential problem with your cash flow and you don't think you can make a payment, immediately sit down with your banker and explain to him the problem—and emphasize that you want to pay off the loan as soon as you can. Ask him to work with you on a new payment plan.

Your banker doesn't want to foreclose on your loan. It might completely blow his chances of your paying the money back. Therefore, he may be willing to do all he can to help you. Ask for an extended payment plan or a lower interest rate. Do whatever it takes to pay off the loan. Bankruptcy should not be an option. Filing for bankruptcy will haunt you for the rest of your life. No bank or lending institution will ever look at you the same way again.

---

### The Least You Need to Know

➤ Before you do anything, make certain you understand your credit history and that you have good credit.

➤ The key to getting yes from a banker is a great loan proposal.

➤ When building your loan proposal, it's best to be thorough and honest.

➤ The perfect loan proposal will tell the banker about your credit history, the collateral backing the loan, your cash flow, the amount of liquid assets, and your personal character.

➤ Submit the loan proposal to several banks, but be sure to get to know the banker by asking the right questions and talking to some of her other clients.

➤ If your loan is denied, do what other wealthy people do and don't give up; find out why, solve the problem, apply again, and consider other bankers.

---

# Chapter 20

# Find Great Talent

---

### In This Chapter

➤ Considering the outsourcing option instead of hiring

➤ How to increase profit margins

➤ Where to find the best employees

➤ Why you should consider paying your new employee a little more than he expects

➤ How to design a net bonus program

---

This chapter has the single greatest potential for catapulting your business forward into profitability. That means that this chapter also has the greatest potential for getting you to Wealth Stages 4 and 5. I know this from experience. My employees have empowered me and my business to grow faster and more profitably than almost all of the money-management firms in the U.S. My profit margins currently exceed 60 percent. The goal was originally to exceed 50 percent. How did we get to 60 percent? This chapter will give you the answer. It wasn't just one strategy that got us there; it was a combination of tactics that my employees and I implemented together along the way. I could not have done it without them.

## Hiring Versus Outsourcing

Before you run out and hire someone, ask yourself first whether you can outsource the work. Outsourcing allows you to hire the best without taking them on your payroll. For example, unless you are a CPA, you're going to need accounting work done for your business. Instead of hiring a CPA and putting him on your payroll, you can outsource your accounting work by paying an independent CPA to do the job for you. Look at every procedure of your business and ask yourself whether it can be outsourced. Then, find someone willing to do the work. You can find help from

➤ Temporary services

➤ Employee leasing companies

➤ Vendors who offer help

# Keep Payroll Costs Under Control

Don't forget that you need to make money in your business, and if you want to make money, you must know how to control your biggest fixed cost, which is probably payroll. One other thing you need to be aware of before you hire is your total payroll costs. Many business owners hire what they think they need well before they look at the budget for payroll. The inevitable result is a poor profit margin or a layoff. Establish a goal to keep your payroll costs at or below 25 percent. My definition of payroll costs includes salaries, payroll taxes, and insurance costs for all employees (excluding you). I've let my payroll exceed 25 percent temporarily as I hire someone new, but within six months, it returns to the 25 percent mark.

# Become a Headhunter

Building wealth using your business is directly tied to the capacity of work your employees can handle. The amount of work they can handle is directly tied to their desire to achieve company goals. The level of desire they have will depend upon their passion for the business and their belief that if they work hard in your company, they can achieve their own personal goals.

How do you find the right employees for your business? First, you have to decide exactly what you are looking for in an employee. Using great detail, describe the best employee you could hire. Write this down before you begin your search. This will help you keep in mind what kind of person you want to hire.

**Treasure Tip**

If you can get payroll costs under control, you are well on your way to being more profitable and wealthier.

Second, look at your competitors and suppliers for possible employees. These people know your industry better than anyone off the street. Their experience will greatly reduce the amount of training they will need. If they are really good at what they do, they'll be known by all the primary business people in your industry. This means that you can ask others (in confidence) about these people before you hire them.

# Ask for Referrals

If you don't specifically know anyone in your industry whom you can hire, ask key people you know for referrals. Explain exactly what you are looking for. Ask who the best candidate would be.

### That Reminds Me...

After one year in business, I asked around in my industry and found out that the best support person in the state was unhappy with her employer. Her name is Linda, and I had worked with her before for over 4 years. I knew she was the best in the office, and it would be a coup to have her on board with my company. I called her and asked her to come in for an interview. She later accepted my job offer and has been working with me for over 7 years.

# Find the Dissatisfied

If you have to, visit other similar companies or get your friends to visit and ask around. Find out who might be unhappy with their current position. Look for someone who wants a bigger challenge and more responsibility.

### That Reminds Me...

When I need a new employee, I ask a few key people to "bird-dog" for me. In fact, I myself become a bird dog. A bird dog is a dog on a mission. He has one thing on his mind—birds, birds, birds. He'll go without food, without water, and without sleep just to get a chance of seeing a bird. If you're looking for a key employee (all of mine are), you stand a better chance of getting a good quality person by doing some sniffing around. It may take time, and you have to be patient. Great employees don't grow on trees. The best ones are loyal and slow to leave their current employer.

# Exceed Your Employees' Expectations

Wealthy business owners know the value of paying employees a little more than they expect. It's a great way of telling your new employee that she is worth the extra money. This not only builds self-confidence in the employee, it also builds loyalty and trust. Show me a company with loyal, trustworthy, and confident employees, and I'll show you a wealth-building machine. If at all possible, pay your new employee a little more than he expects. First, find how much you can afford to pay him. Then, ask exactly what he needs. You want to find the smallest amount of salary he needs to feel comfortable coming to work for you. If he is really excited about working for you, he will probably give you a relatively low figure to begin with. Once you've established this amount and you're ready to hire him, offer him a little extra and tell him it's because he's worth it. If you've really done your homework and you're face to face with a great potential employee—it will be worth the extra salary to get the talent. The little extra could be a net bonus program.

# Establish a Net Bonus Program

Wouldn't it be nice to get your employees to focus on things such as expenses and profit margins? If you've been in business at all, you know how tough this is to accomplish. The secret is a net bonus program. A net bonus program is an incentive pay program based upon a certain percentage of the net income from your business. It is the key to motivating your employees to help achieve your company (and therefore your wealth-building) goals.

The first bonus program I installed was based upon gross income. This motivated my employees to grow, but they had no incentive to spend money efficiently. During our weekly meetings, they had little interest in saving money. All they could think about was growth. The day I changed the bonus program to be based upon net income, the entire company changed! My employees instantly became interested in reducing overhead expenses. It was like magic. Suddenly, they thought like I did. They became interested in reducing every expense they could find. They also began to take more of an interest in planning for the company's future.

It's imperative for you to understand how powerful this concept of a net bonus is for your business. I will never run a business again without it. Overnight, it can change your business forever.

The easiest way to calculate net bonuses every month or quarter is to build a computer spreadsheet that can calculate it for you. Once your monthly financial statements are produced, all you have to do is enter the data, and, presto, you have everything done.

**Treasure Tip**

I give my employees 15 percent of my company's net income. This lump of money is then divided and distributed according to each employee's percentage of payroll.

The net bonus program is designed to allow your employees to share a predetermined percentage of your net income. Once you have decided upon the percentage and calculated the net bonus total, you then divide the bonus dollars according to each employee's percentage of payroll. Half is paid immediately, and half is placed in a pool to be distributed at the end of the year. However, an employee must still be employed by the end of the year in order to receive the other half.

You should include all employees in your bonus program. However, there should be an initiation period for new employees. Mine is currently six months. All new employees must wait six months before they are placed in the bonus program. Here's how I calculate my bonuses:

**Operating Income**

| | |
|---|---|
| Subtract | **Overhead expenses** (minus depreciation) |
| Subtract | **Loan payments** (for capital expenditures) |
| Subtract | **Money for cash reserves** ($2,000, for example) |
| | **Net Income** |
| Multiply by | 15 percent |
| | **Net bonus amount** |
| Multiply by | 1/2 |
| | **Immediate bonus** |
| Multiply by | **Percentage of payroll** = Employee's bonus |

# Delegate and Succeed

Most wealthy people will tell you that delegating is initially difficult to get accustomed to. However, if you can do it successfully, you dramatically increase your chances of achieving Wealth Stages 4 and 5. It took me several years to understand this concept. It wasn't a natural transition for me. During the first few years of my business, I had to do just about everything myself. Slowly, I recognized the need for help and began looking at all the options. I could hire someone without experience for little money, but I would have to train them. This would take time. Therefore, I decided to spend more money and get someone with experience—someone who could walk right in and go to work. I hired the best person in the state and began delegating all my administrative work to her. This lady turned my

**Treasure Tip**

Do all you can to make your company an exciting and fun place to work. The results will amaze you. Your employees will be more efficient, effective, and loyal.

business around. The day I hired the best employee in the state and began to delegate work to her is the day my company's growth took a turn upwards.

The lesson that I learned is that you can't do it alone; you need help. In the early years of starting a business, you are a manager of activities. Soon, you have to hire help, and you become a manager of activities and people. Eventually, you become a manager of people. If you want to increase your business to any significant size, you must become a manager of people. If this is the natural evolution of a business, wouldn't it be smart in the early years to focus your efforts on hiring the best employees? I say it's absolutely imperative.

Once you've hired the best, the next step is to build systems that can be operated by your employees. These systems or procedures are established ways of doing business. They should be written down somewhere, preferably in a computer so they can be easily updated and improved. These systems should be easy enough for any qualified employee to follow.

Once your business is operating this way, you'll have the necessary time you need to focus on strategic planning, which is really what you should be doing. The best book on this subject is *The E-Myth Revisited* and *The E-Myth Manager*, which are both written by Michael Gerber (HarperBusiness).

### That Reminds Me...

One day, I decided to start a newsletter for my clients. I asked my newest employee, Angie, if she would take on the project, and she gladly accepted. She had absolutely no experience and little guidance from me. I explained the concept, bought her software and training, and then got the heck out of the way. The result was incredible. Now, she is producing two newsletters at the same time. These are her babies, and she's darn proud of them; so am I. When you delegate a task, step back and let your employee figure it out.

# Match People and Jobs

When you hire, make sure the responsibilities you want handled are properly matched with the personality of the prospective employee. Ask your prospective employee what she really enjoys doing. Ask her about her strengths and weaknesses. Find out what she does best and make sure that it matches what you are looking for. If the person you need to hire is going to be in sales, find someone with excellent people skills. If you need an administrative person, make sure she enjoys working with numbers. This match game is an ongoing process, too. You have to stay abreast of your employees' personalities as they develop over time. Personalities do change sometimes, so be sure to meet individually with each employee on a regular basis.

# Truly Get to Know Your People

If you really want to build wealth through the growth of your business, you need to know each of your employees' personal goals and aspirations. If you care enough to help them achieve these goals, they'll be more loyal and dedicated to your vision. Help them and they'll help you. I don't believe in the traditional employee review meeting. Instead, I get to know the employee's own personal goals, and I help her accomplish those goals through the success of my company. If I can show my employee how she can accomplish her personal goal by accomplishing the company's goal, we have both won. There's no need for me to be a motivator. If my employee sees how her personal goal can be accomplished through the success of the company, then she'll naturally be motivated to produce. It's a simple concept.

# Conduct Regular Team Meetings

To build a successful and profitable business that can be sold later, you must hold weekly, monthly, and yearly meetings. Team meetings are vital to the success of a business. They hold together the people and the responsibilities of an organization. They develop and maintain a team spirit that is necessary for success. Weekly meetings should be how you monitor the progress of goals set each month. They shouldn't be any longer than one hour in length. The primary purpose of monthly meetings is discussing the results of each goal in progress and setting new goals. Monthly meetings should be an all-day event. Yearly meetings should be at least two days in length and should be held outside the office. The primary purpose of a yearly meeting is to set goals for the upcoming year.

The basic weekly and monthly meeting agendas should at least include

➤ Old business—Items from the last meeting that need attention.

➤ Goal review—Reviewing the status and results of current goals.

➤ New business—New goals and any other items to discuss.

➤ Calendar planning—Reviewing everyone's calendar.

The great thing about meetings in my firm is the "old business" section. This is a great way to keep everyone (including me) accountable for the

**Wealth Warning**

My last boss "met" us to death. Almost every day, there was a meeting. What made it worse is that he would lecture all of us for the mistakes of a few. We didn't deserve to be treated like that. I learned the value of a weekly meeting, as well as the value of one-on-one employee counseling sessions.

projects that should be in process. If the projects are in process too long, they should be eliminated, delegated, or tabled to later dates.

You must also encourage an open and flexible meeting where anything can be discussed. If your employees are intimidated or afraid to give their opinions, you may have problems for years before you ever see them. Your employees should be your greatest asset. Most employers don't realize their employees' full potential.

## Let Your Employees Contribute

The key to long-term business success and the wealth-building process is getting employees involved in helping you develop the company vision and then letting them run with it. Your role should be to manage and support these people. If you have a big vision, you need qualified, motivated help. The only way to get truly motivated help is to include them in your vision and in setting goals. The technical term for this type of management is participative management.

## Consider an ESOP

An ESOP is an employee stock ownership plan. It is used to give employees of private and publicly traded companies the opportunity to buy stock in a company over time. The employees become owners, which makes them feel more a part of the company. The owner gets motivated employees and an opportunity to sell his stock and raise cash.

All ESOPs require a legal document to set up the plan and trustee. A certain percentage of each employee's salary is expensed as a profit-sharing plan deduction and put into the plan to buy company stock.

Before you do anything, take some time to decide exactly what you want to accomplish with your ESOP. This decision should be your first step. Communicate these goals to your attorney before he begins designing the plan. There may be another way to accomplish your objectives without starting an ESOP.

Second, sit down with your employees and discuss what an ESOP can do for them. Get an attorney to help explain it if you have to.

Third, the ESOP plan must be written and designed properly by an attorney who specializes in these plans. Make sure the attorney is independent of any bank or institution. You want him to be as unbiased in this deal as possible. If he works for the bank, whose best interest will he serve first?

**Treasure Tip**

One of my mottoes in the office is, "If you're not making mistakes, you're not trying."

**Treasure Tip**

ESOPs have made many business owners very wealthy and could be your ticket to Wealth Stages 4 and 5.

Fourth, begin the plan and let it work for you. Your attorney can help you as things change.

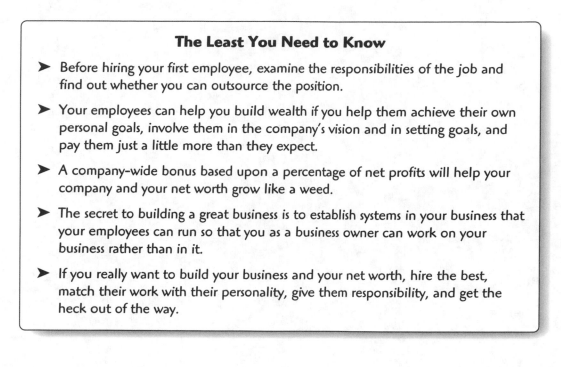

**The Least You Need to Know**

➤ Before hiring your first employee, examine the responsibilities of the job and find out whether you can outsource the position.

➤ Your employees can help you build wealth if you help them achieve their own personal goals, involve them in the company's vision and in setting goals, and pay them just a little more than they expect.

➤ A company-wide bonus based upon a percentage of net profits will help your company and your net worth grow like a weed.

➤ The secret to building a great business is to establish systems in your business that your employees can run so that you as a business owner can work on your business rather than in it.

➤ If you really want to build your business and your net worth, hire the best, match their work with their personality, give them responsibility, and get the heck out of the way.

# How to Sell Your Business

The techniques used to prepare a business to be sold should simultaneously build wealth and cash flow. When you build your business, why not focus on possibly selling the business at a later date? It's like getting a two-for-one deal.

As you know from Chapter 3, "The Five Stages of Wealth," you have achieved Wealth Stage 4 if the market value of your business would produce (after capital gains taxes) enough proceeds to build a portfolio sufficient to support and substantially increase the level of your lifestyle, while at the same time keep up with inflation. Regardless of whether you plan to sell your business in the future, if you plan to achieve Wealth Stage 4 using your own business, you need to understand the theory of preparing your company for a sale.

One of the benefits of owning your own business is the opportunity to build wealth at a much faster pace in relation to the traditional method of monthly investments in the stock market. Because the equity value of your business is tied to its growth and profitability, the key to building wealth is maximizing earnings growth. This not only makes you money, but it also makes your business worth more to a buyer. What I've learned is that what makes your business worth more to a buyer also makes you money in the process. Therefore, you should run your company as if you were going to sell it some time in the near future. Whether you can sell your business or not, you can at least save part of your earnings. If you actually sell your business in the future, your efforts will be further rewarded at the time of the sale.

This chapter will teach you how to build a company that will not only make you a lot of money, but will also make a buyer salivate.

# 23 Ways to Build Your Business and Get Rich

Are you ready to learn how to get to Wealth Stages 4 and 5? These are all common-sense measures to help you increase profits, build your equity value, and make your company more attractive to buyers. Every business is different, which means that a few of these might not apply to your situation. Therefore, use what you can and leave the rest:

1. **Maximize your profit margin.** Take steps to improve your earnings enough to produce a profit margin that exceeds industry standards. Your trade organization should have some data on this. This can be done two ways: cutting your overhead expenses and maximizing sales or gross income. Many business owners try to minimize taxes so much that they inevitably forget about profits. If you plan to sell your business, you need to focus on maximizing profits because that's what the new owner is looking for. Eliminate anything that hides profits.

2. **Get audited financial statements.** Have your financial statements audited by a reputable CPA firm. The first thing a potential buyer will want from you is your company's financial statement. Accurate financial statements will build trust between you and your potential buyer. Plus, the buyer will want to have your statements audited anyway. Having them done in advance will save you a lot of time.

3. **Maximize sales and earnings growth.** Focus on maximizing your company's sales and earnings growth. Your goal should be to achieve a growth rate that exceeds industry standards. Call your trade organization and ask about the average sales and earnings growth rates in your industry. You might also ask who the most successful firms are in your industry. Call them and ask if you can visit in order to share ideas.

4. **Show the potential for more growth.** Build a case that illustrates for the new buyer more potential for growth in sales and market share. If your company dominates the market with a 60 percent market share, the buyer will be worried about the prospects for further growth. Show him how your market may be growing. Illustrate for him how he can achieve a 70 percent market share. Make it easy for him to visualize success.

5. **Design written systems and procedures.** If you and your employees take the time to design and maintain written systems and procedures, your company will

not only run more smoothly and efficiently, but also your prospects for a sale will greatly improve. Empathize with a potential buyer, and imagine yourself making a buying decision between two businesses. If everything else is held constant, except that one had a written procedures manual for all operations and all employee positions in the company, which one would you choose? You'd choose the company that can operate the best with the least supervision—the one with written systems and procedures that anyone can follow. That's every businessperson's dream.

6. **Clean house.** Do you find yourself cleaning your house prior to company coming over? Well, you need to do the same thing when prospective buyers start to visit. Implement a procedure to keep your facility as neat and tidy as possible. You might even consider painting or other improvements that might be attractive to a buyer. If it were your house on sale, what would you do?

7. **Smiling, happy people.** If you want to really impress your prospective buyer, show him a group of happy, enthusiastic, team-oriented employees. If you haven't taken the steps to create this, I suggest you do it now. You can't produce this overnight, but you can at least get started.

8. **Keep it confidential.** You might not want to tell your employees about your interest in selling. It could create unwanted confusion and fear. If your employees think they might lose their jobs as a result of a sale, they will immediately begin to look elsewhere.

9. **Always take time to plan.** Few people take time out to plan. They get so caught up in their work that they never have time to plan. It's like the lumberjack who was so busy sawing that he didn't take time to sharpen the saw. Every six months, my friend Ted and I escape to the wilderness and spend a day planning. What I enjoy the most is his enthusiasm in the planning process. This makes it easier and a lot more fun.

**Treasure Tip**

One thing my father taught me by example is that a clean and organized place of business is more attractive to the customer and more enjoyable for the employee. It also cuts down on injuries and the resulting insurance costs. Thanks, Dad.

**Treasure Tip**

Trade shows and conventions held for your industry are one of the greatest learning tools available to you. Few people understand their value. I asked an advisor friend of mine if he was attending the annual financial advisors convention sponsored by Charles Schwab & Co. He said, "No. I never really get anything out of those conventions." I said, "That's because you don't ask enough questions."

10. **Find the best at your business.** If you want to leap completely over your competition and experience exponential growth, find the best people in your business today and imitate them. Some people are reluctant to help others, especially if you are in their town. Therefore, focus on those who are out of your geographic area. Ask if you can visit with them about their business.

11. **Do what you love to do, and delegate everything else.** I covered this in Chapter 17, "Be Your Own Boss," and Chapter 22, "Taxes Made Easy," but it's important enough to repeat.

12. **Always have a big vision.** To build a better business, you must have a vision of what you want to build. This vision must be big enough to drive you and challenge you. I have found that if my vision is too small, it eventually bores me. However, if it's big and wonderful, I naturally become motivated. The only way you'll know whether your vision is big enough is to try to achieve it first. Remember to expect set-backs and to use the tools in Chapter 17 to get you back on track.

### That Reminds Me...

When I was young, my friend Brandon and I built a tree house. We spent weeks building what we thought was the best tree house in the world, and in our little world, it was the best! It was our escape. However, within a week, we got bored. We thought of all the things we'd do differently and all the things that needed improvement. We wanted a bigger, better house—so we built another and then another. It took me many years to understand the moral of that adventure. I learned that you must have a dream big enough to challenge you all your life. Otherwise, you end up building one tree house after another.

13. **Focus on what you're good at.** What are you better at than most people? What do others say you're good at? If you'll identify your strengths and use them, you might find yourself with a natural competitive advantage that will speed you on to success. If you're really good at something now, just imagine how competitive you'd be if you focused on improving that skill even more. Use your natural strengths to build your business and beat your competition.

14. **Eliminate the fear of failure.** Fear of failure will kill your business. You should always ask yourself, "What is the worst thing that can happen?" Next, you should

ask yourself, "Can I handle the worst thing?" If the answer is yes, then don't worry about it any more. Make plans to handle the worst thing, and then eliminate the fear.

15. **You must work hard.** The average executive work week is about 60 hours. However, if you have an exciting vision and a plan to achieve it, you might find yourself wanting to work more than 60 hours.

16. **Avoid negative people.** If you want to ruin your vision, spend time with problem oriented, negative, and jealous people. If you want to build a better business, focus your social efforts on associating yourself with positive people who are also success oriented. Successful business owners associate themselves with others who appreciate win/win relationships. They celebrate each others' victories and are eager to help after the defeats.

   The same is true with business relationships. If you know that a potential or existing client is going to be a problem in the future, you might want to give him to your competitor. Explain that you feel his objectives will be better served by the other company.

17. **Be an information sponge.** In today's world of computers, the Internet, and fast-paced business transactions, you have to keep track of changes. If you want to learn new ways to improve your business, you must become a Curious George and ask a lot of questions. You also need to be able to read a lot of information in a short amount of time. Where should you focus your attention? The following list gives the most common fast-paced changes that will affect your business:

    ➤ Improved computer systems that improve your efficiency

    ➤ Internet software that can connect you to your customer

    ➤ Changes in your industry and the economy

    ➤ Changes in the needs of the customer

    ➤ Changes in your competition

**Treasure Tip**

If you want to be an efficient information sponge, subscribe to *Audio-Tech Business Book Summaries* (800-776-1910). This company will provide you with written and audio cassette summaries of business books each month. A one-year subscription is $135 and worth every penny.

18. **Keep a good attitude.** If you want to build a better business, you must develop an air of confidence, enthusiasm, and humility. For example, if you try to make a sale with a fearful or hungry attitude, the prospective buyer will probably run away. You have to be confident in yourself, your product, and your business. You also have to be optimistic and see the opportunity in every problem you encounter.

271

19. **Focus on helping others.** Customer service is simply the art of helping others and exceeding their expectations. The most successful companies in the world don't try to merely meet their customer's needs; they try to exceed them. This should be part of your company's core policy. One way to start this process is to examine your marketing efforts. If you exceed the expectations of a prospective buyer, you increase the odds of his becoming a client. For example, after the first 12 months of my business, I changed my marketing focus from selling to teaching. The rewards have been outstanding. During the following three years, my company grew more than 100 percent each year. I changed my marketing to focus on helping others learn how to invest. The more I helped other people learn, the more my business grew. If every company understood this one single principle, the world would be a better place to live.

20. **Develop your genius.** Genius is not knowledge. My definition of genius is someone who can single-mindedly focus on one thing at a time. This might sound easy to you, but with all the hats you're going to wear as a business owner, it ain't easy! Make it easy on yourself, and don't do more than one thing at a time. If you have to leave the office to think, do it.

21. **You must be a decision maker.** First, ask yourself this question: "Am I a decision maker?" If your answer is yes, then proceed. If your answer is no, ask yourself this question again until your answer is yes. To be a good decision maker, you must understand two things. First is the principle of the worse-case scenario. As I said earlier in this chapter, if you can handle it, then don't worry about it. Second, list all the pros and cons of the decision. Weigh each alternative and select the best alternative. Accept the fact that you'll be wrong some of the time.

22. **Make sure you need it before you buy it.** Within six months of starting my own business, I spent more than $10,000 on software that I never used. I honestly thought I needed it, but when I narrowed my focus from financial planning to money management, the software became obsolete. This was an expensive lesson in planning. I could have spent that money on so many other things. It still drives me crazy to

### Treasure Tip

I learned a valuable lesson in customer service from the man who takes care of my laundry. Raymond is by far the most customer-service–oriented person I know. What's his secret? When I asked him, he replied, "Basically, what I do all day is try not to say 'no' to any of my customers."

### Treasure Tip

Any software package worth buying will offer you a trial period. If the software offers no trial period, I suggest you shop around for one that does.

know that I spent that much money on something that wasn't needed during a time when every penny counted. Learn from my mistake. Before you buy anything—especially a big-ticket item—think about it for a while and make sure you need it.

23. **Establish some barrier to entry.** Do whatever it takes to set up as many barriers to entry as you can. A barrier to entry is simply something that deters or prevents other people from competing against you. The best barriers are licenses, patents, copyrights, and professional degrees. If none of these apply to your business, then consider other tactics such as

   ➤ Advertise and dominate your market.

   ➤ Be willing to do what others won't do.

   ➤ Establish yourself in the local media as the expert.

   ➤ Establish an outrageous customer service program.

## Why Sell?

Everyone is different, and every business owner has his own reasons for selling. Your reason might be to build a liquid portfolio that would provide more than enough income for you to live—Wealth Stage 4. The most common reasons business owners sell their businesses (or a part of it) include the following:

   ➤ Retirement

   ➤ Desire to diversify into other businesses

   ➤ Need for additional capital to continue growth

   ➤ Strategic alliance with larger company, allowing economies of scale and new markets

**Treasure Tip**

Before you sell your business, make sure you're ready. Spend some time imagining what you'll be doing after the sale. What will your goals be? What will you want to do next? Do you want to continue working with the new owner?

## How to Value Your Company

To know when you've reached Wealth Stage 4 or 5, you need to know how your business is valued. Putting a price on a closely held business is a difficult process. To put it bluntly, the value of a business is equal to the most amount of money anyone is willing to pay for it. It's not like selling a house where you have comparable sales transactions within the same neighborhood. In contrast, sale prices of closely held companies aren't usually public information, and that makes the valuation process difficult. Therefore, you often have to calculate an estimate of fair market value based on vague criteria. The fair market value is only an estimate. In the end, the real value is whatever price the buyer and seller agree upon at the time of the sale.

Some business owners jump to the conclusion that their companies are worth 16 times their earnings, just like some companies traded on the New York Stock Exchange. They fail to recognize that publicly traded companies have several advantages over most closely held companies:

➤ Easier access to capital.

➤ Ability to use stock for acquisitions.

➤ Highly scrutinized financial reporting to the SEC.

➤ Diversified group of management and directors.

➤ The company's success doesn't rely on one person.

The most common methods of valuation involve mathematical models that take into consideration the company's assets, past and future earnings, industry outlook, strength of management, and uniqueness of the product or service. The three most common valuation methods are described in the following sections.

## The Asset Method

The easiest valuation method is the asset method. The asset method simply sums up the fair market value of the company's underlying assets minus the liabilities. This approach is considered best when valuing a company with significant tangible assets such as real estate and commodities. This is not a good valuation method for a service business with few tangible assets.

**Wealth Warning**

It is imperative that the companies chosen for comparison are in the same business and similar in size. Factors are used to compare each business with yours in order to come up with a price that's fair to both parties.

## The Market Comparison Method

The most common method of valuation is the market comparison method, which is similar to the methods used in valuing real estate. Using this method, the company's financial performance and operations are compared to other similar companies recently involved in a sale transaction.

Factors for comparison are ratios that divide the price of the company's stock with other financial numbers. The most common factor is the P/E ratio, or price to pretax earnings ratio. If you knew the average P/E ratio of the last five companies in your industry that were sold recently, you could easily multiply that average factor to your own pretax earnings to produce an estimated fair market price. You can do the same thing with these other common factors, if you have the following information about other companies that have recently been sold:

➤ Price/pretax earnings

➤ Price/cash flow

➤ Price/book value

Unfortunately, because privately held business transactions are not disclosed to the public, the financial information you need to make these comparable measurements is difficult, if not impossible, to find. However, you might find that your industry's trade organization keeps up with these factors. Maybe it can give you a rule of thumb. The alternative is to do the research yourself by calling the new owners of companies that have been recently purchased. Explain to the new owner that you don't necessarily need to know how much he paid for the business; you just want to get some relative measurements such as the ratios mentioned. You might even promise to share your ratios after you sell your company at a later date. Some business owners will cooperate, and others will not.

## The Discount Method

The third way to value a company is called the discount method or income capitalization method. This method is based upon estimating the present worth of the future financial benefits your company can offer the new owner. More specifically, this method calculates the present value of a company's expected future earnings over a certain period of time using a discount or present value factor. The calculation is complicated, which is another reason why you might want to get some help from a business broker or intermediary.

You'll also find that every industry has its own unique pricing methods. These are specific valuation measurements that others in your industry have used in past transactions. For example, the beer and soft drink industries both typically use the number of cases sold in a year to come up with an estimated value. They call this the price-per-case method. If a distributorship sold 500,000 cases last year, and the price-per-case factor is $1.25, the distributorship is worth approximately $625,000.

One final note on valuing your business: You can spend time valuing your own business if you like that sort of thing. However, a good CPA would be happy to do it for you.

## Who Can Help

You might ask the owners of businesses in your industry if they know of anyone who specializes in doing valuations of companies in your industry. If you have trouble finding someone, contact these folks:

Management Advisory Services
A Division of MOSS ADAMS, LLP
1001 Fourth Avenue, Suite 2700
Seattle, WA 98154-1199
Phone: 206-442-2600, fax: 206-233-9214

Corporate Finance Association of Northern California
Henry S. James, President
344 Village Square
Orinda, CA 94563
Phone: 510-254-9126, fax: 510-254-2160

# Finding a Buyer

Before you can sell your business and get to Wealth Stage 4 or 5, you must find a buyer
for your business. Buyers can be hard to find if you don't know the players in the
market. Even if you do know the players, will you know how to conduct the sale?
Selling a business involves complex valuation methods, tax considerations, and
strategic negotiations. Can you do all that alone?

➤ **There are people who can help you.** Depending upon the size of your business,
there are basically three types of people who can help you find a buyer and walk
you through the sales process. They will also help you negotiate the sale. If you
own a small business with less than $1 million in sales, you can hire a business
broker. You can find business brokers in the Yellow Pages of most major cities.

If your business has $2 to $50 million in sales, you're considered a middle-market
business, in which case you want to hire an intermediary. Intermediaries are
similar to business brokers but are accustomed to dealing with larger businesses
and more sophisticated negotiations. Intermediaries are hard to find unless you
live in a major metropolitan city. If your business grows to more than $50
million in sales, you might want to consider hiring an investment banking
company. These companies are easy to find in the phone book.

Be sure to do your research before you hire one of these people. At the very least,
ask for references and call them with questions. If you know of a company in
your industry that has been sold recently, ask the seller and buyer who helped
them. Most trade organizations also keep track of intermediaries that specialize in
their industry.

➤ **Maximize your company's exposure to buyers.** Make sure your company is in
all the local chamber of commerce listings. Confirm the way they categorize your
company, whom they list as president, and all other pertinent information. This
includes the membership list, as well as other directories that might apply, such
as the book of local manufacturers.

Ask your state industrial development office for its guide to businesses in your state. Are you listed? Is the information up to date? Think of all the different services your company offers, and make sure you are properly listed in the phone book under these services.

➤ **Talk to local CPAs, attorneys, and bankers.** These people know others who might be looking for a business to buy.

➤ **Offer a reward.** You might want to offer a reward for the person who can bring you a referral that results in a sale.

➤ **Don't list your business in the local paper.** You might not want everyone to know you're selling, and you could have all kinds of people calling you, most of whom will not be qualified. If you do list locally, be anonymous and let your business broker or intermediary help you.

## Construct Your Business Profile

A business profile is similar to a business plan. It is used by your prospective buyers as they begin their research on your company. This profile could make you rich if you design it carefully. Given the right amount of profitability, it may be your ticket to Wealth Stage 5. Be accurate and honest. An outline of a typical business profile follows:

I. Introduction

    A. Summary of operations

    B. Financial summary

    C. History of company

    D. Ownership

    E. Reasons for sale

    F. Company strengths and opportunities

II. Description of business

    A. General business description

    B. Description of market and current market share

    C. Future growth potential

    D. Sales and marketing

    E. Competition

    F. Management and employees

    G. Current customers

    H. Suppliers and contracts

III. Business facilities

    A. Location and facilities

    B. Equipment

IV. List of exhibits

    A. Audited financial statements

    B. Marketing material and brochures

    C. List of major equipment and furniture

    D. Résumés and job descriptions of all key employees

    E. Results of recent client survey

    F. Business advisors and references

## Complete the Deal

Most of the clients I know who have achieved Wealth Stages 4 and 5 have sold their business. They knew what their company was worth, they negotiated with the buyer to agree upon a win/win deal, and they had help all along the way.

## What's Important to You?

The following list of questions should help you decide exactly what you want out of the sale:

1. Would you be willing to finance the sale?

2. Do you want to continue to work with the company after it's sold?

3. If you were required to work for another year or two as part of the negotiation, would you be willing to? How long?

4. If you did work, what hours would you want to keep? Do you need to continue your health insurance? What responsibilities would you want to focus on?

5. How will you structure the deal to achieve your financial goals?

6. Do you have key employees or your children in your business who want to continue working? Will the new owners keep them?

7. What would your employees do if they knew you were thinking about selling? Should you keep it confidential?

**Treasure Tip**

Selling is a lot like dating. If you badly need the buyer, he'll run away. If you don't need the buyer, he'll never leave.

Once you know what you want out of the transaction, prioritize each item by its level of importance to you.

This will make the negotiation much easier because you'll know what you can and cannot compromise. Be sure to let your attorney know these items and make sure he keeps the win/win concept in mind. Many attorneys will fight tooth and nail without compromising anything. Don't let this happen. You must be willing to compromise some things.

## Suggestions for Peaceful Negotiations

The negotiation process takes time and a lot of patience. You and the buyer must both be willing to work hard to make the transaction go smoothly. Here are several tips that will make the process a little easier and less time-consuming:

➤ Know exactly what you are willing to compromise and what you're not.

➤ As long as you know your goals, be flexible as to their accomplishment.

➤ Don't insist on winning every argument.

➤ Empathize with the buyer and his needs.

➤ Don't get too excited if you get a better deal than you expected.

➤ Never hesitate to walk away from a sale that doesn't meet your goals.

➤ Never threaten to walk away unless you are serious about it.

➤ Listen for the buyer's goals.

➤ Listen and find out what exactly the buyer is willing to compromise.

➤ Be honest and strive for win/win.

**Treasure Tip**

Strive for a win/win deal where both you and the buyer are happy with the deal.

## How to Have a Smooth Sale

Make sure you understand, in advance, the tax liabilities of selling your company. Hire a tax lawyer who can help you structure the sale to minimize taxes.

Don't procrastinate or be unprofessional in the transaction. Be patient and understand that this is a difficult process. However, don't allow your buyer to stall for no reason.

The personality of the buyer is important, especially if you plan to continue working with the company. If you have more than one attractive

**Treasure Tip**

Be sure to research your buyer. Make sure you know who you're dealing with. Does she have adequate capital? Is she capable of running the company? Make the research for the buyer easy. Do the homework for him in advance. Be honest, and don't hide anything that can surprise your buyer later.

offer, be sure to give a lot of consideration to the nature of the person or people you'll be working with. Spend some social time with the buyer and get to know him personally. This can improve the level of trust and rapport necessary for a good transaction.

Allow the new buyer to get to know your employees on a social level. If your employees are happy with the new owner, things will run more smoothly for both you and the buyer.

Make sure the buyer has enough money after the sale for working capital and emergencies. You might get your business back if he runs out of money. If the buyer says he plans to make up for the lack of cash through net earnings from the business, make sure your company is profitable enough to accomplish this. You also want to make sure you get enough money up front to cover two things: any commission you might have to pay your broker or intermediary and any expenses you might encounter if you happen to get the business back.

Make sure your company is profitable enough to cover the debt payments for the buyer. If your buyer can't pay the debt on the business, he'll have to give it back to you.

# Taking Your Company Public—the Initial Public Offering

If your heart is set on achieving Wealth Stage 5, you must understand how to take your company public. When you make an *initial public offering (IPO)*, you sell a certain percentage of your company's stock to the public for money. You usually sell only a minimal amount of stock so that you can still maintain control. The *underwriter* helps the company decide upon the price of the new shares and the timing of the IPO. The reason behind an IPO is to raise money for expansion and growth in the business. If your company is growing fast and the amount of money you need for expansion is too large for a bank to consider, an IPO might be in order.

**Words of the Wealthy**

An **underwriter** is a brokerage firm that handles the process of offering a company's stock to the public through an **initial public offering**.

Taking your company public gives you the opportunity to cash in on your company's success without giving up control or selling your majority interest of the shares. The benefits of taking your company public include

➤ You sell only a part of your company.

➤ You can still be the largest shareholder and maintain some control.

➤ The value of your company is much higher as a public company.

➤ Your stock is more liquid.

➤ Publicly held stock can be used as collateral more easily.

All these benefits come with a price:

➤ You have to give up some future profits.

➤ You must fully disclose financial information on your company.

➤ Your company will be highly regulated by the SEC.

➤ You must answer to shareholders.

➤ You must answer to your board of directors.

# Additional Resources

If you decide to start you own business, be sure to check out *The Complete Idiot's Guide to Starting Your Own Business*. It is filled with great tips and all the ideas you need to get started. Your library and local bookstore might also have other titles that will help.

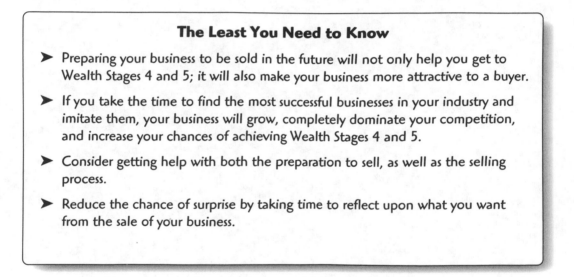

### The Least You Need to Know

➤ Preparing your business to be sold in the future will not only help you get to Wealth Stages 4 and 5; it will also make your business more attractive to a buyer.

➤ If you take the time to find the most successful businesses in your industry and imitate them, your business will grow, completely dominate your competition, and increase your chances of achieving Wealth Stages 4 and 5.

➤ Consider getting help with both the preparation to sell, as well as the selling process.

➤ Reduce the chance of surprise by taking time to reflect upon what you want from the sale of your business.

# Part 4

# The Advanced Strategies for Building Wealth

*In the earlier chapters, we covered most of the basic strategies for building wealth. Part 4 is all about the advanced strategies. This is a summary of things you'll need to focus on if you are serious about building significant wealth. Part 4 covers more strategies that you should be aware of as you approach Wealth Stages 3, 4, and 5.*

*First, wealthy people must pay close attention to the amount of taxes they pay. Second, they live their lives with certain rules or paradigms that seem to prolong their wealth. Third, they use planning methods that allow them to achieve extraordinary goals. The last three chapters in this book will teach you these habits so you can maintain wealth for yourself and generations to come.*

# Chapter 22

# Taxes Made Easy

## In This Chapter

➤ The last of the great tax shelters

➤ The most common tax-related mistakes and how to avoid them

➤ The basics of estate planning

➤ Why you need a tax attorney

As you build wealth, just how important is the subject of taxes? Consider this: The process of minimizing taxes is directly related to the size of your wealth and the amount of taxes you pay. The theory sounds simple: The more you can reduce your tax burden, the more net income you'll take home. All you need to do is know the basics and hire a good CPA to help you. However, most people wait until they have a tax problem before they do anything. By then, it's often too late. My accountant estimated the amount of taxes I would have to pay by April of next year, and I nearly had a heart attack. Suddenly, I'm motivated to do everything I can to fight taxes. However, I know from experience that certain tools and strategies work and others do not. This chapter focuses on the habits and strategies that do help, as well as the habits that don't. Unfortunately, there aren't a lot of tax shelters or loopholes left any more. However, this chapter does cover several strategies you can still use.

As a small business owner you are also responsible for a slew of withholding taxes, unemployment taxes, and other important requirements. A CPA is indispensable for meeting these tax deadlines in a timely fashion.

What about your heirs? If you died today, would your assets be distributed to the right people? Who would be your executor? This chapter will also help you understand the basics of estate planning as well as get you started on your own plan.

# The Last of the Great Tax Shelters

Back in the late 1970s, limited partnerships were the hottest tax shelters around. They lured billions of dollars from investors who were looking for tax breaks. What the majority of these investors got instead was big losses. They thought tax savings was more important than making money.

Things are different now, and the real tax shelters for the most part no longer exist. What remains now are a few tools that allow you tax-free income, such as municipal bonds. Other tools allow you to defer taxes until retirement, and these are the last of the great tax shelters. I've mentioned them before, but here is a complete list along with the key benefits they offer:

➤ **IRAs.** This account is one of the most common things I see wealthy people use to build their wealth. The main attraction here is the benefit of having an invest-ment account that can grow tax deferred for many years. You can only deposit up to $2,000 annually, but over time, this can compound quickly. Not until you are 70 $1/2$ do you have to begin taking withdrawals based upon your life expectancy.

➤ **SEPs.** This is just like an IRA, but it's designed for small business owners who want to put more than $2,000 in their IRAs. This account is often combined with an IRA and is sometimes referred to as a SEP/IRA. You can put up to 15 percent of your salary or $30,000 annually, whichever is less. The real benefit of this plan is that there are no end-of-the-year tax forms to file, and there's no need for an attorney to write a plan document.

➤ **Keogh plans.** These plans have made many physicians very rich, but you don't have to be a physician to start one. You just need a business. These plans are somewhat complicated. However, they allow you to defer paying taxes on as much as 25 percent of your salary, which in turn can be placed in this account and invested just like an IRA or SEP. This is a SEP on steroids! I say that because this plan allows you to deposit so much more each year into the account. Unfor-tunately, there are end-of-the-year tax forms to file on this plan as well as a legal document to maintain that can be somewhat expensive.

➤ **Profit-sharing plans.** This plan is actually part of a Keogh plan and can be set up on its own. You can only deposit up to 15 percent of your income (just like the SEP), but you do have the ability to establish a vesting schedule. This schedule will allow you to phase your employees into the plan over time. For example, after one year, your employees may only be 20 percent vested, which means that if they left your company, they could only take with them 20 percent of their share of the profit-sharing plan. This acts as a golden handcuff that often makes employees think before leaving the company.

➤ **Money-purchase plans.** These are also a part of the Keogh plan and can be set up on their own. The key difference between this plan and a profit-sharing plan is that a money-purchase plan requires that you, the employer, establish a set percentage of your payroll to be deposited into this account. There is no flexibility here. You can deposit as much as 25 percent of your salary, but you have to stick to that percentage. The profit-sharing plan has more flexibility, but the maximum contribution is much lower (15 percent). Everything else is about the same.

➤ **Defined benefit plans.** If you are over the age of 40 and you are the oldest person in your company (or the only employee), this plan might be right for you. It is unique from all the other plans because the deposits you make into the account are based upon your life expectancy and a target (defined) amount of money toward which you are aiming for when you retire. The deposits each year can be much higher than the set limits of a Keogh, SEP, or any other plan. Just like the other plans, the deposits are made pretax and the account grows tax deferred.

➤ **Annuities.** These are not my favorite tax shelters, but they do offer tax-deferred growth of your investment. There are fixed annuities and variable annuities. I explained these in more detail in Chapter 7, "Stay Away from This Stuff." The problem with fixed annuities is that they come with big commission penalties if you withdraw your money within the first several years. The problem with variable annuities is that they offer so few investment alternatives within the annuity plan. Therefore, I don't recommend them often. The only variable annuity I would ever consider is a true no-load annuity such as those offered by Vanguard or Charles Schwab & Co.

➤ **Life insurance policies.** I'm hesitant to list these as a tax shelter because they should never be considered for investment purposes. However, they are excellent for estate planning, which I discuss in more detail later in this chapter.

Let me stress one important observation: Just because an investment is tax free or tax deferred doesn't mean that it's a good investment. *Qualified*

**Words of the Wealthy**

A **qualified plan** is an account into which pretax dollar contributions are made with the intent of using them later during retirement. The primary benefit is that all assets within the plan grow tax deferred until taken out at a later date. These accounts include the IRA, SEP, profit-sharing, money-purchase, Keogh, and defined contribution plans.

**Wealth Warning**

Don't let an insurance salesmen talk you into using a life insurance policy for the purpose of accumulating cash value during your lifetime for investment and retirement income purposes. It's way too expensive and far too complex for these purposes.

*plans* are great, but I don't suggest annuities or life insurance policies for the sole benefit of tax-deferred growth. Refer to Chapter 7 before you use annuities or life insurance products for investment purposes.

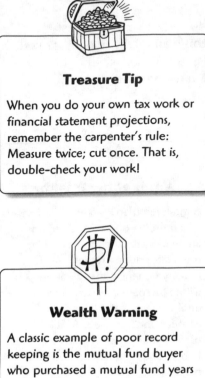

**Treasure Tip**

When you do your own tax work or financial statement projections, remember the carpenter's rule: Measure twice; cut once. That is, double-check your work!

**Wealth Warning**

A classic example of poor record keeping is the mutual fund buyer who purchased a mutual fund years ago but has no statements or records of all the dividends that have been reinvested. Every reinvestment of dividends creates a new cost basis for the purchased shares.

Starting a business and expensing your hobby might seem like a great tax shelter. However, the IRS says you must have a profit motive. How do they determine this? The *Federal Tax Handbook* says that you must show a profit for any three or more out of five consecutive years. There is one exception: If you breed, show, or race horses, you have to be profitable only two out of seven years.

# The Most Common Tax-Related Mistakes People Make

One of the most common characteristics I see among wealthy people is their knowledge of taxes and their tenacity to eliminate tax-related mistakes. They hate mistakes, especially when it means paying more taxes than they should. They do everything in their power to pay the least amount of taxes. A large part of this effort is eliminating the silly mistakes most people make.

## Is Saving Taxes Priority Number One?

For those people who make building wealth a priority, the most common tax-related mistake is maintaining the belief that saving taxes is more important than making money. Believe it or not, this happens every day. Don't let this happen to you. Always use due diligence before you attempt to save taxes. Remember that your first goal is to build wealth. Saving taxes must be, at best, your second goal.

## Silly Mathematical Errors

One of the best ways to reduce your tax is to reduce mistakes. In fact, a number of CPAs all said that the most common mistakes are simple mathematical errors. These mathematical errors can continue to affect your numbers, especially if you've designed your own spreadsheets for estimating your taxes and financial statement projections. I know this from the silly mistakes I've made in the mathematical formulas I use while doing my financial statement projections. Once the mistake is made, it can continue to be a problem forever until it's detected.

## Poor Record Keeping

Failing to keep good records of expenses will cost you a lot of money, but it is easy to correct. If you can't correct it, hire someone who will. Set up a system of records and maintain it well. Keep track of all contributions to charity, cost basis of investments, confirmations of buys and sells from your brokerage firm, and all check registers. Otherwise, you are going to overlook deductions, lose important records, and pay your CPA and the IRS more money than you should.

**Treasure Tip**

Don't be afraid to question your CPA's work, ideas, or actions. Remember, he's human and can certainly make mistakes too.

## Trying to Do It All Yourself When You Know You Need Help

I see this all the time—people trying to do their own taxes and financial statements just to save a dime. Why not hire a specialist who can do all this for you? Here's a list of reasons why:

1. A CPA is a specialist who knows the tax code.
2. One person dedicated to this task will do a better job.
3. Other people may be more objective than you.
4. Hiring help should eliminate any possibility of procrastination.
5. The cost is nothing compared to the potential mistakes and sleepless nights of worry.

## Overlooking Deductions

The following is a list of some of the most overlooked deductions:

➤ Fees for tax preparation services and IRS audits

➤ Amortization of taxable bond premiums

➤ Appreciation on property donated to charities

➤ Business gifts of $25 or less

➤ Cellular telephones and charges

➤ Cleaning and laundering services when traveling

➤ Commissions on sales of property

➤ Contact lenses

➤ Depreciation of home computers

➤ Fees for a safe-deposit box to hold investments

## Incorrect Withholdings

If your tax refund is large, you are withholding too much money, and consequently, the IRS is getting a tax-free loan from you. Don't let this happen too long. You'll lose the power of compounding over time that's so important to building wealth. However, be careful not to withhold too little money. Have your CPA calculate your estimated quarterly taxes for you each year, and adjust your withholding or quarterly tax payment accordingly. A penalty for underpaying your taxes is a total waste of money.

## Not Capitalizing on Qualified Plans

As I said earlier in this chapter, a qualified retirement plan is one of the best tax shelters available today. They are just about the only shelters left.

## Using the Wrong Kind of Debt

Using the wrong debt is such easy mistake to correct. If you are able to itemize expenses each year on your personal tax-reporting form, you can use your mortgage interest as an itemized deduction. Therefore, you should focus on using a home equity loan for any personal debt you have. For example, if you have a credit card with a consistent balance of $5,000 or more, call your bank and arrange for a home equity loan, and use the loan to pay off that credit card. You'll probably get a lower interest rate, and you'll get to deduct your interest.

**Wealth Warning**

Don't fall victim to a slick municipal bond salesman over the phone. I know bond salesmen who can make a bond sound so delicious that you'll have to pry yourself off the phone to keep from buying it. Do your homework on the salesperson and yourself before you buy one.

## Improper Use of Bonds

Municipal bonds are IOUs issued by city, state, and local municipalities. The interest they pay is not taxable at the federal level. Therefore, they don't have to pay the bond holder as much interest as other taxable bonds to be attractive. Sometimes, I see investors in the lowest tax bracket buy these bonds. This is an easy mistake to make if you don't know your tax bracket or understand how municipal bonds work. It's even easier to make this mistake if you fall victim to a slick bond salesman. Make sure you're in a high enough tax bracket to make the tax-free income worth investing in.

Before you buy a municipal bond, take the time to estimate your income and tax bracket if your income has increased this year, or simply look back at your tax forms from the prior year. If you are in the 15 percent bracket, do not buy a municipal bond.

# You Can't Take It with You

It is important to recognize the fact that at your untimely death, you can't take any of your wealth along with you. Therefore, it is imperative that you plan for the distribution of your wealth well in advance of your death. This brings us to one of the most important habits of the rich—estate planning.

# What Exactly Is Estate Planning?

*Estate planning* involves the accumulation and disposition of property (or the estate) for the owner and his family or other heirs. The term "planning" implies the existence of goals. The goals in the case of estate planning can include one or more of the following:

➤ Provide security for the direct surviving family.

➤ Make sure your assets go where you want them to go.

➤ Minimize the financial cost in the transfer of assets, especially estate taxes.

➤ Simplify the transfer of assets at your death.

➤ Minimize family conflict, hardship, and emotional stress.

➤ Provide for the valuation and transfer of a closely held business.

Estate planning is also useful in preventing the worse-case scenarios such as

➤ Direct family members left with financial insecurity

➤ Improper distribution of assets to beneficiaries

➤ Property transferred to minors who aren't old enough to manage it

➤ High estate taxes with only illiquid assets available to pay

➤ Unnecessarily high administrative expenses

➤ Family bitterness and jealousy

**Words of the Wealthy**

**Estate planning** is simply the art and study of preserving wealth for family and future generations to come. It involves planning tools and techniques that cannot only reduce estate taxes, but can also make things a lot simpler after your death.

# The Estate Planning Toolbox

The will is the most important tool in estate planning. It is used primarily to maintain wealth for the next generation. It can

➤ Designate the primary and secondary beneficiaries.

➤ Establish trusts through which assets are transferred.

➤ Identify how estate taxes will be paid.

➤ Appoint guardians for children.

➤ Appoint executors, trustees, and fiduciaries as well as how they are to carry out their respective duties.

**Wealth Warning**

Life insurance commissions are usually equal to at least the first year's premium or at least 7 percent if you pay a lump sum premium. Insurance is important and not all life insurance agents are bad; you just need to be aware of the huge influence the commission creates. Shop around before you buy.

The unified credit against gift and estate taxes is a rule that says you can give your family up to $600,000 after your death without the recipients having to pay estate or gift taxes. Estate taxes are levied on any amount above this. The federal estate tax rates range from 37 percent to 55 percent.

Trusts are also important tools. They are written documents that appoint a trustee and provide beneficiaries the benefit of property ownership without the responsibility of managing that property. They are used in addition to wills to take full advantage of the tax laws regarding estate planning. The typical trust sets up an account in the name of the trust into which assets are placed for the benefit of the owner or her heirs. Inter vivos are trusts that are created by the estate owner before death, and testamentary trusts are created in the estate owner's will and go into effect at death.

**That Reminds Me...**

It's common practice to use an insurance trust to help pay the estate taxes your heirs must pay after your death. This can be a wonderful strategy, but it can also be a waste of money. There are other strategies that might offer the same tax savings without having to pay insurance premiums. Be sure that the person helping you with your estate plan doesn't benefit from the commission on the sale of insurance. Make sure you have an unbiased source of advice. Who knows—the government may eliminate estate taxes someday.

Gifts are common estate-planning tools that wealthy people habitually use to reduce their potential estate tax burden. You can transfer or gift up to $10,000 per person per year without the recipient paying gift or estate taxes. Because only $600,000 in assets can be transferred tax free after your death, you can use $10,000 gifts before your death to help transfer additional assets out of an estate prior to death. These gifts can be larger than $10,000, but you have to either pay taxes on the amount over $10,000 or let it be considered part of the $600,000 tax-free transfer.

Life insurance can also be important for two reasons. First, if you don't have an estate to leave your family, life insurance can provide them with one. This in turn helps ensure their financial security after your death. Second, life insurance can be used to pay the estate taxes at your death.

Retirement plans are also a tool for estate planning. All qualified plans require a designated primary and secondary beneficiary. At the account holder's death, the proceeds are paid directly to the primary beneficiary or the secondary in the case where the account holder and primary beneficiary die at the same time. Because the proceeds go directly to the beneficiary, they can sometimes provide instant liquidity for the estate, which may be needed for various reasons.

# Getting Started

You must first realize that estate planning is not a one-time thing. After you get the basics set up, you must make it a habit to maintain your estate plan. The first step to estate planning is deciding what you want to happen after your death, where you want your assets to go, and how your heirs will be able to pay any estate taxes that might result. Almost all tax attorneys will provide you with an estate-planning questionnaire that will make the planning process smoother.

The second step involves hiring a tax attorney to help you design the plan as well as the right tools you need to make it all happen. How can you find the best attorney? Ask other successful business friends whom they recommend. You might also ask your CPA for a referral. Talk to several attorneys before you select one. Ask for client references and call them.

The third step is getting the plan in place and maintaining that plan. This involves yearly check-ups with your attorney to make any changes that are necessary.

Remember, I am not a tax attorney nor a CPA, and no book can take the place of either. Therefore, be sure you check with your CPA and tax attorney before you use any of the tax or estate planning ideas in this book.

**Treasure Tip**

If you need an insurance agent, I suggest you work with an independent chartered life underwriter. This will ensure that you get some experience and objectivity, along with several quotes from different insurance companies.

## The Least You Need to Know

➤ The only great tax shelters that have survived tax reforms are retirement plans such as IRAs, SEPs, profit-sharing, and money-purchase plans.

➤ Just because an investment product offers tax-free or tax-deferred income doesn't make it suitable for you or worth investing in.

➤ The best place to find the right CPA for you is from a referral from another business owner whose business is growing and experiencing the same problems you will be.

➤ If you make a personal loan, consider using mortgage debt first because it's usually cheaper and you can write off the interest expense.

➤ A good tax attorney can save your family a lot of money and time.

# The Paradigms of Wealth

As in all aspects of life, your mind is your biggest asset, as well as your own worst enemy when it comes to building wealth. If not managed properly, your mind can be your biggest liability. Most wealthy people understand this concept and use it to their advantage. They understand the mindsets or mental habits, otherwise known as paradigms, necessary for building wealth, which I've discussed in detail throughout this book.

What you need to examine are your own paradigms. First, you have to understand the definition of paradigms. Second, you need to know how they work and how they can affect you in your everyday life. Once you understand them, you can use all the habits and strategies in this book to build your own wealth paradigms.

## Eleven Obstacles to Wealth

There are hundreds of reasons why people fail to build wealth. Take a look at the following list, and if any of them sound familiar, do all you can immediately to correct the problem and change the way you think:

➤ They work hard but not smart.

➤ They're not willing to delegate.

➤ They accept self-imposed limitations.

➤ They don't live within their means so they don't have enough to save, and they are too proud to scale back their lifestyle.

➤ They're waiting for an inheritance.

➤ They're not willing to take risk.

➤ They don't do enough homework to protect themselves from scavengers.

➤ They don't channel their efforts in the direction of their passion.

➤ They lack single-mindedness of thought.

➤ They let pride get in the way.

➤ They expect and accept entitlements (such as welfare).

Realistically, this list is endless. However, each of the items has something in common. Every one of them involves a mental belief or mindset that ultimately prevents the person from building any significant wealth. These are paradigms. If you understand what paradigms are and how they work, maybe you can improve your chances of building your own wealth.

# The Study of Paradigms

In my attempt to fully understand the human mind and the tendency to develop mindsets, I was led to the study of *paradigms*. This single subject has been one of the primary catalysts for my success in business and my achievement of Wealth Stage 4. Without the knowledge of paradigms and how they affect my own life, I don't think I would have ever achieved what I have in the last five years. I'm not exaggerating one bit. My business would have probably failed, and I would not have had the opportunity to write this book. Paradigms are incredibly powerful. If you're not aware of your own paradigms and how they control your life, you're destined to fail. Take my advice: Learn all you can about your own paradigms immediately. You'll never make it to Wealth Stages 4 or 5 without this knowledge.

### Words of the Wealthy

The word **paradigm** (pronounced pair-a-dime) originates from the Greek word *paradeigma*, which means model or pattern.

*Future Edge* by Joel Arthur Barker is the greatest contemporary book written on paradigms. It will certainly forever change the way you look at your world—and for the better.

A paradigm is a set of rules that people perceive as their reality. This same set of rules tells you what can and cannot happen. It also defines success and failure. It's like playing cards. Someone years ago decided upon the rules of the game, and therefore, that's how to play the game. For some unknown reason, no one really ever questions the rules. They just play the game.

Take a minute to let me illustrate the power of paradigms using an example. Look at the nine-dot diagram, and draw one like it on a piece of paper.

The objective is to connect all nine dots using four straight lines, without picking up your pen. Take your pen and begin on one dot. You can only draw four straight lines, and remember, you cannot take your pen off the paper. Each line must be continuous from the last. If you really want to understand how the human mind thinks, you'll try this exercise. After you try the exercise, flip ahead to find one way to solve the puzzle.

*Nine-dot diagram.*

This exercise is more than just a game or puzzle. It's a lesson in life, at least it was for me. Take a look at the completed puzzle. Ask yourself this question: What had to happen for the puzzle to be solved?

After sharing this with thousands of people in my workshops, the most common reply I get is, "You had to get out of the box," or "You had to go out of the boundaries." My reply is simply, "What box? What boundaries? I drew nine dots."

Did you see a box or boundaries when you first saw the nine-dot diagram? If you drew a box in your mind and limited yourself to its boundaries, you never could have solved the puzzle. If you did not draw a box in your mind and were open-minded enough not to limit yourself, how many times did you try to solve the puzzle?

There are two things to learn from this exercise. First, your ability to achieve wealth is directly influenced by your ability to identify and control your own personal paradigms. The only way you will be able to do this is through honest reflection and self-examination. Constantly ask yourself these three questions:

1. Why did I react the way I just did?
2. What happened in the past to cause me to react that way?
3. Do I need to reexamine any of my beliefs (paradigms)?

**Treasure Tip**

A paradigm is simply a mindset or way of perceiving the world. It's the smile of a mother to a baby, it's the forest to the deer, it's the water to a fish, and it's the New York Stock Exchange to the broker on the floor as he screams out a trade.

**Treasure Tip**

One thing that will hold you back from building serious wealth in your life is a self-imposed limitation. They are usually easy to set up but often difficult to notice and eliminate.

This examination is important because to the degree to which you can open your mind and see outside your box (your imagined boundaries or paradigms), you'll be able to achieve all the wealth you dream of.

Second, think about how many times you tried to solve the puzzle. Why was this important? Your ability to achieve wealth is directly influenced by your own level of tenacity or "stick-to-it-ness." Your path toward wealth will more than likely involve some obstacles, and if you don't have the passion to stay with the process, you might not achieve your goal.

*One answer to the nine-dot exercise.*

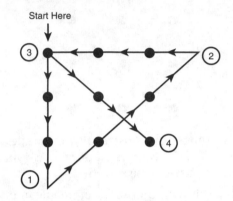

How many times will you try? How much faith do you have in your ability? Will you give up and surrender, or will you continue until you achieve your goal? Your creativity, faith, and tenacity are directly related to the level of wealth you are capable of achieving.

When Galileo proved Copernicus' theory correct that the Earth revolved around the sun, he was exiled for years. The world was not ready for this new idea. All the books on the subject had to be changed. What irony. This guy was exiled for a theory that happened to be correct.

### That Reminds Me...

I saw a T-shirt recently with a rodeo scene of a cowboy riding a bull. It said, "Guts, cuts, and sore butts." It reminded me of what I encountered in starting my own business to pursue my path to wealth. I worked 7 days a week to get started and even pulled 2 overnighters every month. When you work from 8 a.m. until 3 p.m. the next day, you really get sort of silly. I remember losing my key client during the second year who represented over 25 percent of my business. That hurt, but I pulled up my boot straps and worked even harder. No matter what business you start, it does take a lot of hard work. Make sure you enjoy the work before you get started!

As you develop your plans to build wealth, are you ready to test your willingness to accept new ideas? Are you ready to look at conventional wisdom you have used for years and accept the fact that it may no longer work? Will you let conventional wisdom intimidate you?

# The Wealth Paradigms

For more than 10 years, studied investors have built their wealth using wealth paradigms. In fact, this entire book is based upon these paradigms. Each of these paradigms has been taught in the context of habits, investment-selection tactics, and laws. There's no point in repeating them all, but it is important to understand how they work. Therefore, I've selected three paradigms that have helped me build the foundation of my investment strategies, which you'll recognize from Part 2, "Becoming an Investor—Wealth Stages 3 and 4."

Most of the wealth paradigms I've found usually fly directly in the face of conventional wisdom. The ones I'm about to discuss are certainly no exceptions. Therefore, it is important to understand not only the wealth paradigms, but also the conventional wisdom it goes against, which I call the "anti-wealth" paradigms. In each of the descriptions, I begin with the anti-wealth paradigm and finish with the wealth paradigm. You'll notice that most of these involve the concept of investing, but each one can be applied to other situations in life.

## Past Performance Versus Hockey Puck

What criteria do you use when selecting a mutual fund? Most investors use a 1- to 10-year track record. That's not surprising, considering the fact that almost all the books ever printed on the subject of mutual funds state past performance as the key criteria for selection. Peruse any extensive magazine rack in the U.S., and chances are you will find one if not two magazines addressing the issue of "Top Performing Funds," or "The Best Mutual Funds." All of these funds address one primary issue—past performance and its use in selecting a mutual fund. What makes this concept ironic is the disclaimer you see with each of these ads and articles: "Past performance is no indication of future returns."

A friend of mine once said to me, "Hey, why not use past performance? If you want to predict the top passers in the NFL this year, I'd be willing bet you would find that 8 of the top 10 were in the top 15 during the previous season." He might be right about the NFL, but the mutual fund world doesn't work that way. I've studied this stuff for years, and it has been proven in many different studies that the top performers last year (or the past 5, 10, or 15 years) are seldom the big performers the next year (or the next 5, 10, or 15 years). If what they say is correct and past performance can be used to predict next year's winners, we could put together a quantitative model and build a winning portfolio consistently over time. Unfortunately, the stock market and mutual fund market don't work like the NFL. If that were true, I'd pick the very best players each year and beat everyone else. It's simply not that easy. If you have ever read any of the magazines in your local grocery store, you'd certainly think it was—but it's not. Just about every book ever printed about mutual funds says the same thing my friend did, but I'm telling you that it just doesn't work. If it were that easy, everyone would own the very best funds every year.

### That Reminds Me...

If that's not enough to catch your attention, consider this: How far would you get in your car (in a forward direction) if you had to look in your rearview mirror 95 percent of the time? If markets repeated themselves, past performance would give you an indication of future returns. Unfortunately, the market changes on a daily basis. Therefore, no matter how well a fund did last year, it is a new year now, and everyone (including the fund manager) is faced with completely different circumstances—completely different markets.

Barker said in his book *Discovering the Future*, "Your past guarantees nothing." He explains that it doesn't matter how good you are at the old paradigm. When the new paradigm begins, everyone starts all over at zero. Barker's statement holds true when investing. The first and most common investment paradigm is what I call the *past-performance paradigm*. This is one of the most devastating and misunderstood of all investment-related paradigms.

When I see a list of last year's best performing funds, I think, "Wow! What a waste of paper!" It reminds me of when I watch a football game and the play-by-play announcer starts talking about last year's game, who won, and all the statistics and then uses the information to comment on the possible outcome of the current night's game. How completely crazy is this? You have totally new teams, maybe even a new coach, new plays, a new quarterback, and probably a whole new field!

### Words of the Wealthy

The **past-performance paradigm** is the mindset and belief that the past performance of an investment should be the primary justification for purchase.

The proper paradigm to use is what I call the hockey puck paradigm, which I described earlier in the book using the story of Wayne Gretzky. He said he skates to where he thinks the hockey puck is going to be while everyone else skates to where the hockey puck is (or used to be). The best way to select any investment, whether it is a mutual fund, stock, bond, real estate, or a business, is to determine where the market is going and invest in that direction.

## Fear Versus Contrarian

Another one of the most interesting paradigms concerning investment psychology is the reaction most investors have to sudden heavy market declines. One of my clients panicked when Gorbachev was kidnapped and the market dropped suddenly. He wanted to sell everything, and I could not talk him out of it. His paradigms prevented him from seeing any other alternative. Consequently, we sold at the lowest prices that day. Of course, the market suddenly reversed, and most funds went increased in price quickly before he changed his mind. His mindset was, "Get out before we lose everything." He fell victim to the *fear paradigm.*

The opposite of the fear paradigm is the *contrarian paradigm.* A contrarian is someone who invests when everyone is selling. Sudden heavy losses in the market are common and will occur randomly with great intensity. A contrarian views this as an opportunity to purchase investments at lower prices. If you refer to a chart of the stock market over its history, you will notice that all bear markets are followed eventually by a bull market. The contrarian completely understands this. For example, how could anyone be more afraid of owning one of the tobacco companies today? The contrarians who own the stock today are betting that their company could split off the tobacco-related business and unleash a perfectly good company uninhibited by the litigation. It might be a stretch, but it could happen.

**Words of the Wealthy**

The **fear paradigm** is the mindset and belief that when everyone is afraid of an investment, it should be avoided. The opposite is the **contrarian paradigm,** which is based on the belief that if everyone hates an investment, it should definitely be considered.

## Greed Versus Philanthropy

Victims of the greed paradigm focus single-mindedly on building their wealth without any plans for sharing with others or contributing to charity. This is a terrible trap that will inevitably result in loneliness and horrible self-esteem.

The most successful and happiest wealthy people I know contribute regularly to their favorite charities. They find that they ultimately get back more than they give. It may be direct, or it may be indirect, but personally, I do get back more than I give away to charities. I call this my philanthropic paradigm. It's not that you should expect anything back, and I think that's important to understand. You must give unconditionally. If you do, you'll be rewarded many times. Call it divine intervention or synchronicity, but it does work. You reap what you sow. Everything goes full circle in the balance of life, and charitable giving is no exception.

I urge you to give this paradigm a chance in your life. Once you experience it, share it with others. Be a role model for giving in your community. Encourage your friends and business associates to contribute to their favorite charities and to become role models for philanthropy. Your contribution doesn't have to be monetary. You could simply offer hands-on volunteer work.

### That Reminds Me...

One of the most philanthropic people I know told me recently that his parents had given to numerous charities anonymously. They had also funded college educations for local children who couldn't afford tuition. They did almost all of their giving on a private basis. This might seem generous, but my friend said the privacy was unfortunate. He wishes now that his parents had been more public with their giving. They could have been excellent role models for the community throughout the year.

# One Last Word

There are too many paradigms to cover. Now that you understand how they work, it will be easier to develop your own set. Throughout your journey toward building wealth, the most important thing to remember is that some paradigms will help you and some will hurt you. The key is to continue reexamining the paradigms you pick up. Identify them, isolate them, and make sure they are based upon beliefs that coincide with truth and reality—not just the past.

### The Least You Need to Know

➤ To achieve great wealth, you must establish paradigms that naturally encourage you to maintain the necessary habits and mental attitude for building wealth.

➤ The reason why most people don't get rich is their negative mental paradigms related to wealth, finances, and self-imposed limitations.

➤ Once you understand paradigms and how they can affect every aspect of your life, you'll then be able to achieve anything you can think of, including Wealth Stages 4 and 5.

➤ As you build your wealth, you must adopt a philanthropic paradigm to ensure your contribution to society and your value to your community.

# Chapter 24

# The Last Word on Wealth

---

### In This Chapter

➤ Your mind—the key to planning and achieving goals

➤ Finding the best time- and life-management systems—personal and business

➤ Yearly planning retreats for brainstorming, mind-mapping, and project planning

➤ Writing a mission statement

➤ How to make better decisions

---

Setting goals, managing time, and planning regularly are all keys to wealth. If all you do is write your goals on a piece of paper, you significantly improve your chances of achieving them. What if you not only wrote them down, but also did some research and planning related to the goal once you set it? Wouldn't you again increase your chances of achieving your goals? What if your goals were based upon your most important values in life? Wouldn't that even encourage you more to achieve the goals?

If you want to build great wealth, you must learn how to set goals that align with your most important values in life. All wealthy people plan regularly. Every great accomplishment of mine has been the direct result of planning skills, which are simple to learn and develop. After using over 11 different time- and life-management systems, I've developed what I consider to be the best planning system available. Use the ideas in this chapter to design your own system that works best for you.

I've learned that whatever you plan for is achievable to the exact degree to which you believe you can achieve it. Therefore, it is imperative that you believe in yourself and your ability to realize the goals you have. The planning secrets in this chapter will help you do just that. You'll learn both the tools and the strategies necessary to acquire great wealth.

# Unleash Your Mental Power

Before I discuss the actual planning process, you must first understand and appreciate the power of your mind. It is the most important wealth-building tool you have. For example, did you know that your mind doesn't know the difference between reality and imagination? That makes your ability to imagine quite a powerful tool. It allows you to actually live (or practice) every experience in advance. This is called mental imagery.

Mental imagery is the most important tool in the planning process. You can use mental imagery to go through the motions before you actually attempt your task. This will give you the opportunity to capture every step so that you can plan for it and improve it prior to actually executing the plan. You'll be able to know in advance exactly what to expect. You'll know the resources necessary, what needs to be delegated, the possible obstacles to overcome, and the key people you'll need helping you.

Try this exercise. Have someone read the next paragraph to you while you close your eyes. For this exercise to work, you must keep your eyes closed. Ask the helper to carefully read the paragraph aloud at a fairly slow and gentle pace:

> Imagine that you have a nice, fresh, bright yellow lemon in your hands. Feel the rough, almost oily texture. Bring it up to your nose and smell it. (Pause a few seconds.) Smell the wonderful lemony scent. It smells clean and fresh. Now, take the lemon and slice it in half. Bring one half up to your nose, and smell it once again. (Pause a few seconds.) Now, take a deep breath and bite it! (Pause a few seconds.) Is your mouth watering?

Maybe I'm crazy about lemons, but the first time I did this my mouth was watering like crazy. I wanted a lemon so badly that I almost drove to the store to get one. It proved to me the power of my imagination.

## That Reminds Me...

The world's greatest golfers probably understand the concept of mental imagery the best. Before they drive their balls off the tee or take any other shot, they go through every little motion in their mind as if they were actually making the shot. Most of them do this more than once. The mental practice helps them perfect the shot before they even swing the club in reality. You can also do this in your own life. It doesn't matter whether you mow yards or perform brain surgery, mental imagery can help improve your performance.

# Tools for a More Productive Life

I've used more than 11 different time and life-planning systems. I've concluded that they all have their own strengths and weaknesses. Everybody is different, and what works for me might or might not work for you. Here are the four best systems:

➤ **Priority Management, 800-221-9031, Bellevue, WA.** This system involves a half-day workshop and at least a one-hour personal consultation from one of the company's 300 representatives throughout the world. The cost of all this and the planner is approximately $500. I personally recommend this system. Parts of it are based on Dan Stamp's book *The Invisible Assembly Line*, published by AMACOM, New York, NY.

➤ **Seven Habits Organizer, 800-331-7716, Provo, UT.** This system is based on Stephen Covey's book *The Seven Habits of Highly Effective People.* It comes in three different sizes and includes a quick-start guide and an audio tape to teach you the system. The cost is between $65 and $90, depending on which size you prefer.

➤ **Franklin Day Planner, 800-869-1776, Salt Lake City, UT.** This system is based on information contained in Benjamin Franklin's autobiography. He carried a book in which he listed 13 values and goals and incorporated them into his day. His system of self-improvement was used to design the Franklin Day Planner. The system costs between $36 and $50, depending on the size you prefer, and includes a catalog through which you can order training tapes or register for training seminars.

➤ **The E-Myth Academy, 800-551-3312, Santa Rosa, CA.** If you are a business owner and you want to make your business the best it can be, I highly recommend this program. Author and lecturer Michael Gerber wrote the books *The E-Myth Revisited* and *The E-Myth Manager.* If you want to get an idea of this guy's theories, read his books first and then consider his mastery program. The mastery program will provide you with a consultant who will work with you on a monthly basis. This program is extensive and somewhat expensive, but there is nothing like it that I've found. It's worth every penny.

Before you spend money on a system, do a little research. Call each of the four companies and request information. No matter how good a system is, don't hesitate to customize or improve the system for your needs.

**Treasure Tip**

If you really want to build wealth, you must write down exactly what you define as wealth. Describe what you define as being wealthy. Refine this further and make it your goal. This alone more than doubles your chances of achieving wealth.

The planning steps within the rest of this chapter are my own personal favorites. They are best implemented using one of the systems mentioned. You can certainly design your own system; however, it would take away from the valuable planning time you'll need to accomplish your own goals. My point is that these systems do cost money, but they are worth every cent.

# Yearly Planning Retreats

Yearly planning is a key wealth-building habit. This section will describe the most important elements of the yearly planning session. Use these to design your own session. I highly suggest a natural setting of solitude if at all possible. Make sure your surroundings encourage and motivate you.

## *Write Your Mission Statement*

Have you ever asked yourself this question: Who am I? Take a minute and think. What are the most important values in your life? What do you value the most in life? Look back at your answers to the three questions in Chapter 5, "The Secrets of Millionaires." Your answers will help you start your list. I've listed my value categories. Yours will be different, but maybe the categories will be similar:

| | |
|---|---|
| Spiritual | Financial security |
| Physical well-being | Knowledge improvement |
| Family | Fun and recreation |
| Friends | Career |

**Treasure Tip**

A personal mission statement will help you increase your chances of achieving whatever it is that you want in life. All you have to do is be honest when you write it, be disciplined when you follow it, and be consistent when you read it.

For each of your value areas, write a mission statement that explains exactly what is important to you, as well as your primary goal regarding that area of your life. Below the mission statement, begin listing your dreams and goals within that particular area. Keep this list handy so you can add more dreams and goals later. It should be considered a working list that will change regularly. Any time you think of something you want to accomplish, write it down and add it to the list. Be sure to check off each goal as you accomplish it.

## *Traditional Brainstorming*

Few people understand how to brainstorm properly, and even fewer appreciate the power that can come from it. To be successful at brainstorming, you need only a few guidelines. If you take the time to follow these guidelines for brainstorming, you will immediately increase your chances of achieving your desired wealth level. The objective of a brainstorming session is to produce the largest number of ideas possible. You're looking for quantity first and quality second. Here's how it works.

First, start with an open-ended question. For example, your question might be, "How can I reduce my monthly expenses?" Perhaps you want to address a problem or paradigm that's holding you back in your wealth-building activities. Put it in the form of a question: "How can I eliminate this mindset and think more objectively?" Your goal is to write down as many answers to the direct question as you can possibly think of within an hour.

Second, write down the first things that come to your mind without concern for grammar or spelling. Just write whatever you think about—no matter how ridiculous or crazy the answer seems. (If you brainstorm in a team setting, make sure no one criticizes any answers.)

Third, sit in solitude with no possible interruptions from other people or the phone. Fourth, do this outdoors or be as close to nature as you can. Sit by a house plant if you have to. If you can't get close to nature because it's dark and cold outside and there are no house plants, find a quiet place or put on some soothing music. Your goal is to create a peaceful atmosphere free from distraction that will open your imagination. Fifth, don't stop until you have at least 20 answers.

Return to the section "What Business Will You Start?" in Chapter 16, "Start with Your Hobby." The three questions are great brainstorming questions to work on. They should also be part of your yearly planning sessions.

## Mind-Mapping

My favorite way to brainstorm is called mind-mapping. It was taught to me by my business consultant, Roger Lane, who teaches the priority management course. In fact, every chapter in this book was written initially using a mind-map. I'll explain how they work using the mind-map I drew to brainstorm the topics for this chapter.

First, in the center of a blank piece of paper, I wrote the name of the chapter and circled it. In your case, you would write down the idea or yearly goal you want to brainstorm about. Second, from that circle, I drew a line out to the upper-left corner, and wrote down the first thing that came to my mind, which was my "communications book." Below this, I wrote the categories within that book. I continued to write down all the ideas that came to mind without any concern for order. You would do the same when creating your own map, getting related thoughts about the question down on paper as they occur to you.

Once you've completed your mind-map, use it to organize and plan your goal—which in my case was to write this chapter. Take your mind-map and identify the main topics or tasks. Then, list all the steps necessary to accomplish each task in chronological order. The end result should be an organized list of tasks and an organized plan that can actually be used to accomplish a goal. I wrote every chapter in this book using mind-maps. Almost every great goal I've achieved in the last several years began with a mind-map.

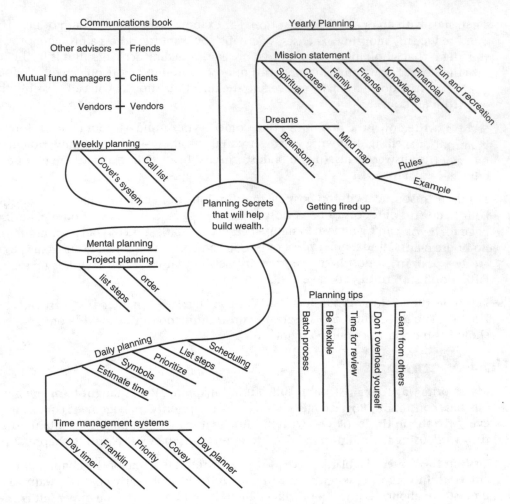

*A mind-map example.*

Why is mind-mapping better than conventional brainstorming? According to the research I've studied (as well as my own experiences), the human brain doesn't necessarily work chronologically. It produces thoughts randomly instead of logically. The people who understand this and allow their minds to create ideas in this fashion are more effective planners. Because mind-mapping gives the brain the opportunity to express ideas naturally, it is the tool of choice for planning and brainstorming.

# Monthly Planning Sessions

Your personal monthly planning sessions should be conducted mostly in solitude. I often bring a friend to bounce ideas off of, but most of the time, I sit in solitude. These sessions allow me to think freely without interruption. This section points out the primary elements of my monthly planning session.

## Prioritize Your Goals

From your categorized list of dreams and goals, decide which goals you want to work on now and which ones you want to save until later. Continue this process until you've prioritized the entire list. Don't be surprised if your priorities change occasionally. Select the most important goal and proceed to project planning. For example, let's assume that your goal is to achieve Wealth Stage 3 in 10 years.

## Project Planning

Once you decide on a goal, your goal or dream becomes a project for you to plan. The first step is to state your objective and expected results as specifically as possible. Write it down; you want to achieve Wealth Stage 3 in 10 years. Add any more specifics that come to mind. Second, use a mind-map to list all the steps necessary. Write your goal in the middle of the page and begin writing down anything that comes to mind. One part of your mind-map might be to set up budget. Another might be to follow the steps in Chapter 4, "How to Become a Saver," and calculate your target savings goal. Part of this mind-map should include the resources, equipment, and facilities that will be needed. It should also include the key people who can help. Be sure to include possible obstacles, as well as solution ideas. Once the mind-map is completed, the tasks should be prioritized, and a project plan should be written.

This project plan is primarily a prioritized list of all the necessary tasks that need to be completed. Each task should be in chronological order and include

➤ Steps necessary for completion

➤ Estimates of time each task will require for completion

➤ Estimated starting date

➤ Deadline for completion

The project plan should also include several lists, such as

➤ Key contacts and phone numbers

➤ Resources, equipment, and facilities needed

➤ Possible obstacles and how each one can be resolved

➤ What tasks can be outsourced

➤ What tasks can be done in-house

➤ Estimated costs

Once you have all the steps and resources listed, use your calendar to identify when you plan to accomplish the tasks. Select the days you plan to focus on each specific task.

## The Project Notebook

One way to keep up with all your projects is to build a project notebook, which is a three-ring binder with dividers for each project. This tool will help keep your life, as well as your planning sessions, better organized. Use dividers to separate key elements of your project. For achieving Wealth Stage 3, you might set up the following dividers: investment account, retirement plan, budgeting, and business ideas. You might want to include your mind-map for future reference.

### That Reminds Me...

My project notebook is a large three-ring binder with dividers for each project. Under each divider is my project plan along with all the supporting documents. If a project begins to take up too much space, I make a separate project notebook specifically for that project. This book, for example, became a separate project notebook. If you are comfortable with a computer and can compose on a keyboard, you may want to build a computer file instead of a notebook. It's the same idea, only it's much easier to change things in the computer.

## Assess and Adjust

Each month you might want to take some time to reorganize your tasks if necessary. Things do change, and you must be flexible. I guarantee that you're going to constantly come up with new ideas that will require you to change your path. Therefore, you must review your plan once a month. Review your wealth-building plan at least once a month, and keep it in order so that you can keep a close eye on your progress.

# Weekly Planning

Weekly planning is not as important to the wealth-building process as daily planning, but it is still a great habit. Some people like to plan their weeks in advance. Others like to plan one day at a time. If you like the idea of weekly planning, Stephen Covey's system has a weekly planning sheet that's handy to use. It allows you to organize your tasks according to your list of values. The key to any plan is prioritization. First, you should spend most of your time prioritizing the tasks needed to accomplish your monthly goals. Second, you should spend a little time planning the tasks you've selected for this week. What days will be dedicated to these tasks?

I still make a weekly call list that I use each week. For years, I listed people to call for the day, only to recreate more than half of the list the next day because they were unavailable and never called me back. Finally, I wised up and began making a weekly list. I keep track of my daily call progress using symbols like LM, which stands for "left message" or WCB for "will call back."

# Daily Planning

Daily planning is vital to the wealth-building process. The more you can accomplish in one day, the faster you can build your wealth. The best planned days produce the most results. One of the most powerful planning strategies in the world is planning for tomorrow one day in advance. Why is this so powerful? Your mind is given ample time to imagine accomplishing all that you need to accomplish. Subconsciously, your mind has time to work through all the tasks, as well as identify all the potential conflicts or problems. This enables you to awaken the next day knowing exactly what you are going to accomplish that day. You not only know what you are going to do, but you also know exactly how you're going to do it. The steps to planning your day are simple:

1. Read your goals for the month (or week), and list the necessary steps you want to accomplish that day. Record any appointments listed in your monthly calendar.

2. Prioritize the list of steps.

3. Identify which steps must be accomplished that day using the letter A or number 1.

4. Identify the steps that can wait until tomorrow using the letter B or number 2.

5. Estimate the time it takes to accomplish each of these tasks, and schedule time to work on them.

➤ The following is a list of strategies I've learned over the years that have helped me be more successful. I tend to dream big. If you're the same way, this list will help you achieve much more than most people ever thought about.

➤ Stick to your plan, but be flexible. Things do change unexpectedly, and you might have to find a better way to achieve the wealth level you desire.

➤ Batch-process your work and control your interruptions. Batch processing just means that you are going to single-mindedly focus on one project at a time for a given time period. You can control your interruptions by closing your office door or going to a private place with no phone. Wealthy people understand the power of their own office doors.

➤ Everywhere you go, keep paper and pen ready. You might want to carry a mini-cassette recorder. It sure makes it easy to record thoughts, especially when driving.

➤ Don't forget to learn from others and their mistakes. You don't build wealth by reinventing the wheel. Save some effort, time, and money by finding others who have done what you want to do. Copy and improve their successful actions, habits, and so on.

➤ The secret to great wealth is not to get overloaded. Do one thing at a time. Don't try to accomplish too many goals at one time. Select the most important one, and focus on it. Then, move to the next one.

➤ Take time to review your progress toward building your wealth. Find new ways to accomplish your goals more quickly. Find someone who will hold you account-able for your goals. Accountability can be important to the accomplishment of your goals. You can be accountable to yourself, but you might also want to ask a friend to be an accountability coach. He may also be a great source of ideas.

# How to Motivate Yourself

If you really want to get fired up about a particular goal or project, take a piece of paper and list all of your greatest accomplishments in life, including the year you accom-plished them. Spend as much time as it takes to fill at least one page. These accom-plishments can include anything that was important to you at that time. You could even include the day you learned how to tie your own shoe! I remember the first time I ever drove a car. Boy, was I excited and proud. I'm an avid water-skier and remember vividly the first time I made it through the six buoys of a water-ski slalom course. After that, I felt I could accomplish anything, including Wealth Stage 5!

Any time you need some inspiration, pull out this list. Pick one of your accomplish-ments that you're really proud of, and think back to that time. Close your eyes and relive the excitement and feeling of accomplishment. Now, imagine yourself today accomplishing your current goal or project. Whether it's Wealth Stage 1 or 5, imagine feeling the same way as you achieve that next wealth level. Keep that feeling with you and draw power from it.

# Become a Better Decision Maker

Building wealth requires an enormous amount of decision-making ability. If you approach every major decision with the same decision-making procedure, you'll find that decisions become a lot easier to make. Here are the steps I take when making a critical decision:

➤ Describe the primary goal. What am I really trying to accomplish?

➤ Identify all the issues related to this goal.

➤ Gather all the information necessary.

➤ List all the alternatives to choose from. For example, doing nothing may be an alternative.

➤ List the pros and cons of each alternative.

➤ Identify the alternative that best achieves your goal in the least amount of time with the least amount of cost.

➤ Use the answers to prioritize the alternatives and select the best alternative.

If your decision involves another decision made in the past, you might want to consider using the same strategy I mentioned earlier in the book regarding sell decisions. It's called zero based thinking. Ask yourself this question, "Knowing what you know now, would you have made the same decision in the past?" If the answer is no, you might want to reconsider your current situation.

# Communications Book

One of the most powerful tools in my wealth-building arsenal is my communications book. I learned this idea from consultant Roger Lane and the priority management system he taught me. In this book, I have categorized and listed all the names, addresses, and phone numbers of all the people I know and work with. Here are the categories listed in my book:

➤ Friends and family

➤ Clients

➤ Vendors

➤ Other advisors

➤ Mutual fund managers

➤ Business advisors

Each of these people are also listed in a database so that I can sort, list, and mail them whenever I need to. The printed copy serves as a back-up for the database, and the database copy serves as a back-up for the printed copy.

It seems I add another person to the list every day. Therefore, it is important that you keep your communications book near your workplace or home. Mine is more than three inches thick, so I can't very well carry it everywhere I go. If yours is small, you might want to incorporate it in your daily planner.

## The Least You Need to Know

➤ The most powerful planning tool toward building wealth or anything else is the mind because it doesn't know the difference between imagination and reality—which means you can use mental imagery to practice accomplishing your goals in advance.

➤ The first step in the planning process is the identification of your values, which will represent the core of your entire planning process.

➤ To plan efficiently and effectively for the accomplishment of your next wealth level, you must learn how to mind-map and brainstorm properly.

➤ If you want to really achieve the highest wealth levels possible, build a project notebook and communications notebook that can accompany you on planning sessions outside your office and home.

# Software to Help Make You Rich

**Advanced Business Valuation** (Chapter 21): 20 comprehensive business valuation methods, 3D graphics, financial statement analysis, and forecasting abilities to help you determine the true value of your business.

**Business Basics** (Chapter 17): More than 100 of the most essential business documents, agreements, spreadsheets, checklists, forms, and templates needed to run any business. Can be customized to fit any business.

**Easy ROR** (Rate of Return) (Chapter 13): Exact calculations of time-weighted return on investment using minimal data input. Shows your true investment performance in just minutes. Monthly, quarterly, annual, and cumulative returns can be reported before or after tax and gross or net of fees.

**Ernst & Young's Total Financial Planner** (Part One): Helps assess insurance needs, fund retirement plans, and diversify investment portfolios. Also makes quick calculations, such as whether to buy or lease a car or home.

**E-Z Legal Credit Repair** (Chapter 19): Provides full instructions and contains ready-to-use forms to correct every type of credit problem. Also works for businesses.

**Fundbuilder** (Chapter 11): Shows how to take advantage of price fluctuations in your mutual funds to maximize returns. Calculates cost per share, compares it to the current fund price, and makes specific management recommendations based on the investment parameters you set.

**Instant Investor** (Chapter 10): Offers a massive amount of historic stock, index and commodity prices, economic time series, and financial software. Economic time series include data from as far back as the 1940s and market price data for all major markets for the past five years.

**Market Skill Builder** (Chapter 10): Provides users with realistic trading and market simulations. Using theoretical money, users make their own investment decisions and sharpen their market skills. Offers a wide variety of markets, including stocks, stock index futures, interest rate markets, currency markets, and agricultural and metal markets.

**Master Investor** (Chapter 11): A portfolio manager with charting and technical advice. Allows users to strategically plan investments for short-term or long-term needs. Produces 37 different portfolio reports for more than 1,000 different portfolios. Data can be easily exported into any spreadsheet or database.

**Microsoft Money 98** (Chapter 4): Instant access to your financial information. Allows users to manage accounts, track expenses against a budget, prepare tax information, and print checks. Includes online banking services, financial planning wizards, and investment management.

**Monocle** (Chapter 11): Covers more than 1,000 funds with daily pricing. Designed for ease of use, offers push-button simplicity, one-step data updates, multi-fund comparisons, and advanced charting tools.

**Mutual Fund Manager** (Chapter 11): Allows investors to research, track, and analyze their mutual fund and stock investments and also calculates tax gains and losses. Provides summary information regarding your mutual fund and stock transactions using graphing features. Includes a comprehensive mutual fund database that can be queried to find a fund that meets your exact needs.

**Quickbooks** (Chapter 16): Invoicing: Software does the math and calculates sales tax, creates customer statements, and displays old invoices onscreen instantly. Accounts Receivable: Always know what customers owe and for how long. Prepares deposits and reports overdue accounts. Accounts Payable: Shows what you owe which vendors and when and reminds you when bills are due.

**Quicken ExpensAble** (Chapter 4): Enter receipts in any order and ExpensAble does all the work. Organizes, analyzes, itemizes, and graphs expense reports. Allows you to always know what you are owed. Includes 30 preprinted forms that can be easily customized to meet your needs.

**Quicken Financial Suite 98** (Chapter 2): Quicken Financial Planner helps you plan for retirement with a whole new level of control. Action Steps report will show exactly how much money you need to save each month and where you should invest the money to achieve your long-term goals. **Quicken Deluxe** V5.0 allows you to track your savings and investments, create a home inventory, manage small business finance, do online banking, and get advice on mutual funds and other investments. **Quicken Family Lawyer** has more than 70 personal and business documents to protect your family and assets. Includes everything from wills, trusts, and estates to sales and leases.

**Smart Business Start Up** (Chapter 16): Simplifies the startup process by guiding you through the four most important steps of business startup: researching markets, writing a business plan, incorporating a business, and locating capital.

**Simply Money** (Chapter 4): Check-writing and personal finance program that organizes and simplifies your checkbook. Offers eight financial calculators, enhanced tax support, and electronic bill payment.

**60-Minute Estate Planner** (Chapter 22): Shows the way to informed and easy estate planning with simple-to-use plans for virtually every type and size of estate. Includes real-life case histories, forms, graphics, charts, and worksheets to help lessen the tax bite on your estate.

# Web Site Index

**Bank Rate Monitor**      **http://www.bankrate.com**

A lot of useful news, calculators, and up-to-date interest rate quotes for mortgages, credit cards, auto loans, home equity, and banking. (Chapter 2)

**The Dollar Stretcher**      **http://www.stretcher.com**

"Living Better for Less." This site offers helpful suggestions on how to reduce expenses, as well as general tips for financial success. Stories, tips, searchable archives, and a newsletter. (Chapter 5)

**Freeedgar Database**      **http://www.freeedgar.com**

Real-time access to SEC filings at no charge. (Chapter 12)

**Home Path**      **http://www.homepath.com**

Sponsored by Fannie Mae, this site offers online help in buying or refinancing a home. Interactive calculators and references help users in a wide array of situations. (Chapter 5)

**InvestorGuide**      **http://www.investorguide.com**

Research, news, quotes, and a lot of great links. (Chapter 12)

**Invest-O-Rama**      **http://www.investorama.com**

One of the best financial sites available for investors. A huge directory of financial Web sites, portfolio tracker, research, company information, charting, market commentary, quotes, and a free electronic newsletter. (Chapter 12)

**Investools**                          http://www.investools.com

Rated in top 10 sites for investors by *Barron's*. Newsletter, quotes and graphs, reports and data, and access to research. (Chapter 12)

**Lombard Institutional Brokerage**     http://www.lombard.com

Brokerage services, quotes, and graphs. (Chapter 12)

**Microsoft Investor**                  http://www.investor.com

A huge site offering an online portfolio monitor, MSNBC and Reuter's news offerings, and company information research. (Chapter 12)

**Money Magazine Online**               http://www.money.com

News, links, searchable archives, free downloads, tips, and market commentary. (Chapter 2)

**Money Talks**                         http://www.talks.com

"The daily investment magazine for the serious individual investor." Weekly columns, daily tips, news, related links, and free annual reports. (Chapter 8)

**Morningstar**                         http://www.morningstar.net

Statistics on more than 6,500 mutual funds, information on more than 8,000 individual stocks, and a portfolio analyzer. (Chapter 12)

**Mortgage Net**                        http://www.mortgage-net.com

Shopping for mortgages made easy. Mortgage reference desk, calculators and tools, and interest rate trends. Economic calendar, forums, and articles. (Chapter 2)

**The Motley Fool**                     http://www.fool.com

News, tips, research, quotes, and graphs. Offers a wealth of general personal finance advice. (Chapter 10)

**Pawws Financial Network**             http://www.pawws.com

Brokerage services, news commentary, and market analysis. (Chapter 10)

**Quicken Online**                      http://www.networth.galt.com

Investment news, quotes, book reviews, and columns. (Chapter 12)

**Stock Detective**                     http://www.stockdetective.com

Protects investors by listing Web sites and radio and TV programs that are known to carry promotional advertising that is supposedly research. Has a history of pointing out bad investments. (Chapter 7)

**The Wealthy Way**                     http://www.wealthyway.com

Money-saving and wealth-building techniques and a newsletter. (Chapter 5)

**Yahoo! Finance**   http://quote.yahoo.com

Provides free services that other sites charge for. Market monitor, an excellent portfolio tracker, and Reuter's news on individual companies. (Chapter 14)

**Zacks Investment Research**   http://www.zacks.com

Both fee and free services, including investment advice and professional information on 6,000 companies. (Chapter 12)

# Words of the Wealthy— the Whole List

**12(b)1**   A securities regulation that allows mutual funds to charge a fee in addition to the management fee for such things as "marketing expenses, distribution expenses, or sales expenses." These expenses, in essence, disguise a commission. Be sure to avoid 12(b)1 fees in excess of .25 percent.

**Asset**   Property with a market value that can be sold for cash. This can include stocks, bonds, real estate, and privately held stock. Liquid assets can be sold quickly, whereas illiquid assets, such as real estate or a small business, usually take some time to sell.

**Capital Ratio**   A ratio that is calculated by dividing the bank's capital by its total assets. This ratio measures the bank's availability of capital and financial strength.

**Certified Financial Planner (CFP)**   Someone who has completed comprehensive courses and passed the CFP exams administered by a company in Denver, Colorado, called the College for Financial Planning. CFPs can be brokers, insurance agents, salespeople, or fee-only advisors.

**Collateral**   Something of value that is pledged against a loan in case of default. When you list collateral such as furniture, equipment, property, or accounts receivable, you should also include documents that will evidence the value of these items.

**Contrarian**   Someone who invests contrary to everyone else, buying when the market is correcting and selling when the market reaches new highs. Contrarians welcome bad news because they know investors will overreact, and as a result, certain stock prices will fall lower than they should.

**Estate Planning**   The art and study of preserving wealth for family and future generations to come. It involves planning tools and techniques that can not only reduce estate taxes, but also make things a lot simpler after your death.

**Fear Paradigm**   The mindset and belief that when everyone is afraid of an investment, it should be avoided. The opposite is the contrarian paradigm, which is based on the belief that if everyone hates an investment, it should definitely be considered.

**Fee-Only Advisor**   A money manager or financial planner who receives a fee for service, which is usually based on a percentage of assets under management or time. Fee-only advisors do not receive any commissions for recommended investments.

**Fiduciary**   An advisor who has been authorized to buy and sell securities on behalf of the client. This authorization is given in the form of a limited power of attorney signed by the client. An advisor has fiduciary responsibility when he is responsible for buying and selling securities for the client.

**Fixed Annuity**   A contract with a life insurance company whereby you give a sum of money, and based on your age, life expectancy, and current interest rates, you'll eventually receive monthly payments for as long as you live. You decide when you want to receive payments, and until then, the money grows tax deferred.

**Full Service Brokerage Firm**   A firm that offers its clients securities as well as advice. The firm is compensated by commissions, which are paid at the time transactions are made. A discount brokerage firm offers the same selection of securities, but because it does not offer advice, the commissions are usually lower.

**Fundamental Analysis**   The study of the basic facts that determine a security's value. A fundamental analysis of a mutual fund includes the study of the securities within the fund, the manager, the philosophy, expenses, and average p/e ratio.

**Gross Domestic Product (GDP)**   The total value of goods and services produced by a country during a year. The GDP's rate of growth is more popular in the news than the actual total GDP number. When plotted on a graph, this growth rate illustrates the economic cycle.

**Growth-Oriented Manager**   Someone who searches for stocks with high earnings growth. Investors are willing to pay relatively higher prices for growth stocks for the chance that they may rise even higher later.

**Haggle**   From the Old English term "heawan," meaning to beat or cut. Haggling is the process of negotiating the lowest price possible in a purchase transaction. The U.S. is one of the few countries where haggling is not a normal part of everyday shopping.

**Harvesting**   An unconventional way of deriving income from a portfolio that includes not only dividends and interest, but also capital gains.

**Hodad**   Describes people who are generally fake or phony. Hodads may look and smell like they're rich, but if you take a close look, they owe a lot of money and lease everything they have.

**Inflation**   An increase in the volume of money and credit relative to available goods, which results in a substantial and continuing rise in the general price level. Inflation is not a simple rise in prices, as most people believe. The rate of inflation is measured by the month-to-month percentage change of the consumer price index (CPI).

**Junk Bond**   An IOU issued by a company whose ability to repay its interest and principal in a timely manner depends on the economy and the company's ability to sell its products or services. It is also known as a high yield bond. Standard & Poor's as well as Moody's offer corporate bond ratings, and a junk bond is any bond with a rating below BBB or Baa.

**Letter of Engagement**   A document prepared by a CPA that outlines in detail what he or she will do for you. The letter should also illustrate how the CPA will be compensated and at what rate.

**Liquid Assets**   Those assets that can be instantly converted into cash. Illiquid assets are just the opposite; they are not easily converted into cash.

**Micro-Delegation**   Simply the delegation of micro-view business responsibilities to other professionals. This strategy enables you to focus on the big picture for your business. It also allows you to delegate the tasks to other people who are often better at them than you.

**Money Manager**   Another name for a fee-only investment advisor.

**Multi-Level Portfolio Management**   A term I use to describe the use of many different mutual funds in a portfolio. These funds add additional layers of diversification and together produce a certain synergy unachievable by any one investor alone.

**Net Asset Value**   The actual true value of each share of a mutual fund. This is calculated by dividing the total value of the fund by the number of shares outstanding.

**No-Load Funds**   Mutual funds that can be purchased, sold, and owned without any commission charges. The only charges involved are management fees. Shares are sold at the net asset value price, and no salesperson is paid to sell the shares.

**No Transaction Fee (NTF)**   A program started by Charles Schwab & Co. that gives investors the ability to buy hundreds of different no-load funds within the same account without paying any transaction fees. The program is so popular that even full-service brokerage firms are beginning to follow in their footsteps.

**Outsource**   A new term that simply means to pay someone outside your firm to do a job for you. It's an alternative to directly putting someone on your payroll.

**Over-the-Counter Market**   A secondary market where securities are traded by phone and computer. The NASDAQ market is the largest and most popular over-the-counter market.

**Paradigm**   From the Greek word "paradeigma," which means model or pattern.

**Past-Performance Paradigm**   The past-performance paradigm is the belief that the past performance of an investment should be the primary justification for purchase.

**P/E Ratio**   The price of a stock divided by the yearly earnings per share. It compares the price of a stock relative to its earnings, which is important to know when you compare one stock to another. It is also important in determining if a stock is underpriced or overpriced relative to other stocks.

**Privately Held Company**  A company whose shares are not publicly traded. Privately held stock is issued to a small number of shareholders, and the value or price of the stock is usually determined by comparisons with other similar companies using factors such as earnings and gross income.

**Pro-Forma Financial Statements**  Used to project the estimated financial results of a new company. They consist of an income statement, balance sheet, and cash-flow statement.

**Qualified Plans**  Plans such as 401(k)s and SEPs that allow employees to deposit part of their own salary into the plan. The deposit is made pretax and the account grows tax deferred. Each employee has their own individual account in which they can select from a number of different investment alternatives.

**Quantitative Analysis**  The study of numerical information for the basis of decision making. Under the idea of quantitative theory, everything is expressed in measurable form and therefore is also predictable. Investors who use this theory believe that by studying specific market data, they can accurately predict the market's movements.

**Relative Strength**  A graphic illustration of the percentage (or fractional) difference between the price of a security and an index (or any other security). If the security and index rise and fall equally at the same time, the graph is a straight line.

**Return on Investment (ROI)**  Calculated by dividing the net income by the amount of capital invested in the company. There are two ways to increase ROI: reduce expenses or increase sales.

**Secondary Market**  Any market where previously issued securities are traded. The New York Stock Exchange (NYSE) is the most well-known example. There, investors can buy and sell stocks from each other through the designated traders on the floor of the exchange.

**Soft-Dollars**  An indirect way many advisors are paid a commission for using the services of a particular brokerage firm or mutual fund. The brokerage firm or mutual fund company usually provides the advisor with research, software, or quotation machines that are normally part of the advisor's overhead expenses. Therefore, soft-dollar payments tend to be the equivalent of commissions.

**Stock**  What you hold when you invest in and become part owner of a company. Shares of stock can build your wealth by paying you dividends and by rising in price.

**Target Savings Goal (TSG)**  The amount of money required each year to build a portfolio large enough to support your preferred standard of living at retirement.

**Technical Analysis**  Using charts to read the price history and other statistical patterns of stocks or mutual funds. Many investors and most professionals use these charts to make investment decisions. A technical analyst is also known as a "chartist."

**Total Return**  The percentage return of a portfolio, which includes dividends, interest, and capital gains. Total return is also known as portfolio performance.

**Underwriter**   A brokerage firm that handles the process of offering a company's stock to the public through an initial public offering.

**Value-Oriented Manager**   A manager who searches for undervalued stocks that are priced below what he actually thinks they're worth. The goal of the value manager is to sell at a profit once the market realizes the stock's true value.

**Variable Annuity**   An annuity that works like a fixed annuity except its value and pay-out amount varies according to the performance of a portfolio of mutual funds from which the contract holder can select. Typically, these policies offer a stock fund, a bond fund, and a money market fund.

**Wealth**   Defined by *Webster's Dictionary* as an "abundance of valuable material, possessions, or resources." The word wealthy is defined as "extremely affluent." The definition of affluent sounds even better, "having a generously sufficient and typically increasing supply of material possessions." However, your own definition of wealth is whatever you choose.

# Index